T0303293

Foxhunting
with Meadow Brook

Foxhunting
with Meadow Brook

JUDITH TABLER

THE DERRYDALE PRESS

Lanham • Boulder • New York • London

THE DERRYDALE PRESS

Published by The Derrydale Press
An imprint of The Rowman & Littlefield Publishing Group, Inc.
4501 Forbes Boulevard, Suite 200, Lanham, Maryland 20706
www.rowman.com

Unit A, Whitacre Mews, 26-34 Stannary Street, London SE11 4AB

Distributed by NATIONAL BOOK NETWORK

British Library Cataloguing in Publication Information Available

Library of Congress Cataloging-in-Publication Data Is Available

ISBN 978-1-58667-151-8 (cloth : alk. paper)
ISBN 978-1-58667-152-5 (electronic)

♾™ The paper used in this publication meets the minimum requirements
of American National Standard for Information Sciences—Permanence of
Paper for Printed Library Materials, ANSI/NISO Z39.48-1992.

Printed in the United States of America

Contents

Preface

MEADOW BROOK HOUNDS
MASTERS OF THE HOUNDS

A. Belmont Purdy	May 27, 1881–Jan. 24, 1882
Francis R. Appleton	Jan. 24, 1882–Jan. 23, 1883
Edwin D. Morgan	Jan. 23, 1883–Jan. 22, 1889
Thomas Hitchcock, Jr.	Jan. 22, 1889–Dec. 31, 1892
Frank Gray Griswold	Jan. 24, 1893–Apr. 30, 1895
Ralph N. Ellis	Apr. 30, 1895–Jan. 27, 1903
Foxhall P. Keene	Jan. 27, 1903–Sept. 27, 1904
Peter F. Collier	Sept. 27, 1904–Jan. 23, 1907
Hunt Committee	Jan. 23, 1907–Jan. 28, 1908
(Robert Potter, R. L. Stevens)	
Samuel Willets	Jan. 28, 1908–Jan. 26, 1909
Malcolm Stevenson	Jan. 26, 1909–Jan. 25, 1910
Hunt Committee	Jan. 25, 1910–Apr. 25, 1910
(Ralph N. Ellis, H. F. Godfrey)	
Joseph E. Davis	Apr. 25, 1910–Jan. 30, 1913

Harry I. Nicholas and James Park	Apr. 18, 1913–Jan. 27, 1914
Harry I. Nicholas	Jan. 27, 1914–Jan. 27, 1925
Harry T. Peters	Jan. 27, 1925–May 27, 1931
Harry T. Peters and Jackson A. Dykman	May 27, 1931–May 23, 1933
Harry T. Peters and Harvey D. Gibson	May 23, 1933–July 1, 1946
Robert Winthrop	July 1, 1946–Apr. 27, 1948
Robert Winthrop and Marjorie B. Hewlett	Apr. 27, 1948–Apr. 1, 1951
Charles V. Hickox and Mrs. John J. McDonald (Marjorie B. Hewlett)	Apr. 1, 1951–1953[1]
Charles V. Hickox and William F. Dobbs	1953–1958
William F. Dobbs	1958–1971
Devereux Milburn Jr.	1958–1968
Mrs. Theodorus V. W. Cushny	1967–1971

HUNTSMEN RECORDED WITH THE MASTERS OF FOXHOUNDS ASSOCIATION OF AMERICA

Charles Cullinan (professional)	1880–1881
Franklin Gray Griswold, M. F. H.	1893–1895
E. Robert (Ned) Cotesworth (professional)	1903–1904
John Foster (professional)	1905–1906
James Blaxland (professional)	1906–1907
Edgar Caffyn (professional drag)	1906–1907
Michael Hanlon	1908–1908
Thomas Allison	1910–1951
Charles D. Plumb	1951–1970
Michael McDermott	1970–1971

ONE

Formation

Whelp: (1) A foxhound puppy before weaning; (2) an
unweaned fox cub.

Long Island, New York, is famous for its beaches, lighthouses,
ducks, potatoes, and traffic. A hundred years ago, equestrian
sports—horse racing, polo, and foxhunting—would have been at
the top of that list. While those activities can still be found on the
island, they are mere shadows of long ago. Tens of thousands of
spectators once traveled to watch horse races at Belmont Park
and Aqueduct Racetrack, and polo matches in Westbury. The
history of racing and polo are well documented, but the third,
foxhunting, has been largely ignored. Foxhunting never drew
large crowds. It is not a spectator sport, except in its purest form,
where the riders watch the hounds work. Few statistics are of interest to anyone other than foxhunters. How long the hunt lasts
and how many days a year it went out are hardly burning issues
among everyday readers—or bookies.

Long Island foxhunts have come and gone. These varied from a private pack of just a few hounds to large packs, to which people subscribed. By far the most important of these was the Meadow Brook Hounds. This foxhunt existed for a little over ninety years, from 1877 to 1971, in one form or another. Many of the people who rode with Meadow Brook left a lasting impact on both foxhunting and Long Island.

The wonder is not that this foxhunt ceased in 1971, but how it survived so long amid housing developments, crisscrossing highways, and supersized shopping malls. The Meadow Brook Hounds stubbornly resisted extinction, because the people who rode to these hounds worked so hard to keep it going. From its humble origin with four young men out for a day's sport, Meadow Brook matured into one of the most famous hunts in the United States. The fast pace, frequent runs, and high fences attracted top-flight equestrians from all over the country—and more than a few from other countries. There was an expression in the Meadow Brook community: if you want to see a horse from almost anywhere, just keep hunting with Meadow Brook, because eventually every rider will bring his or her horse to hunt here.[1]

The Meadow Brook Hounds did not spring onto the plains of Hempstead with a ready-made pack of good hounds and beautifully groomed horses; the journey took years and many transformations. In the decade following the Civil War, New York City expanded rapidly, both in financial importance and in population. Wealthy families vied for power and status. New millionaires bragged that they owned the best of everything. "My dog is better than your dog" and "my horse is faster than your horse" were pervasive sentiments. Many current sporting events date back to that period. The Belmont Stakes commenced in 1867 and the Westminster Kennel Club dog show in 1877.

Horses were the sports cars of the time: admired for their sleek lines and shiny colors, and valued for how they handled around curves, on straightaways, or over fences. The young and adventurous riders wanted to test their mettle, but one could only circle Central Park so many times. Just outside Manhattan was a rural country waiting to host outdoor activities. Trains and trolleys carried people to Long Island and New Jersey, but once there, the horse was king.

On November 23, 1875, *The Sun* newspaper ran a front page article, directly below the masthead and next to the column about the death of Ulysses S. Grant's vice president, Henry Wilson.

THE HUNTING OF REYNARD

"It's frozen stiffer than a graven image," ruefully exclaimed out Joe Donahue yesterday morning, as he stepped out of the Mansion House in Hackensack. The stars were twinkling in the cold, clear heavens, and the ground was hard. "It's a poor morning for a hunt, boys; but we'll try it, and when the sun gets up a bit it'll soften the ground." . . . It was, indeed, an inauspicious morning for foxhunting, as Donahue said, but the party of hunters who had ridden out from New York and Jersey City the night before to be in time, seemed anxious to be off to the cover as though they had the "cloudy sky and a dewy morn," that proclaimed a hunting morning. . . . Their horses were well groomed, and their "cords" immaculate, and as at least three of them were old hunters, Messrs. Purdy and Clason having hunted in the south of France and in England, much good riding was expected of them. . . . Harry Blasson put his little horse at almost anything in his way, and "popped him over" like a bird. Sammy Holden tried a two-rail fence with his pony—the pony cleared the fence and Sammy "cleared" the pony; but he landed on his feet, and was in the

saddle in a moment all ready to fall off again at the next jump.
. . . For an hour the hounds hunted the cover until, becoming discouraged, they began to struggle back to the waiting
huntsmen, and then it was high time to look elsewhere. . . .
By the time Garrison's Wood was reached there were over
twenty horsemen in the field, and twice as many gentlemen in
carriages. . . . The hounds put into cover and the huntsmen
waited impatiently for the result. They did not have to wait
long, for soon there came swelling out of the cover the most
attractive music in the world, the cry of hounds. First there
came a deep roar from old *Leader*, the truest dog in the pack,
and then hound after hound took it up, until the whole pack
burst into chorus. Nothing was seen of them, but the sound
indicated that they were headed toward the road on which the
hunters waited. As the cry grew louder and louder, impatient
horsemen spurred forward toward it.

"Keep back, Gentlemen, for God's sake keep back,"
shouted Col. Skinner, standing erect in his carriage, his gray
eyes flaming with excitement, "keep back. You'll head off the
fox." Hardly had he spoken before Ryan shouted, "There
he goes. It's the fox"; and sure enough the red quadruped
came running easily down the road. He was a large dog fox,
and carried his white tipped brush right jauntily. The noise
from the huntsman scared him, and turning short he went to
cover again. In a minute the hounds came up on his track,
and also went out of sight in the woods. Then followed a few
minutes of confusion, inexperienced huntsmen riding hither
and thither, the veterans shouting to them to keep back, and
the men in the woods yelling to the hounds. All this confused
the hounds, and the pack scattered. . . . The fox was lost.
He had got away. . . . At five o'clock in the Mansion House
a hungry table full of huntsmen attacked John Ryan's viands,
and success to Joe Donahue, the father of Jersey foxhunting,
was the toast.[2]

The article was one of many about foxhunts at the time. This one was important, because it illustrated the tone and revealed much about the time and the people of the day. *The Sun*, a conservative newspaper that published from 1833 to 1950, relied on advertising, not on reader subscriptions, and was considered the first paper that did not cater to an upper-class readership. In a day before radio, movies, and television, the goings-on among the "horsey-set" entertained a large audience. The publishers believed their readers wanted to know everything, including the horses' and hounds' names and their histories. There must have been a positive response, because in the years that followed, coverage increased. These articles were then reprinted in smaller city papers throughout the nation. Riders, horses, and hounds became national celebrities of the day.

One name mentioned in *The Sun* article was Belmont Purdy,[3] who earned the title "father of the Meadow Brook Club."[4] On a different day, he and his friends, Robert Center, William E. Peet, and Frank Gray Griswold,[5] were eager participants in Joe Donahue's hunts. "Several riders were quickly on the spot, cheering for the victory. The brush was awarded to Griswold, and Purdy, coming in second, received the head."[6]

In the spring of 1877, Griswold, Peet, and Purdy gathered at Robert Center's rooms in Manhattan determined to organize a foxhunt on Long Island.[7] Griswold believed that true foxhunting was "impossible near New York," so he suggested "the Pau form of sport." Pau was a resort town in Southwest France near the Pyrenees Mountains. Griswold, who had grown up foxhunting in England, had spent a year in Pau drag hunting.[8] In a drag hunt, hounds follow a scent that is laid along the ground rather than live quarry.

The men subscribed $250 apiece and developed their plan. The twenty-three-year-old Griswold was about to travel abroad,

Figure 1.1.   August Belmont Purdy, M.F.H. Charles S. Pelham-Clinton,
"Fox-hunting Near the Metropolis," *Cosmopolitan* magazine, vol. VII,
May–October 1889, 89.

so he was tasked with finding suitable hounds overseas.[9] Peet,
Purdy, and Center explored Long Island and settled on the
Hempstead Plains.

They rented a farmhouse on the A. T. Stewart property in
East Meadow next to Garden City. "It was ideal country for
drag-hunting, and was chosen for that reason. The fences would
have been too big to jump if the turf had not been sound. The
soil is so light that it drains quickly, and it is seldom that the

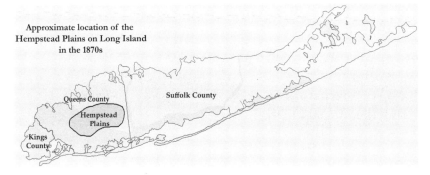

Figure 1.2.   Map of Long Island.

going is not perfect even in the early spring. It is the very worst scenting country in the world for fox-hunting, and carries little scent except on the snow or when the frost is coming out of the ground."[10]

In August, Griswold arrived home with ten couples of well-bred Irish harriers. He had purchased them near Dublin from Thomas Turbett of Scribblestown.[11] Griswold, Peet, Center, and Purdy called the hunt the Queens County Hounds, but newspaper accounts often used variations, including the Queens County Drag Hunt.[12] Kennels were built and servants hired, but Griswold wrote: "The difficulty was to obtain hunters. There were no horses to be found that could jump, and the fences were big and strong. We bought green horses and schooled them ourselves. In fact, we began from the beginning in every way, having much enthusiasm and little money. We personally did everything, even to cleaning our boots and breeches, and thoroughly enjoyed ourselves."[13]

While the men were enjoying themselves, the nearby farmers tilled the soil. Quaker families, such as the Hickses, Jacksons, Seamans, Tituses, Underhills, Williamses, and Willetses, had farmed these plains and established Garden City, East Meadow,

Jericho, Westbury, Hicksville, and Mineola. This land provided wagonloads of poultry, vegetables, and fruit to feed the residents of New York City. The high-fenced fields penned in sheep and cattle that yielded wool, meat, and dairy products. The milk from Westbury dairies was famous for its sweetness, which came from "the richness of the pastures."[14]

Seeing the land more as a recreational area, the young, eager sportsmen posted invitations to subscribe to the hunt in newspapers and mailed out circulars to personal acquaintances:

Q.C.D.H.

September 1st, 1877

Dear Sir:

Having imported a small pack of hounds from Ireland, which we have established at East Meadow Brook, Long Island, where we propose to run a drag twice a week over country well adapted to that purpose, and being unable to maintain the pack properly without the assistance of those of our friends who are interested in our success we should be greatly pleased to receive a subscription from you.

Rob't Center	*Committee*
Wm. E. Peet	*Queens County*
Belmont Purdy	*Drag Hounds*
F. Gray Griswold	
Address	
F. Gray Griswold	
Garden City Hotel	
Garden City, L.I.[15]	

The opening hunt was held Wednesday, October 3, 1877, at one o'clock on the grounds of the Garden City Hotel, where spectators gathered on the piazza. Griswold, as both Master of Foxhounds and huntsman, wore a "pink" (the traditional term to describe the scarlet color) cutaway coat, buckskin breeches, and shiny high boots. Seven couples of harriers led the field. They were white with black and brown spots, about eighteen inches high, and with shorter dewlaps and ears than American foxhounds. An Irish whipper-in, Fitzpatrick, also in a pink coat, assisted in the management of the hounds. Earlier, he had dragged an anise-seed bag for seven miles, laying the scent for the hounds to follow. Not wanting to know the exact direction the hounds would take, Griswold never put down a dragline himself. Mr. and Mrs. Belmont Purdy, Robert Center, William Peet, C. DuBois Wagstaff, Elliott Zborowski (wearing pink), and Harry Blasson rode in the "field" (followers of the hunt). Behind them were numerous and varied dogcarts, traps, and carriages crammed with hilltoppers (spectators who preferred not to jump fences).

The day was not without incidents: Wagstaff and Griswold fell while going over different four- and five-barred fences. Neither was seriously hurt, and they quickly remounted. After Griswold was back in the saddle, Blasson set his horse, Jack Horner, at the five-barred fence. The horse, an experienced hunter from prior outings in Canada and New Jersey, cleared the fence, but then stumbled. Blasson dismounted and discovered that the horse was bleeding from his mouth. Within fifteen minutes Jack Horner was dead, probably from a burst blood vessel. Blasson sought out the landowner, a farmer named Taylor, and asked him to bury the horse. However, since Blasson was exceedingly fond of Jack Horner, he requested that Taylor first skin the horse, so Blasson could have slippers made from the hide. Taylor obliged.[16]

After this successful opening hunt, the Queens County Hounds continued to go out, but not without engendering some displeasure. Henry Bergh, president of the Society for the Prevention of Cruelty to Animals, fired off a letter to *The New York Times*. He addressed it to the farmers of Long Island:

> When your wheat crop is about ripe, the gentry propose to "meet" at a given place of rendezvous, adorned in gorgeous costumes of a suggestive and appropriate color—scarlet—all mounted on fiery steeds, who at a given signal scamper over your fields, to the number of 50 or 100 red-coats, close upon the heels of a score of dogs, in hot pursuit of a terrified fox![17]

The letter ended with a description of the racket hounds and huntsmen make dashing across the farmers' fields and lawns. He said this could be disturbing, especially when, perchance, a farmer's wife or child might lie dying inside the house. Bergh then aimed his ire at the women who foxhunt. He compared them to females who attended horrible spectacles at the Roman amphitheater and chastised them for "social demoralization and national ruin."[18]

The Queens County Hounds members responded with their own letter to the farmers, published in the *New-York Herald* on October 11. They denounced Bergh's letter as a "scare-crow" meant only to terrify the farmers. In fact, the hunt would only take place at the time of year when no harm would be done to the farmers' crops, and if by some chance any damage might occur, the hunt members would recompense the landowners. The authors pointed out that the sport of foxhunting would be of great benefit, because it would attract people to the area who might otherwise travel to England or France to hunt. A local hunt would bring vitality and growth to Long Island.[19]

Other observers saw humor in the sport of drag hunting. One reporter suggested dragging a bag of catnip instead of anise-seed. Then the hunters on Long Island could follow a pack of cats.[20] *The New York Times* published a long article entitled "Hunting the Anise-Seed Bag."

Hunting the anise-seed bag is a manly sport, and in time may become as popular in this country as hunting the fox is in England. As everybody knows, the anise-seed bag is one of the swiftest and most subtle animals. . . . Moreover, the anise-seed bag is fiercer and more courageous than the fox. . . . It would be a sad affair if a huntsman eager to be in at the death were to risk a personal conflict with an infuriated anise-seed bag and be torn into—say, twenty-seven pieces. . . . The substitution of the anise-seed bag for the fox shows not only the fearlessness and the judicious economy of the Queens County huntsmen, but it is evidence of their patriotism. They prefer to hunt a fierce American animal rather than an imported monarchical fox. There will be no trouble in finding plenty of anise-seed bags. It is believed that Hempstead Plains is infested with them, and that they breed in large numbers all over Long Island. They are seldom seen, for they do not feed on farmers' crops, and rarely attack human beings, except when they find it impossible to escape. Hence, there are scores of Long Island farmers who have never seen a wild anise-seed bag, and are familiar only with the tame variety that can usually be found at drug stores. Still, the fact that the hunt, at its very first meeting, struck the trail of what was believed to be a full-grown and dangerous anise-seed bag, shows that the animals are numerous on Hempstead Plains, and is full of promise for future sport.[21]

The next week, the hunt dispensed with the drag. They met at the kennels in East Meadow Brook and set out after a live fox, which was delivered into the area from Greenwood, New York, by Colonel Delancey Kane.[22] The fox was loosed, and the ensuing chase was fast-paced and required jumping over several large fences. Elliott Roosevelt, Theodore Roosevelt's younger brother, rode a black mare and took a "cropper" (a fall), but he remounted and finished the hunt. The Queens County Hounds recorded their "first kill" in forty minutes.

The hunt continued to meet weekly and varied the quarry between anise-seed and live game. The outings were reported in *The New York Times, New York Sun, New York Tribune, New York World, Brooklyn Daily Eagle,* and *New-York Herald.* Much of the attention was spurred on by James Gordon Bennett, editor of the *New-York Herald* and a foxhunter, who supplied a horse for his reporters. The horse, Kaibo Kip, was soon renamed "Herald's Hunter."[23]

The Queens County Hounds enjoyed a strong first season of hunting, at the conclusion of which Belmont Purdy and William E. Peet retired from the committee. Purdy remained a member of the field, but Peet moved to Paris, France.[24] The two vacancies were filled by one man, Count Elliott Zborowski, who was also appointed first whip.[25]

The Queens County Hounds might have pronounced the undertaking a great success, except for a social gaffe. In November, the men decided to hold a hunt ball as a celebration and a "thank you" to the local landowners. The following advertisement appeared in newspaper classifieds:

> The Queens County Hunt Ball
> The annual ball given by the Queen's County Hunt for the farmers of the Queen's County will take place on Thanksgiving Eve in Mineola. The Queen's County Fair Association has offered to allow the hunt a large hall on the fair grounds, and there it will take place. A special train will leave Hunter's Point at 7:30, returning after the ball.[26]

The ball was a huge disappointment, due to the absence of young ladies.[27] A lengthy article in the *Brooklyn Daily Eagle* said that the ladies of the farmers on Long Island were

> hurt far more deeply—hurt beyond all hope of recovery—wounded in their pride by the vulgar invitation printed in the classifieds so that anyone can attend. The invitations should have been mailed and the guest list shaped.
>
> Now anybody who knows anything about country life, especially on Long Island, knows that there are fifteen to twenty grades of society here. . . . In such an indiscriminate gathering of farmers as such of advertisement invited, the various grades saw themselves at once lost in hopeless confusion, merged into almost as common a ruin as their own fields by the huntsmen. Would a Hicks permit his wife and daughters to go to a ball at which she would meet on equal terms the wives and daughters of the Browns? The Brown ladies might stand the Hickses, but would they risk contamination by the Jones girls? Certainly not. The consequence was that the ball was a failure; the object of the ball, namely, the propitiation of the injured agriculturalist, was hopelessly overthrown. . . . Had the youths who hunt the foxes but half the sagacity of their quarry, they would not only capture more brushes, but would win more friends.[28]

It was doubtful that the hunters cared much about the lack of attendance at the ball, but something had happened. Enthusiasm waned, and the number of riders in the field diminished. Some rode with the newly formed Rockaway Hunting Club, which hunted "over the country extending from Far Rockaway to Baldwin and Rockville Center, with occasional meets at Springfield and Jamaica."[29] There was also a dustup between Frank Griswold and August Belmont Jr., which caused them to cease speaking for many years.[30] Griswold packed up his hounds and moved to Westchester County, New York, for fall and spring hunting, and to Newport, Rhode Island, for "cub hunting" (training) during August and September.

The Long Island foxhunting enthusiasts were dismayed. Belmont Purdy, August Belmont Jr., and Thomas Hitchcock Jr. brought over some of Joe Donahue's hounds from Hackensack. But the hounds were a mismatched, ragtag lot and did not provide much sport. Purdy announced they needed to import a new pack from England. With the guidance of Belmont and Hitchcock, who had recently attended Oxford University, Purdy commissioned J. Burke Roche of Ireland to find the best hounds and ship them to their kennel in East Meadow Brook.

When the hounds landed, the *Brooklyn Sunday Eagle* called them "the finest pack ever seen in this country" and published a list with each hound's name and parentage. Accompanying the hounds were huntsman Charles Cullen and whipper-in James Bergen.[31] Cullen only remained with the hunt a short time, and Bergen assumed the role of huntsman.

Purdy's Hounds or, as the *Brooklyn Daily Eagle* prematurely christened them, "the Meadow Brook Hunt," commenced hunting that fall, meeting on Mondays, Thursdays, and Saturdays at 4:00 p.m. At the close of a successful season, William R. Travers suggested that Purdy need not support the entire enterprise on his own, and at a meeting at Delmonico's Restaurant in New York City during the winter of 1880–1881, the followers of the hunt formed the Meadow Brook Club.

POSTSCRIPT

Just before Frank Griswold decided to move the Queens County Hounds to Westchester County, he purchased a big gray hunter named Hailstone in Rhode Island. The horse was a good jumper over timber fences common on Long Island, but "not as clever over stone walls" of Westchester, so Griswold sold Hailstone for $1,500, which he considered a good price. Shortly after this transaction, a friend invited Griswold to meet a man named Thomas Edison in Menlo Park, New Jersey. Griswold toured the "one-story shedlike building," and Edison introduced him to his new method of making electric bulbs and demonstrated the first phonograph. Griswold invested all of the $1,500 from Hailstone into fifteen shares of the Edison Co., which made him a tidy sum years later.[32]

MEMBERS OF QUEENS COUNTY AND MEADOW BROOK HUNTS

Robert Center

Robert "Bob" Center, the son of Edward H. Center, a wealthy cotton merchant, grew up in Manhattan. His uncle on his mother's side was D. D. Withers, one of the founders of the Monmouth Park race course. Robert became an experienced rider. He was described as physically small, but "full of pluck." He rode with Meadow Brook and appeared in amateur races until the early 1890s, when he had a bad fall.[33] After that, he was primarily a yachtsman, serving as commodore of Seawanhaka Corinthian Yacht Club and rear commodore of the New York Yacht Club. His other passion was cycling, and he imported the first Michaux bicycle into the United States. Center died at age fifty-five on April 17, 1895, after his bicycle was struck by a coal cart in New York City. His obituary stated that "Mr. Center was one of the most kind-hearted of men. He was a man, too, whose word was as good as his bond."[34]

Count Elliott Zborowski

Count Elliott Zborowski descended from the New Jersey family of Albert Zabriskie. Elliott's father, Martin, preferred the old Polish spelling of the last name, Zborowski. The family claimed to be related to the Polish king, and this ancestry came with the title of count. Following the death of his father in 1878, Elliott inherited a large estate in Bergen County, New Jersey, and a fortune of five to ten million dollars.[35] Elliott invested in theaters in New York City and London.

He was an early foxhunter with Queens County and probably one of the more experienced, because he wore a pink coat on opening day. Speed was a major attraction, and as soon as the automobile was available, he switched over to the newer variety of horsepower and became a keen motor racer.

Much was written about Elliott's colorful life in the 1890s. In 1892, he was named in a nasty divorce between Baron and Baroness de Stuers, who had been Margaret L. Cary, a New Yorker and granddaughter of William Astor. Court papers claimed that he and the baroness traveled from Paris to London under the name of Mrs. and Mrs. William Elliott. The baroness fled to South Dakota, which was known at the time as the place to get a divorce "while you wait." She testified that she had been "confined" by her husband due to her "unbalanced state" and "nervousness." The baron had also sent their daughter to a convent to keep her away from her mother. Margaret received the divorce on grounds of cruelty, and within hours married Elliott Zborowski. Her custody dispute with her ex-husband raged on for several more years.

Count and Countess Zborowski moved to Europe, where he was often referred to as "the American count." Zborowski began to make a name for himself in auto racing. He finished second in an important race, and on April 1, he entered "an automobile hill-climbing race" between Nice and La Turbie in France. At the first major turn, his car swerved violently and flipped over. The count was thrown headfirst into a stone wall and died instantly. Some witnesses blamed the count's imprudent decision to wear white kid gloves, which prevented a firm grip on the brakes, but others were more fatalistic, remembering the "Zborowski curse." Several generations earlier, an angry Irish lord had sworn that none of the Zborowski men would die in their beds.[36]

TWO

Early Days

Cubbing: preseason training in the late summer or
early fall. The idea is to educate young foxes to run
from the hounds and puppies to hunt in a pack.

CERTIFICATE OF INCORPORATION

Original filed with County Clerk at Jamaica, Long Island, and
with the Secretary of State at Albany, on May 12th, 1881.

We, the undersigned, August Belmont, Jr., Wendell Goodwin, Belmont Purdy, Frederick O. Beach and Francis R.
Appleton, all of full age, citizens of the United States and of
the State of New York, do hereby certify, That we propose to
form a corporation of the class known as "Societies for Social,
Instructive, Recreative and other purposes," pursuant to the
provisions of an act of the Legislature of the State of New
York, passed April 11th, 1865, and entitled "An act for the

incorporation of societies or clubs for certain social and recreative purposes," and the several acts amendatory thereof, and we do hereby set forth:

First, That the name of said corporation is to be the "Meadow Brook Club."

Second, That the object and nature of the business for which said corporation is to be formed is, to support and hunt a pack of fox hounds in the proper seasons, and to promote other out-door sports; and that the Club House, fixtures and principal place of business thereof is to be at Garden City, Long Island, State of New York.

Third, That the number of directors of this club shall be five, who shall also be the Trustees of the Club. The directors for the first year of the existence of this corporation shall be August Belmont, Jr., Wendell Goodwin, Belmont Purdy, Frederick O. Beach, and Francis R. Appleton, all of New York City.[1]

Each man signed the document, dated May 5, 1881, and committed to buy one fifty-dollar share of the one hundred shares available.

By May 27, they had drawn up a constitution with by-laws defining the duties of the president, vice president, treasurer, secretary, Master of Hounds, and governing body—the stewards. The club property was transferred from Belmont Purdy to the Meadow Brook Club. The bill of sale is dated June 1, 1881, and turns over the lease of "valentine farms" on the Stewart estate, as well as the tack; liveries; carts; four sets of servant's bedroom furniture; nine couples of hounds; a chestnut mare, Storm; a roan horse, Tanglefoot; a bay mare, Sally Lunn; and one cow, no name given. In exchange, the club paid Purdy $1,500.[2]

The first president of the club was the esteemed equestrian William R. Travers. At the time, he was sixty-two years old and a

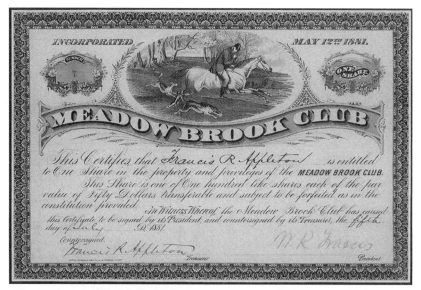

Figure 2.1. Certificate of one share of the Meadow Brook Club. From the Collection of the Meadow Brook Club.

member of twenty-seven clubs. He must have provided a wealth of experience to the younger members.[3] The vice president, Colonel William Jay, was somewhat younger at age forty, but he was a Civil War veteran and active in polo, horseracing, and coaching.

During the first year as the Meadow Brook Club, Master of Foxhounds (M.F.H.) Purdy took the hounds out regularly from September through December, weather permitting. He posted the fixtures (location, times, and dates of meets) in the local papers. These did not always occur on the same days of the week. And the times varied, with 3:30 or 4:00 p.m. the most common.

By then, Griswold had brought his Queens County Hounds back to Long Island and set up his kennel in Mineola. This created some territorial elbowing among the Meadow Brook, Queens County, and Rockaway Hunting Clubs. However, in general the three organizations seemed to have had enough country and days in the week to avoid direct conflicts. Enthusiastic riders participated in all three hunts and could follow the hounds six days of the week. Occasionally, the hunts combined a meet, which then concluded with a "pink dinner" (a social event where men wore their pink coats).

In February 1882, Meadow Brook entered its second fiscal year, and Belmont Purdy relinquished the office of Master to Francis R. "Frank" Appleton. The spring season commenced March 11, and the stewards' report stated that the hunting was successful and attracted very large fields. It also defined Meadow Brook's territory as "east of the Garden City line" and said that

Figure 2.2. *Francis R. Appleton Sr.,* painting by Ellen Emmet Rand, 1925. Courtesy of the Trustees of Reservations, Appleton Farms Collection.

the club had surrendered the country west of that line to Griswold's Queens County Hounds. The spring season ended April
22, with a joint meet with Griswold's hounds in Huntington.

By May 1882, the Meadow Brook Club was expanding. The
stewards added lawn tennis courts and secured twenty acres for
polo fields and pigeon shooting. To differentiate the activities,
the hunting branch of the club was referred to as the Meadow
Brook Hunt or the Meadow Brook Hounds. The actual name
would not be clarified for many years. To add to the confusion,
the proper format of the name was always two words: Meadow
Brook, never Meadowbrook. This detail escaped the attention of
many newspaper and magazine editors. Even some of the members of the hunt wrote it incorrectly in their memoirs.[4]

The new acreage devoted to polo was just a sliver of land
compared to the surrounding farm country that was being
gobbled up by new landowners. In the years 1875 to 1900, farm
acreage in Queens County dropped from 90,738 to 69,357.[5]
The wheat and corn production dwindled and thus idled the
local gristmills. Farmers found a stronger market for flowers and
ornamental trees. The town of Hinsdale provided so many floral
seeds that it was renamed Floral Park. Hicks and Sons nursery
in Westbury became famous for its supply of special trees, vines,
and fruits, which soon decorated the estates of Long Island
millionaires—an area that would eventually become known as
the "Gold Coast."[6] At the time, newspapers, familiar with the
moniker "Newport colony" for the social elites in that section of
Rhode Island, dubbed the hunting area in the Hempstead Plains
the "Meadow Brook colony."

That autumn, hunting commenced in October, and meets
were held on Thursday and Saturday afternoons. So that members could get themselves and their horses fit, stables were
made available for members' horses at the cost of thirty dollars

a month per horse in September. If a member supplied his own groom to manage his horses, the monthly fee was cut in half. The clubhouse offered a kitchen and overnight accommodations for members at three dollars a day or seventy-five dollars per month.[7]

Francis Randall "Frank" Appleton Sr., the hunt's second M.F.H., received a letter from Jack Cheever, Master of the Rockaway Hounds, dated October 29, 1882. It illustrates how the hunts endeavored to settle their territorial disputes.

> My Dear Sir,
>
> My dragman and fence men inform me to-day of several complaints made to them by farmers in *our* country of damage done by the "Meadowbrook" hunt, north of Freeport, Baldwins & Rockville centre. As our line is known to extend from Jamaica East to South Oyster Bay, our country lying in the section South of the air line between those two points it would be merely Justice to the Rockaway hunt, if the other hunts would confine their selves to their proper limits especially as we go to great trouble and expense to make all damages good and to keep on good terms with our farmers. You would be doing me a great favor if you instruct your dragman in future to avoid our country as I presume it is without your knowledge that your drag was laid over it.
>
> Yours very sincerely,
J. D. Cheever
Master of the Rockaway Hounds[8]

There is no extant record of Appleton's response, but he probably handled the complaint with dexterity. He was the successful mediator for many Meadow Brook members' disputes, and although he was only M.F.H. for one year, Appleton

Figure 2.3.   Edwin D. Morgan III, M.F.H. Casper Whitney, ed. *Outing* magazine, April-September 1905, 374.

remained active in the club until 1895, holding the offices of secretary, treasurer, and vice president.[9]

The next Master was Edwin D. Morgan III, and he tackled the hunt's financial debt. On February 1, 1883, he, Richard Mortimer, Stanley Mortimer, and August Belmont Jr. each pledged five hundred dollars for 1883, 1884, and 1885. They signed a note stating that the

> aim of the Club is to place the Meadow Brook Hounds on a par with the best packs of their class in Europe or America, and so satisfy, to its fullest extent, the increasing interest in the sport. In view of this, we, the undersigned, deem it advisable

to raise a sum by subscription, for a term of years, which shall put the Master beyond dependence on the Club treasury and in a position to follow a liberal and untrammeled policy in developing fox hunting in America.[10]

M.F.H. Morgan was a keen hunter and wrote one of the few first-hand records of a day's outing with Meadow Brook in the 1880s:

I had a horse that could jump walls well, and there were some very good ones out at the time. Frank Griswold had a marvelous hunter called Orion and Mid Burrill too had a very good horse, and I remember that Foxie Keene and Jimmie Kernochan of the younger element were always at the top of the hunt and could jump anything, both riding ponies. I have seen them jump a mason wall five feet four inches high. Tom Hitchcock was always well mounted, or appeared to be to me whether he really was or not. Stanley Mortimer had some very good horses indeed, one called Masquerade, a horse of fine quality, and a little mare who was most appropriately named Desperation, but when ridden freely in accordance with Stanley's custom she always got there, although her legs bore scars of many battles with the fences.

At Meadow Brook I found a very good huntsman called Jimmie Bergen, and he on an old roan horse called Tanglefoot was unbeatable. No fence was too big for him. No matter how fast Tanglefoot went between his fences he jumped them very slowly, almost rearing up in front of them and landing on his fore feet on the far side followed by his hind feet. Absolutely safe. I never saw him down but once, and that was in the north country at the end of the season, at a hunt which was given by me. The drag was laid as strongly as possible, by request, in order to have the hounds run at top speed the whole time. Tom Hitchcock on Kathleen got into the field where the hunting stopped at Jericho, and I got into the road bounding it on the north but could not get out. Stanley Mortimer and Jimmie Bergen, the only other riders in the hunt, had fallen about a mile back. It is lucky that it did not happen in the days of prohibition, for the only way I could get my horse home was by buying a pint of gin at the hotel in Jericho and giving it to him. This braced him up until I got him home, and he suffered no bad consequences, although I thought at the time he would never come out again.[11]

During Morgan's mastership, the hunt club celebrated a marriage. A foxhunter and pioneer landowner in the area, Adolf Ladenburg, married Emily Louise "Nellie" Stevens at the Long

Figure 2.4. *Meadow Brook Hunt, 1886.* From left to right: F. R. Appleton, horse's name not given; Thomas Hitchcock riding Kathleen; Mrs. Belmont Purdy riding Doctor; W. K. Thorne, horse's name not given; Elliott Roosevelt, horse's name not given; Edwin D. Morgan riding Atcazar; Mrs. Edwin D. Morgan riding Marksman. From the Collection of the Meadow Brook Club.

Mansion, the home of her parents, Mrs. and Mrs. Alexander Stevens, in Lawrence.[12] A special private car was added to the eleven o'clock train from Long Island City to accommodate the arriving guests.[13] Members from the Rockaway Hunting Club and Meadow Brook Club attended the wedding "clad in scarlet and olive green coats, white breeches, their whips twisted in their hands, while horse and hounds waited on the lawn."[14] Following a reception, the riders formed two lines and shouted "Happy marriage bells" as the wedding carriage departed. Then the riders galloped behind the happy couple a little way before returning to the lawn where the hounds were loosed,[15] and "the hunters among whom were several of the lady guests, were soon skimming over fences and ditches."[16]

One of the wedding guests was Elliott Roosevelt, future President Theodore Roosevelt's younger brother. The Roosevelt family had been coming to Oyster Bay since 1874, when Elliott and Theodore were teenagers. Twenty-three-year-old Elliott was elected to the Meadow Brook Club on June 7, 1883. Theodore Roosevelt joined Meadow Brook sometime afterward; the date is not clear, but he was a voting member in 1885. Elliott was the more active Meadow Brook member. He built his house near the clubhouse and served as a steward and acting club secretary; he sat on the stable, polo, and house committees.

Theodore Roosevelt rode to hounds with Meadow Brook occasionally. He married Alice Lee in 1880 and was elected to the New York State Assembly in 1881, which meant he spent much of his time in Albany. His wife remained in New York City, while the couple's Oyster Bay house, Leeholm, was under construction. When Alice died suddenly on February 14, 1884, two days after giving birth to a daughter, the grief-stricken Theodore headed west, exploring the Badlands of North Dakota to regain his balance. When Theodore returned to Oyster Bay in

Figure 2.5. Early Members of the Meadow Brook Club, left to right, back row: Stanley Mortimer, W. S. Hoyt, Douglas Robinson, W. K. Thorn, Adolf Ladenburg; front row: Elliott Roosevelt, J. F. D. Lanier, Thomas Hitchcock, H. B. Richardson. Courtesy of the Museum of Polo & Hall of Fame.

the fall of 1885, he hosted the Meadow Brook Hunt at Leeholm, which had been renamed Sagamore Hill.[17] *The New York Times* reported the event the following day, October 27.

MR. ROOSEVELT IN AT THE DEATH
    HE RIDES TWO MILES WITH A BROKEN ARM IN PURSUIT OF A FOX.
    A party of about 40 riders left Sagamore Hill, Oyster Bay, at 1 o'clock Saturday afternoon in pursuit of Master Reynard. Among the gentlemen were the Hon. Theodore Roosevelt, August Belmont, Jr., Alfred Morgan, Stanley Mortimer, and Belmont Purdy. Each rider had his crack horse, as the country

was deemed the "stiffest" to be hunted over on either side of the Atlantic. Mr. Roosevelt rode his horse Frank, a powerful thoroughbred, which, with distended nostrils, led the cavalcade about one-third of the distance, when he suddenly began to go "lame." As the hunt approached a stone wall about five feet high Frank hesitated. Mr. Roosevelt drove his spurs into the animal's sides and Frank sprang into the air. His lame leg bothered him, however. He tripped on the wall, and the horse and rider rolled together over a small pile of stones. Mr. Roosevelt sprang to his feet and remounted the animal as it arose. Dashing ahead the plucky rider soon regained the hounds, although he felt that something was wrong with his left arm. Two miles further on the fox was run to cover. Mr. Roosevelt immediately became the object of interest to his companions. His face was covered with blood, while his left arm hung nerveless at his side. Upon examination it was found that the ex-Assemblyman had received a simple fracture of the left forearm, while a piece of court plaster about an inch square was required to cover an abrasion on the gentleman's nose. "It's a mere trifle," said Mr. Roosevelt yesterday, and he refused to talk about the matter.[18]

Shortly thereafter, Roosevelt wrote a lengthy piece, which appeared in the July 1886 issue of the *Century Magazine*, in which he discussed "Riding to Hounds on Long Island."[19] He explained that Meadow Brook did not prefer drag hunting because of a lack of foxes, but because it took less time and businessmen in a metropolitan area could only devote a few hours in the afternoon to recreation. Also, he mentioned that live foxes, both red and gray, were hunted once or twice a week by Meadow Brook. Some of the country was described as wooded and hilly, except on the plains in the middle of the island. Most fences were timber, and many were mortised so rails would not fall. He personally measured several jumps and found that they varied in height from four to five feet. Roosevelt concluded the article with a defense of foxhunting, but not about animal cruelty. Instead, he refuted the argument that the activity was too English. "To say the sport is un-American seems particularly absurd to such of us as happen to be in part of Southern blood, and whose forefathers in Virginia, Georgia, or the Carolinas, have for six generations followed the fox with horse and hound."[20]

Roosevelt's hunting gave the newspaper columnists a chance to jibe the budding politician. When the Meadow Brook Hounds attended a joint meet on Staten Island with the Richmond County Hunt Club, the *Boston Post* reported that Roosevelt rode hard and was in "at the finish." The article concluded with "judging from his recent utterances," this occupation is better suited to Roosevelt, who is "more foxy than wise."[21] Perhaps

Figure 2.6. Meadow Brook Hunt Meet at Sagamore Hill. Roosevelt 560.15-001, Theodore Roosevelt Collection, Houghton Library, Harvard University.

THE

Meadow Brook Hounds

MEET.

NOVEMBER, 1884.

SATURDAY, 1st,   Ridgewood,   at 4.00 P. M.
MONDAY, 3d,   Garden City,   " 3.30 P. M.
TUESDAY, 4th,   Kennels,*   " 10.45 A. M.
       Point to Point Steeple Chase.
WEDNESDAY, 5th, Westbury Station, " 3.30 P. M.
SATURDAY, 8th, Hempstead,   " 3 30   "
    The Master's, Luncheon at 1 o'clock.
MONDAY, 10th, New Castle Wood, at 3.30 P. M.
WEDNESDAY, 12th, Brookville,†   " 3.45   "
SATURDAY, 15th, Huntington,‡   " 11 45 A. M.
    "   "   Syosset,   " 3.00 P. M.
    Luncheon at 1 o'clock.
MONDAY, 17th, Mineola Fair Grounds, " 3.00 P. M.
WEDNESDAY, 19th, Wheatly,   " 3.30   "
   Lower Duck Pond. Mr. W. P. Titus.
SATURDAY, 22d, Hempstead,   " 3.30   "
    Mr. Barnum's.
MONDAY, 24th, East Meadow Toll Gate, " 3.30 "
WEDNESDAY, 26th, Woodbury,   " 3.30   "
SATURDAY, 29th, Jericho—Horton's, " 3.30 "

MEADOW BROOK,
   Oct. 25th, 1884.

* For a Silver Cup presented by several members.
† A wagon will leave Meadow Brook with the luggage of those desiring it at 1 P. M., and with a servant of the club in attendance, will meet the 2.05 train from Long Island City at Locust Valley, 3 miles from Brookville, the nearest point by rail to the meet.
‡ Two box cars will be attached to the 9.05 train from Long Island City at Westbury. Luncheon at Syosset at one o'clock.

Figure 2.7. Fixture Card, November 1884. From the Collection of the Meadow Brook Club.

we might have had a Teddy Fox instead of a Teddy Bear, if the press had written more about Roosevelt's foxhunts than his bear hunt in 1902.

In 1884, Edwin D. Morgan, M.F.H., took a leave of absence for one year, and August "Augie" Belmont Jr. was appointed as acting Master. Belmont was thirty-one years old, and he had joined the Meadow Brook Club in his twenties. He played polo, rode in amateur horse races, and foxhunted. He was a natural choice for acting Master in 1884, and he seems to have performed his duties well. Belmont commissioned a popular animalier, Gustav Muss-Arnolt, to paint "The Meadow Brook Hounds Meet at the Old Westbury Pond on Long Island." This work shows Belmont as M.F.H., and the huntsman, staff, hounds, and field, including Theodore Roosevelt.

It was not until November 1885, when Belmont was a steward, that his famous temper caused problems.[22] On Election Day, the Meadow Brook Club hosted a posthunt dinner, and,

Figure 2.8. *The Meadow Brook Hounds Meet at the Old Westbury Pond on Long Island*, painted by Gustav Muss-Arnolt for Mr. August Belmont Jr., Acting Master of the Meadow Brook Hunt, Fall Season 1884 and Spring 1885, dated 1885. From left to right: Col. William Jay's drag, Mr. Adolf Ladenburg on the white mare, Mr. Stanley Mortimer in his trap, Mr. J. F. D. Lanier on Gertrude, Mr. E. T. Cushing, Mr. W. R. Stuart on Dublin, Hon. Theodore Roosevelt on Frank, Mr. S. S. Sands Jr. on Trojan, Mr. T. Hitchcock Jr. on his gray horse, Mr. H. L. Herbert on Laurelwood, Mr. W. E. D. Stokes on Jericho, Mr. Alexander Dongan on Phantom, Mr. W. Thorn Jr. on Kitty, Mrs. A. B. Purdy on Lady Evelyn, Mr. August Belmont Jr. on Mineola, Mr. Elliott Roosevelt on Mohawk, Mrs. August Belmont Jr. on Carmelite, Miss Oelrichs on Spinnecock, Mr. A. B. Purdy on the colt, Miss Lucy Work on Death, Mr. H. B. Richardson on Don, Mr. O. H. P. Belmont and the Lepper, Mr. F. R. Appleton on Lord Harry, Mrs. S. S. Sands Jr. on Ah, Sin. Long Island Museum of American Art, History & Carriages. Gift of August Belmont, IV, 1978.

for the first time, they invited women. About fifteen to twenty men and six women attended, including Mrs. Belmont Jr. When the men decided it was time for the women to withdraw to a separate room after the meal, as was traditional, several members began to sing a well-known tune, "Goodnight Ladies." August exploded, claiming the song was an insult to the female guests. The language became heated, and Belmont stomped out of the room. The remaining members felt that their honor had been attacked. A duel was proposed—first with guns, but then downgraded to a fistfight. Finally, the men cooled down and agreed that all that was necessary was for Belmont to present a written apology. If none was given, he should resign his stewardship and other offices in the Meadow Brook Club.[23] Frank Appleton convinced Belmont to write the letter.

Later that same month, Belmont complained vociferously that Frank Griswold had brought his Queens County Hounds into Meadow Brook territory. Griswold replied with an angry letter demanding that Belmont make these remarks to his face, rather than to others. Belmont fired off a missive detailing Griswold's offenses. The argument became nastier, and more harsh words were exchanged. The Meadow Brook stewards attempted to intervene, but that further outraged Belmont. Again, he submitted his resignation as a steward and member of the club. This time his resignation of stewardship was accepted, but conciliatory letters from Frank Appleton and Elliott Roosevelt persuaded Belmont to calm down, write another apology, and remain a member of the club.[24] Eventually, Belmont would be fully reinstated and go on to become a president of the club. But he was never elected M.F.H. again.

Edwin Morgan was still M.F.H. on February 10, 1886, when a tragedy occurred at the club. The hunt was between fall

Figure 2.9. Old Meadow Brook Clubhouse. From the Collection of the Meadow Brook Club.

and spring seasons, and Mr. and Mrs. Morgan were vacationing in Pau with Stanley Mortimer and Thomas Hitchcock.[25]

According to newspaper reports and entries in the stewards' records, it seems that Meadow Brook had at least two stables for the horses used for hunting, polo, and general transportation. The upstairs of the larger stable (the "club stable") contained rooms for the stableboys and kennel helpers. Nearby were several other wooden buildings: the smaller hunt stable, the main clubhouse, the kennel-man's house, the kennel, and perhaps a carriage house. Steward John G. "Jack" Beresford's handwritten notes recorded the events of February 9–10.[26]

Three of the boys Wm. Flearn, George Kyle of Club stable and John Gaynor of Hunt Stable state that they all went to bed leaving very little fire in the stove before nine o'clock—Wm. Flearn states he was the last to go up, and put out the lamps.

Mr. Kernochan's man John Stevenson and Club helper,
Wm Nickells, went to a Party or Performance at Hempstead
without permission—and although they deny it, it is believed
that they went into the saddle room on their return, and either
raked out by accident some live ashes from the stove, lit a
pipe, and threw the lighted match down, or in some way were
the cause of starting the fire accidently.

The boys were awakened at 2:30 am by the noise the
horses were making and escaped with very little belongings
on them.[27]

The account described how the boys ran for help and alerted
several club members who were staying either at the clubhouse
or lived nearby. The men opened the west door, and Elliott Roosevelt's horse, Mohawk, galloped out. But when they tried to enter the stable, the smoke was too thick. They dashed around the
building to the northeast door, but again, the smoke drove them
back. Beresford found an axe and hacked a hole through the wall
into the nearest stall, where his own pony was housed, but he
found the animal already dead from suffocation. The stable boys
rushed to the smaller hunt stable and released seven horses into
the nearby orchard field, where they also placed the hounds.

The club stable became fully engulfed in flames, and concern
grew that fire would spread to other buildings. The men doused
the ground and sides of the buildings with water while the stableboys threw snowballs on the roofs, successfully extinguishing
the sparks that landed there. Beresford stated that the clubhouse
was in great danger, but a shift in the wind helped them to finally
contain the blaze.

Twenty-four horses died that night, including Jimmie Bergen's Tanglefoot and the celebrated steeplechaser Hobson's
Choice. Mohawk was the sole survivor from the club stable.

Beresford surmised that someone had not fastened the stall door properly, and that the mistake had saved the horse's life.

Elliott Roosevelt lost two other horses that night, but Mohawk seemed to have been a favorite. This was the horse he

Figure 2.10. Elliott Roosevelt on Mohawk. Roosevelt R500.P69a-006, Theodore Roosevelt Collection, Houghton Library, Harvard University.

bestrode when posing for a formal hunting photograph. And in 1893, shortly before his death, Elliott took his daughter Eleanor (the future Mrs. Franklin D. Roosevelt) for a carriage ride in Central Park, and he selected Mohawk to pull them along. Elliott bragged that "if he just said 'Hoopla' to Mohawk, he would try to jump over all the carts around us." Eleanor wrote that "I tried to hide my fears as I murmured, 'I hope you won't say it.'"[28]

Following the fire, the hunt soldiered on. Beresford's report ended optimistically—he jotted down the dates for the hunt meets in March. For Meadow Brook, 1886 was a year to forget, and things did improve the following year. With the assistance of insurance money, the club built bigger stables, refitted the kennel, and paid a long outstanding club wine bill for five hundred dollars.[29]

Elliott Roosevelt took a leave of absence from the club and sailed to Europe. Thomas Hitchcock Jr. filled his vacancy on the Stewards' Committee.[30] The stewards had some difficult decisions to make in the next few months. The club buildings remained on land rented from the A. T. Stewart estate. Stewart had died in 1876, but his estate had been tied up in litigation for years, and when his widow died in 1886, Meadow Brook was left without a clear landlord. The stewards discussed the matter, including the purchase of nearby acreage. However, they stayed where they were and, in 1889, signed a new ten-year lease.

In 1888, two years after his wife's death, M.F.H. Edwin Morgan remarried. While he and his wife still rode to hounds and kept steeplechase horses, he spent more and more time sailing. Eventually, his yacht, the *Columbia*, would defend the America's Cup, and he would become commodore of the New York Yacht Club. With a new wife and yachts on his mind, Edwin Morgan resigned as Master in January 1889 and was succeeded by Thomas Hitchcock.

This was the same Thomas Hitchcock who years earlier had aided Belmont Purdy in his purchase of the original Irish harriers for Meadow Brook. The club honored their new M.F.H. that fall by hosting a Thanksgiving eve dinner and by presenting Hitchcock with a large silver bowl. On Thanksgiving morning, the group celebrated with a hunt that found and killed a fox near Westbury. The party then attended a luncheon given by Mr. and Mrs. Elliott Roosevelt, followed by a gallop back to the Meadow Brook clubhouse for an unusual race.

The names of twenty-six types of animals were printed on slips of paper, which were randomly drawn by the guests. Each guest was given a ribbon and a stick that could be used to pull, guide, or prod his or her animal over a one hundred-yard race course marked out on the polo field. The animal assortment included pigs, calves, monkeys, sheep, chickens, roosters, turkeys, ducks, geese, guinea hens, parrots, cockatoos, poodles, goats, and peacocks. The spectators cheered on their favorites and feigned shock at the bawdy vocabulary exhibited by a parrot, who disliked being out in the cold and damp. First place was awarded to James F. D. Lanier with his guinea hen, second place to Henry Van Rensselaer Kennedy and his turkey, and third to Charles Wright with another guinea hen.[31]

These were the huntsmen and -women whom Thomas Hitchcock led into the next decade.

MEADOW BROOK MEMBERS

Francis Randall Appleton, Sr. and Jr.

Francis Randall Appleton Sr., the hunt's second M.F.H., came from Ipswich, Massachusetts. His family's one-thousand-acre homestead, Appleton Farm, exists today and is one of the oldest

continuously operating farms in the country.[32] Appleton graduated from Harvard in 1875 and moved to New York City, where
he worked as a lawyer and banker. He served as president of the
Harvard Club and on the boards of banks and businesses alongside other Meadow Brook members, including Theodore Roosevelt. Coincidently, Appleton's younger brother, Randolph,
remained in Massachusetts and became the fourth M.F.H.
(1893–1900) at the Myopia Hunt.

Francis Appleton Sr. was a quiet but influential voice in the
world of high finance. When J. P. Morgan died, his will dis-
closed the existence of the secretive and selective Corsair Club.
"Other clubs have been called exclusive and others have represented great wealth, but never has such a social organization
of men called together such powerful, active financial geniuses.
They were Mr. Morgan's choice comrades; they represented the
kind of brains which the great financier admired most." Appleton was one of only twelve members.[33]

Francis Appleton Jr. was born in 1885, and he followed the
family pattern of attending Harvard University, graduating with
both a bachelor's degree and law degree in 1910. He moved to
Manhattan, where he practiced law, until World War I commenced. He enlisted and fought in France during World War
I, earning the rank of colonel. After the war, he returned to his
international law practice in New York and to the foxhunt.

In the hunting field, Frank Appleton Jr. was always called "the
Colonel." He was a fixture at Meadow Brook, riding to hounds
into his seventies. The Colonel showed up at almost every meet,
regardless of the weather. He was a tall, wiry man, and always
turned out in perfect order—pink coat, top hat, well-polished
boots, and immaculately groomed chestnut horse. He was a sin-
cere supporter of Meadow Brook, including its steeplechases,
hunter trials, and point-to-points.

Figure 2.11.   Francis R. Appleton Jr. Acting M.F.H. 1914. From the Collection of the Meadow Brook Club.

The Colonel and his wife, Joan, preserved boxes of ephemera and official correspondence related to the Meadow Brook Hounds from 1881–1971 at their Appleton Farms in Ipswich, Massachusetts. This material is housed in their research department in Sharon, Massachusetts, and provides much insight into the early years of the hunt. The Colonel died in 1974, and Joan in 2006.

Frederick O. Beach

Frederick O. Beach was an original member of the Meadow Brook Club. His good looks earned him the nickname "Beauty." In 1899, he married Camilla Moss, who was the widow of

Charles O. "Carley" Havemeyer, who had died of a self-inflicted gunshot the year before. Both Camilla and Frederick foxhunted at Meadow Brook and in Aiken, South Carolina, where he was also active in coaching.

In 1912, there was a mysterious attack on Mrs. Beach in Aiken, which resulted in a somewhat sensational trial. Mrs. Beach said she had been accosted in the yard by a stranger, who then ran away. The police investigated the scene and questioned witnesses. Their suspicions were aroused by several discrepancies and because afterward the Beaches immediately sailed to Europe. Upon arrival, Mr. Beach received word that he must return at once, because he was charged with attacking his wife. After much delay and many consultations with his friend William K. Vanderbilt, Frederick and his wife returned to America where he was indicted. The trial took place in the summer of 1913, and every detail was covered by the national press—most of it on the front pages. Frederick was eventually cleared of all charges, but doubts remained about him and the motives of the Aiken police. No one else was ever charged.

The couple remained married, and their son John A. Beach seemed to inherit some of his father's good looks. In the 1930s, he appeared in a few westerns with John Wayne, and as a minor but regular character on television in the *Hopalong Cassidy* series. Frederick died in 1918, and Camilla died in 1934.[34]

August Belmont Jr.

Following his graduation from Harvard in 1874, August Belmont Jr. joined his father's successful financial business in New York City. The powerful family's interests included banking, politics, and horseracing. When his father died in 1891, August

Jr. took over August Belmont & Co. and financed, among other ventures, the New York subway and the Cape Cod Canal.

Belmont's hobbies included both dogs and horses. He raised prize-winning fox terriers at his Blempton Kennels on his Hempstead estate, served as the fourth president of the American Kennel Club, and founded its magazine, the *AKC Gazette*.[35] But Belmont was primarily a turfman. He built Belmont Park and raised many great horses, including Man o' War, which his wife named in his honor. She deemed it appropriate, because at the time of Man o' War's foaling in 1917, Belmont, age sixty-five, was headed off to World War I and becoming a "man of war." Belmont had joined the Army to assist the United States in

Figure 2.12. Paul Cravath and August Belmont Jr. (left to right). Library of Congress, Prints & Photographs Division, LC-DIG-ggbain-14604.

getting aid and supplies into Spain. The war was the reason that Belmont had decided to dispose of a large number of his race-horses. Years later, he said that his biggest regret was selling his favorite yearling, Man o' War, to Samuel Riddle.[36] Man o' War (1917–1947) won twenty of his twenty-one races and became one of the greatest racehorses of all time.

Wendell Goodwin

Wendell Goodwin signed the club's certificate of incorporation, but only occasionally rode with the hunt. He had grown up outside of Boston and graduated in 1874 from Harvard, where he was praised for his athletic prowess, especially in crew.[37] He moved to Brooklyn, New York, where he formed a partnership (Goodwin-Swift) to promote and build electric railroads (trolleys) in the area.[38] He planned to fill his trolley cars with spectators for his other venture, a Brooklyn baseball team. Goodwin served as president of the Players' League and worked to bring his team to Brooklyn.[39] The businesses were codependent, and when the Brooklyn team joined the National League, the Player's League failed, as did Goodwin's trolley business.[40] By 1894, Goodwin was ruined financially and, perhaps, mentally. He suffered from "incurable paresis" and was moved to an institution in Litchfield, Connecticut, where he died at age forty-five on March 1, 1898.[41]

However, Goodwin did leave his mark on baseball. During the early years, Brooklynites tried out many names for their local team: the Grays, the Bridegrooms, the Grooms, and the Robins. Nothing stuck. To get to the ball field, spectators had to cross Goodwin's trolley tracks, which was daunting to many, because the electric cars moved so much faster than the old horse-drawn ones. Spectators and players alike dashed between trolleys, and their antics gave them the name "Brooklyn Trolley Dodgers." This was soon shortened to Brooklyn Dodgers, a team name that did stick. The Dodgers part stayed with the team when it relocated to Los Angeles. Who knows what they would have been called without Goodwin's trolleys?

Colonel William Jay

William Jay was a descendant of John Jay, a founding father of the United States. The family homestead is preserved in Katonah, New York. When the Civil War broke out soon after his graduation from Columbia University, William joined the Union Army. He served on General George Meade's staff and rose to the rank of lieutenant colonel. After the war, he graduated from Columbia Law School and established a successful legal practice in New York City. He was also vice president of the *New-York Herald*, which might have been a reason for the newspaper's detailed coverage of foxhunting. Jay married Lucy Oelrichs in 1878, and they had a daughter, Eleanor, in 1882, who years later became Mrs. Arthur Iselin, a name much associated with Long Island.[42]

While both Jay and his wife rode with Meadow Brook, Mrs. Jay's name appeared more often than her husband's in articles about the hunt. The colonel's interests lay primarily with polo and coaching. He and his friend, Colonel DeLancey Kane, were co-owners of the first four-in-hand coach to be imported to America from England and founders of the Coaching Club. In the time of railroads, electric trolleys, and eventually automobiles, these few enthusiasts sought to preserve the historic coaches and to breed quality horses to pull them. The annual parade of coaches down Fifth Avenue and coaches' appearances at racecourses and horse shows were festive and popular for many years.

Edwin Denison Morgan III

Edwin Denison Morgan III was a Harvard graduate, class of 1877. His grandfather was the governor of New York and one of the founders of the New York Republican Party in the time of Abraham Lincoln. In his memoir, Morgan revealed that he became interested in foxhunting when he was returning from Europe with Tom Hitchcock in 1881. After he joined Meadow Brook, he house-hunted with August Belmont Jr. as his real estate guide. Together, they found his first house, which he called The Alcazar, located on Front Street and Hendrickson Avenue in Hempstead.

In his *Recollections*, Morgan recounted his reluctance to install a telephone at the house, because he did not want any ugly poles. He swore that his people "would cut them down as fast as they go up." However, when the telephone salesman informed him that they already had permission to put the poles on the other side of the street, Morgan readily agreed.[43] The story is humorous, because when Morgan decided to build his grand estate a few years later, he needed electricity for it, so he founded Nassau Light & Power Co.[44] The company was later sold to Long Island Light Company, which has been responsible for many poles (ugly or otherwise) all over Long Island.

Morgan purchased more than six hundred acres of land on a rise called Wheatley Hill just outside Westbury and hired McKim, Mead, and White to design a house. He called the estate Wheatly. (The name is spelled without the second *e* throughout Morgan's memoir.) The house was the first really large construction in the "colony." It stood three stories high and two hundred feet wide, and the estate included stables for hunters, polo ponies, and carriages; a chapel; a swimming pool; and many farm buildings.[45] The grounds were planted with mature trees from

Hicks Nursery; a photograph of moving these huge trees was included in Morgan's memoir. The house was demolished in the 1950s, but some of the acreage still exists as the Glen Oaks Country Club.[46]

In 1886, Morgan became a bit of a celebrity, when he and Mrs. Morgan, Stanley Mortimer, and Thomas Hitchcock were sailing home from Liverpool, England. They were onboard the SS *Oregon*, considered the fastest ship afloat at that time. On March 6, before sunrise, an unidentified schooner struck the *Oregon* fifteen miles from New York, off the coast of Fire Island. The schooner sank at once, and the *Oregon* soon followed. The steamer was not equipped with an ample number of lifeboats, and the passengers and crew were only saved by ships that raced to their aid.[47] Meadow Brook's M.F.H., Morgan, was proclaimed a hero for the selfless assistance he rendered.[48] His young wife, Mary Penniman Morgan, became ill later that summer. Some suggested the stress of the shipwreck had caused the illness.[49] When she died in Newport in August, the official cause of death was typhoid fever.[50]

August Belmont Purdy

A. Belmont "Bob" Purdy came from a family of horsemen. Both his grandfather, Samuel, and father, John F. Purdy, were famous horsemen in their day. By profession, Samuel Purdy had been an architect, but he was known as "a gentleman rider and known throughout the country as an expert judge of horseflesh and a trainer of marked ability." He owned American Eclipse (foaled May 25, 1814), one of the most important racehorses of his day.[51]

His son, John F. Purdy, was a stockbroker, wine merchant, and horseman. He was also a close friend of August Belmont

Sr., who, according to his biographer, was the "King of Fifth Avenue" and one of the wealthiest men in the country.[52] Years earlier, in 1841, John F. had served as Belmont's second in a duel, the outcome of which left Belmont shot in the hip and John F. Purdy stretched out on the ground in a faint.[53] However, the friendship endured, and John F. named his only son August Belmont Purdy. John F. was famous in the equine world. He held the record for driving his trotting mare, Kate, one hundred miles in 9 hours 49¾ minutes (including rest stops). Kate lived to be thirty-six years old, so it must be assumed that the race did her no harm.[54]

Bob Purdy took after both his grandfather Sam and father John. He was a professional wine merchant and a noted horseman. In his youth, he and other future Meadow Brook members made names for themselves as gentlemen (amateur) riders in steeplechase races held throughout Maryland, New Jersey, and New York in the 1870s and 1880s. In the hunting field, Purdy was reported to be an excellent rider using the English style, "with a long rein and short stirrup."[55] His wife, Bertha Gillet Purdy, rode with him, following both the Queens County and Meadow Brook hounds. She was the first of several ladies to be crowned a Meadow Brook "Diana," after the goddess of the hunt, noted for her skill and beauty.

By 1889, she was a mother and became more cautious. She told a newspaper reporter that she no longer wanted her husband to ride, because of the danger.[56] Within two years, Bob Purdy resigned from the Meadow Brook Hunt, and over the next decade he suffered many unrelated reverses of fortune. Details of his divorce and bankruptcy were splashed on gossip and financial pages.[57] Little more was heard about him, except when he officiated at a horse race or dog show. He escorted his daughter and only child, Bertha, down the aisle when she married William Beers in October 1911. But even that was short-lived happiness; the bride's obituary appeared in *The New York Times* on June 1, 1912.[58]

Throughout his life, Bob Purdy wrote articles on hounds, horses, and riding. In 1905, he championed the cause of women who rode astride.[59] Much of his work was never published, and Purdy boasted of a room screen in his apartment with its panels covered with rejection letters, which, he bragged, were from every extant magazine and newspaper.[60] Purdy's name came up in a libel case against *Collier's Weekly*, and it was revealed that he was a secret source of gossip for the magazine.[61] After, Purdy vanished from the news columns. He died after a short illness on May 23, 1919, at his sister's home in Hempstead. The notice appeared in *The New York Times* and contained no mention of his relationship to Meadow Brook.[62]

Elliott B. Roosevelt

Elliott B. Roosevelt was President Theodore Roosevelt's younger, and only, brother. When Elliott married Anna Hall in 1883, the couple set up two households—one in the city and another in a rented house in Hempstead. Their daughter, Anna Eleanor, who would grow up to be the wife of Franklin Delano Roosevelt and First Lady of the United States, was born October 11, 1884. When she was three, Elliott built his country estate, called Half Way Nirvana, in the Salisbury section in Hempstead. The house has long since been torn down and the acreage dissected for housing developments, but the town of Hempstead designated the location of Eleanor Roosevelt's childhood home a historic landmark in 2014.[63]

Half Way Nirvana was in the thick of the foxhunting and polo country, perfect for Elliott's favorite pastimes, but perhaps not so beneficial for his well-being. Elliott suffered from alcoholism and probably an addiction to drugs. In 1888, Theodore wrote to their sister, Anna, that he was worried about his brother. "I do hate his Hempstead life. . . . It is certainly unhealthy, and leads to nothing."[64] Shortly after, Theodore delivered the same message in a speech about "The American Boy."

> There is, of course, always the risk of thus mistaking means for ends. Fox-hunting is a first-class sport; but one of the most absurd things in real life is to note the bated breath with which certain excellent fox-hunters, otherwise of quite healthy minds, speak of this admirable but not over-important pastime. They tend to make it almost as much of a fetish as, in the last century, the French and German nobles made the chase of the stag, when they carried hunting and game-preserving to a point which was ruinous to the national life. Fox-hunting is very good as a pastime, but it is about as poor a business as can be followed by any man of intelligence. . . . Of course, in reality the chief serious use of fox-hunting is to encourage manliness and vigor, and to keep men hardy, so that at need they can show themselves fit to take part in work or strife for their native land. When a man so far confuses ends and means as to think that fox-hunting, or polo, or foot-ball, or whatever else the sport may be, is to be itself taken as the end, instead of as the mere means of preparation to do work that counts when the time arises, when the occasion calls—why, that man had better abandon sport altogether.[65]

Elliott Roosevelt died at age thirty-four on August 14, 1894.

William R. Travers

William R. Travers was one of the founders of Saratoga Race Course, and the Travers Stake, a prestigious horse race, was named to honor him. In 1881, Travers had a great deal of experience and guided the younger members of the Meadow Brook Club. He died in March 1887, and *The New York Times* said he was "the most popular man in New York" because of his wit and good humor. The obituary illustrated this by retelling an exchange that took place in New York City when Travers bumped into a childhood friend from his hometown, Baltimore:

The friend said, "Why Bill, you stutter worse now than you did in Baltimore."

"H–h–have to," answered Mr. Travers laconically; "b–b–b–bigger city."[66]

THREE

The Second Decade

Master: The Master of Foxhounds (M.F.H.), the
person (male or female) who is responsible for the
hunting and the organization of the country. Much
like the captain on a ship, the Master's word is law for
those in the hunting field. He or she is responsible for
making sure rules and traditions are upheld, and that
everyone is under control and safe.

In 1889, the Meadow Brook Club records listed seventy-two
active members, five honorary members, and twenty couples of
English foxhounds.[1] Thomas Hitchcock Sr. served as M.F.H.
at Meadow Brook for four years, and later the club's annual
reports incorrectly credited him with initiating live foxhunting.
Throughout the 1880s, the Meadow Brook hounds hunted
foxes and chased after the anise-seed bag.

The appointment of M.F.H. was voted on each January,
and Hitchcock had only held the position a few weeks when he

Figure 3.1. *The Meadow Brook Hunt at Westbury, Long Island, 1892. Thomas Hitchcock, Master.* **From the Collection of the Meadow Brook Club.**

had to deal with the hunt's first fatality. The hunt met Monday, March 18, 1889, at the fairgrounds in nearby Mineola. The hounds had been running about an hour and a half when, crossing Mr. Titus's land near Westbury, Samuel Stevens "Sammy" Sands Jr.'s horse fell and rolled on his rider. Sands's thigh was broken. He was transported to his home in Garden City, but on Thursday, he died from "congestion of the lungs." Club Secretary Frank Appleton recorded that the fatality was "supposedly due to the fall and the subsequent exposure" in the hunt field. Appleton noted the club's lament over the loss of such a young and active member. Sands had been captain of the polo team and an avid foxhunter who never missed a meet.[2]

The day after Sands's funeral, a letter appeared in the *New-York Tribune* protesting the dangerous sport of foxhunting and the waste of such a young man. The author repeated a long-standing criticism about upper-class Americans only liking the sport because it was so British.[3] Sands's death altered the tone of future newspaper accounts. While reporters continued to cover the hunt, there was less glamorization of the sport and more detail of accidents and falls ("croppers").

There was no response from Meadow Brook. In his memoirs, Foxhall Keene praised Master Hitchcock, who "kept the hunt at concert pitch" with many fine runs "over the rolling North Shore Country." Keene delighted in jumping fences that were "ungodly big."[4] Sensing that members wanted more hunting, not less, Hitchcock took them off the Hempstead Plains as far east as Smithtown and claimed that country for Meadow Brook.[5] He negotiated invitations for them to hunt on Staten Island with the Richmond Hunt Club.[6]

On August 27, 1891, Thomas Hitchcock married Louise "Loulie" Eustis from Washington, District of Columbia, daughter of the late Louisiana Congressman George Eustis Jr. and granddaughter of William W. Corcoran, philanthropist and founder of the Corcoran Gallery of Art in Washington. Like her husband, Loulie was an outstanding rider and devoted to fox-hunting. The Hitchcock marriage took place in Beverly, Massachusetts, and was "a modest affair, with no display of jewels." The newlyweds traveled to Newport and Long Island before embarking on an extended trip to France.[7]

The Hitchcocks settled in Old Westbury, in the heart of Meadow Brook country, and called their estate Broad Hollow Farm. Surrounding them were the Belmonts, Beaches, Birds, Whitneys, Morgans, and other households who enjoyed foxhunting, polo, shooting, sailing, tennis, and golf. In the summer, many of these families relocated to Newport, Rhode Island. But after a while, some of the vacationers tired of swimming, tennis, sailing, and golf. Society pages were filled with details of parties where hosts and hostesses competed in providing the most innovative entertainment. During a Fourth of July celebration, Meadow Brook members Eloise and James P. "Jimmy" Kernochan brought in a large cow that the delighted guests milked.[8] Cows were fine, but the foxhunters wanted to ride, so the Meadow Brook hounds were brought up for some preseason training.

The Hitchcocks were part of the summer Newport colony, but Loulie Hitchcock soon introduced her husband to another part of the country. As a child, she had been considered frail, so in the winter her aunt whisked her off to Aiken, South Carolina. When M.F.H. Hitchcock visited the Aiken area, he realized its foxhunting and polo playing potential. Long Island weather dictated that the hounds could only hunt from October through December and from March to April. But in Aiken's milder climate, he could continue hunting in January and February. In December 1891, Hitchcock requested permission to take the Meadow Brook hounds south for two months. The stewards called an emergency meeting.[9]

Could the hounds and all the related equipment be loaned out to a member, even if the member was the Master? What sort of precedent were they setting? On the other hand, the hounds did travel to Newport in the summer. After much discussion, they agreed that half the pack could go. Edwin Morgan, Francis Appleton, and Robert Stuart were charged with sorting and ensuring that an adequate number of hounds, horses, and hunting equipment remained on Long Island.[10]

Throughout January and February 1892, Hitchcock and William C. Whitney hunted the Meadow Brook hounds in Aiken. The English foxhounds did not meet their expectations, and Hitchcock became an advocate for hunting with American foxhounds. Some felt that this criticism was unjustified, because the borrowed Meadow Brook hounds had primarily hunted the anise-seed bag.

Meanwhile, back on chilly Long Island, the Meadow Brook foxhunters wanted their hounds back. The stewards called a second special meeting. At Delmonico's Restaurant in New York City on January 28, 1892, they rewrote a section of their constitution. Article II was revised: "The Meadow Brook Club is organized in order to support and hunt in the proper season a pack of foxhounds, exclusively on Long Island, and to encourage and furnish for its members and the community at large the means of drag-hunting and other out-door sports and games." The phrase "exclusively on Long Island" was new.

Hitchcock returned with the hounds and resumed his duties as M.F.H. for the spring season. He and his wife were often complimented for the handsome picture they made on their matched chestnut thoroughbreds, Good Times and Hard Times. The newspapers regarded Mrs. Hitchcock as the "first lady" of the hunt and "the best woman rider in the country."[11]

During Hitchcock's mastership, a group of young men garnered attention when they created a club within the club. They called themselves "The Bulldags," and their hunting days were dominated by a single rule: any member who could not keep up with the Meadow Brook Drag, unless he had two falls or was badly hurt by one, had to buy dinner for the whole club at the end of the day. This resulted in competitive and, occasionally, reckless racing in the field. The Bulldag membership consisted of J. D. R. Baldwin, Rawlins L. Cottenet, Charles L. Cottenet, W. C. Hayes, Harry S. Page, C. Albert Stevens, and William Tiffany. Later, they added the somewhat younger "Bull Pups" Columbus Baldwin, Belmont Tiffany, Maxwell Stevenson, and Henry W. Bull.[12] Most of the Bulldags had rooms in the Meadow Brook clubhouse. They took their meals and drank together,

Figure 3.2. *"Bulldag" Charles Albert Stevens, Member of the Board of Stewards, 1895–98.* From the Collection of the Meadow Brook Club.

bellowed out songs composed by "their bard" Rawlins, held impromptu sparring matches, and took horses out on wild rides. One night, garbed only in their pajamas, the Bulldags saddled up and steeplechased through the countryside. Their escapades were not appreciated by the senior membership.[13]

Two of the best riders in the Bulldags were the Cottenet brothers, Rawlins, Meadow Brook's first whipper-in, and his older sibling, Charles, nicknamed "Little Minch" due to his short stature. On October 12, 1892, the Meadow Brook hounds met at Syosset. M.F.H. Hitchcock was home tending a sick daughter, so Rawlins took over the Master's duties. John Abdale was the whipper-in.[14] At the Syosset-Woodbury crossroads, the hounds turned southeast and headed across a field. At the far side was a fence line with several jumpable panels, so the riders fanned out. Stanley Mortimer was on the right, next was Henry L. Herbert on the high jumper Transport, and then came Harry Page on The Heeler and Charles Cottenet on a fast gray called Dixie.

"Bulldags forever," shouted Charles. "Which first?"

Harry Page replied, "My horse rushes; I'll go first."

Harry spurred on The Heeler, who jumped high and cleared the fence, but as he jumped, Harry spied a strand of barbed wire about three inches above the top rail. He landed and turned in his saddle to warn Charles, but it was too late. Dixie's forelegs snagged the wire. The big mare somersaulted, flipping over and crashing down on her rider.

Harry, Stanley Mortimer, and Rawlie rushed over.[15] Charles was unconscious and bleeding from his mouth and nose, so they carried him to a nearby farmhouse. Two doctors arrived, but the internal injuries were too severe.[16] Cottenet died a few hours later on his thirty-first birthday.[17]

The front page of *The New York Times* screamed, "Time to Call a Halt: Danger in Reckless Riding to Hounds." The article cited disgust among members of the Union, Knickerbocker, and Calumet clubs, where Charles had many friends. It was "high time for the hunting set" to stop the wild riding over rough and unsuitable country.

Meadow Brook members countered that there had only been two deaths in the club's eleven-year history. But, the opponents pointed out, there had been no fatalities with the Rockaway, Richmond, or Essex Hunts. And, it was not only the deaths that gave cause for concern. Within the last few weeks, Robert Center, Ralph Ellis, and Frank Appleton had each received severe injuries. Whenever anyone arrived at his club limping or bandaged, all he had to do was mutter, "The Meadow Brook Hunt," in lieu of explanation.

Reporters interviewed some of the ladies. Mrs. Sidney Dillon Ripley said she objected to her husband hunting with Meadow Brook, because of the danger. As for the women themselves, only a few expert riders, such as May Bird and Eloise Stevenson Kernochan, still hunted. While the club roster boasted seventy-four members, only about twenty-five comprised the "hunting set." The article ended with this: "It seems such a crying sin that a brave young life should be taken away in pursuit of what even the most amateurish sportsman cannot help but feel is, to a certain extent, a childish and foolish pastime."[18]

Other articles followed. Some were more evenhanded, mentioning that this particular accident was not due to reckless riding, but to the dangerous placement of wire atop panels in the hunting field.[19]

The stewards decided to cease hunting for a short time out of respect, but then bad weather and "dissensions within the club" stopped all hunting until March. During the hiatus, Hitchcock resigned, stating that he had to devote his attentions to forming his own pack in Aiken. The stewards of Meadow Brook looked about and found Frank Gray Griswold.[20]

Griswold had left his position as M.F.H. at the Rockaway Hunting Club in 1888 following a financial dispute. He claimed that he'd underwritten at least fifteen thousand dollars of the hunt's expense during his five years as Master. When Rockaway proposed to further decrease the monies allotted for the hunt, Griswold picked up his hunting horn and took his horses and hounds home to nearby East Williston.[21] Meadow Brook had been providing its M.F.H. with 50 percent (recently reduced from 60 percent) of the total hunt subscription income, not to exceed five thousand dollars per annum. The Master had total control of this money, allocating it to maintain horses, hounds, and servants necessary for general hunting.[22] The stewards of-

fered these conditions, and Griswold agreed. He was listed as
Master of Meadow Brook in the first listing of hunt clubs in the
Steeplechase, Hunt, and Pony Racing Association in 1894.[23]

Griswold "was the perfect type of sportsman . . . with a long
handle-bar mustache and twinkling eyes that seemed to mock his
exaggeratedly sporting manner of dressing."[24] He had been edu-
cated abroad, receiving his college degree in Dresden, Germany.
While he was always interested in horses—showing, hunting,
riding, jumping, and racing them—they weren't his sole pursuit.

Figure 3.3.   Frank Gray Griswold, M.F.H. Meadow Brook Hounds 1893–95,
Queens County Hounds 1877–93. From the Collection of the Meadow Brook
Club.

From 1879 to 1893, he worked as a director of the Lorillard Tobacco Company. During foxhunting season, he would hunt in the morning, catch a train to New York City by 8:30 a.m., and be at his Jersey City office by 10:00 a.m.[25]

Griswold's return attracted people. James F. D. Lanier, Mr. and Mrs. Cooper Hewitt, Mr. and Mrs. Edward Potter, Anna Sands, Mr. and Mrs. Egerton Winthrop Jr., William Jay, Henry L. Herbert, Charles Grenville Peters, E. Willard Roby, Oliver W. Bird, J. W. Stevens, Henry S. Field, Kinsley Magoun, Rawlins Cottenet, and Mr. and Mrs. James Kernochan returned to the field.

On Saturday, April 1, the meet was set for Roslyn. Eager hounds and ready horses were brought by grooms to the railroad station at around 2:30 p.m. At 3:30 p.m., the Long Island Rail Road train pulled into the station. Thirty riders, who had changed into their hunting apparel in the baggage car, mounted up. The hounds were put on the scent of an anise-seed bag, which led them over a course of two miles through several fields, where angry farmers yelled at them to leave. Unabashed, the hunters headed toward the Roslyn Tower, where their kennelman waited with a "bagged" fox. When the hounds approached, he released the fox, and a live chase ensued. After a brief, fast run, the hounds killed.[26]

News articles covering hunts using bagged foxes such as this highlighted another problem for Meadow Brook. Long Island residents complained loudly and often about the importation of foxes, which the hunt brought in from upstate New York and Pennsylvania. These foreign reynards were decimating their poultry businesses.

A bagged fox gave a good chase for the hunters, because the disoriented animal had no idea which way to run. All it could do was run fast from the trailing hounds and provide an exciting

Figure 3.4. Meadow Brook Hounds meeting at the Roslyn Clock Tower. From the Bryant Library Local History Collection, Roslyn NY.

gallop for the riders.[27] While the practice weighed the outcome in favor of the hounds, over the years many foxes escaped and settled down to enjoy the good life on Long Island. Stephen Underhill of Jericho claimed that he'd lost one hundred ducks to

foxes during the summer of 1890.[28] Residents in Locust Valley
and Oyster Bay complained that their poultry flocks had been
decimated. By 1894, the outcry was so loud that the Queens
County Board of Supervisors made it (1) illegal to import foxes,
(2) imposed a two-hundred-dollar fine per imported fox or other
varmint, and (3) offered a five-dollar bounty per dead fox.[29]

Griswold returned to drag hunting, with the provision that
the hounds could pursue a live fox if they came upon one. A
friend of Griswold's, an Englishman and well-known foxhunter,
Captain E. Pennell-Elmhirst, visited Meadow Brook in 1892
and in 1894. He described his experiences for *The Field* magazine using the nom de plume "Brooksby." He noted that the
Meadow Brook meet was fast, challenging, and populated by
much younger riders than in England.[30] At the opening meet in
1894, he estimated that twenty riders and a coterie of carriages
and carts followed the hounds. Brooksby guessed that the chari-
oteers had been informed of the route, because they sped along
the unpaved roads and managed to keep up with the hounds and
horsemen, who jumped through the fenced fields.

> Now for a sense of Long Island. Look right and look left. No
> escape. Each twenty acre field is bound round with these
> great mortised fences; and gates are as little known. . . . One
> spot is altogether the same as another; our leader follows in
> the track of hounds; and the first four-footer is flown without
> rap of hoof or even refusal. The second is like unto it—but can
> claim a few inches more, with the advantage or otherwise of
> a slight drop. Ah, what a delicious sensation!—the bound of
> a freegoing horse, eager for his jump and careful of his stride.
> 'Tis like a gasp of mountain air again, that one breathes in the
> few seconds of that voyage aloft. I have always held that a fair
> pace at strong timber is best and safest—as it is certainly most

pleasurable. I find my theory indorsed [*sic*] again and again among these timber jumpers of America.[31]

All this praise and good hunting could not entice Griswold to stay. He resigned as M.F.H. in the spring of 1895, explaining that he wanted to hunt in England for the next two years.[32] However, later he wrote that "I had much trouble with Rockaway and Meadow Brook," and "I stuck it out 20 years. It ended in my being elected Honorary Member (1887) of the Meadow Brook Club and later made Master. They offered me the Mastership several times in later years also. It was one grand fight though and disgusted me with human nature."[33]

Many thought the next Master would be James L. "Jimmie" Kernochan.[34] He was active in all areas of the club and experienced. He had a private pack of Hempstead beagles, which he occasionally hunted alongside the hounds.[35] However, some judged him too young at twenty-seven, and when votes were tallied, he received only three and Ralph Nicholson Ellis, seventeen.

Ellis was a thirty-seven-year-old bachelor from Cincinnati, Ohio, who was ready and willing to devote all his time to hunting. He undertook a serious study of the sport and traveled abroad to observe long-established hunts. He researched and wrote on the topic. In *The Book of Sport*, he recorded the history of drag and foxhunting in America and professed that the American red fox was larger, wilder, and more difficult to hunt than its English cousin.[36] In addition, the North American country necessitated longer and harder gallops. He concluded that American foxhunting needed time to evolve. Great hunting would only develop when huntsmen attained more skills, available only through experience and study. The same applied to the foxhounds; they needed to be bred selectively for traits best

Figure 3.5.   Ralph N. Ellis, M.F.H. William Patten, ed. *Book of Sport* (New York: Taylor, 1901), 193.

suited for the locale. For example, most American foxhounds must "range wider" than those hunting in the English countryside. An American foxhound often needed to run a long distance to support its fellow hounds, much farther than foxhounds in England. Finally, Ellis concluded, the varying soils and climates in the United States required foxhounds bred for specific regions.

While foxhunting was in this stage of flux, Ellis pronounced drag hunting as the temporary, acceptable alternative. He berated the newspaper stories that mocked the chase of the aniseseed bag. In fact, he felt that drag hunting should be encouraged as the most democratic sport in America. Less time was wasted when the hunt's path was predetermined, and that convenience enabled both the rural population and city professionals to participate side-by-side as equals.

Finally, Ellis condemned the press for its coverage of accidents in the hunting field. Misleading and exaggerated reports had hurt the sport, specifically the Meadow Brook Club. He said that not one in ten of the reported falls ever occurred. He knew many accounts were fabricated for sensationalism, and some had incited unnecessary fear in family members. He knew of articles written by ignorant scribblers and, even worse, liars. He had read detailed descriptions of entire hunts that had, in reality, been canceled that day due to bad weather.[37]

Ellis began his first season at Meadow Brook with panache. He contacted hunt and riding clubs throughout New York, Massachusetts, New Jersey, Pennsylvania, Maryland, Virginia, and Canada. They were invited to join Meadow Brook for a drag hunt on October 19. About seventy riders from a dozen different hunts accepted. The largest and showiest contingent came from the Richmond Club on Staten Island. Their riders, horses, and a four-in-hand break (large open carriage) arrived on a hired boat that docked in Roslyn Harbor. The whole party disembarked and paraded to the clubhouse amid much fanfare.

That day, the Meadow Brook Club was also hosting a golf tourney between Winthrop Rutherford, representing Newport Golf, and Charles E. Sands, from St. Andrew's, Scotland.[38] About two hundred riders, golfers, and spectators enjoyed a festive lunch before setting out on their separate ways. Reports of the day described the clubhouse as "quaint," but with "no pretensions to architectural beauty."[39] It consisted of two wooden buildings whose second stories were linked together by a covered bridge, under which one passed to reach the stables.[40]

The blue sky and autumn leaves on the trees created a picture-perfect backdrop for the many "huntsmen, horsewomen, stylish traps, and well-groomed horses" gathered on the grounds.[41] At 3:15 p.m., Master Ellis readied the field of riders. The huntsman blew his horn, and the hounds moved off. The large field followed Ellis for about ten miles "of the prettiest bits of the northern country" and over many "formidable jumps." The only mishap occurred when William C. Hayes had a cropper, in which he broke two ribs, but it "was not deemed of great consequence." Additional onlookers followed in their traps and carriages. The chase ended about a mile east of Roslyn.[42]

When the riders returned home to the clubhouse, they discovered another hunt underway—for two-legged varmints. Two men, disguised as late-arriving huntsmen, had shown counterfeit invitations and displayed much anguish at missing the chase. The servants permitted them inside to wait for the hunt's return. Once there, the thieves entered the men's changing rooms and stole more than five thousand dollars' worth of jewelry, cash, and clothing.[43] The robbers were never apprehended.

The foxhunters were not deterred. The following Thursday at 3:00 p.m., Ralph Ellis greeted another large field on the club grounds. Many were there to view Mr. and Mrs. James Kernochan's houseguest, the ninth Duke of Marlborough. Lord Spencer-Churchill was passing a few days on Long Island before his marriage to Consuelo Vanderbilt, the daughter of Alva and William K. Vanderbilt. The duke rode the Kernochans' big chestnut horse, Rebel, and he kept up with the best of them, racing through East Williston, Roslyn, and circling back to Old Westbury. He finished second only to Thomas Hitchcock and in plenty of time to catch the 4:50 p.m. train to the city.[44]

M.F.H. Ellis was probably more interested in English foxhounds than dukes. The next year, 1896, he imported a new pack of English hounds and used them to chase live foxes. Ellis admitted that they performed with moderate success,[45] but a year later, they seemed to be working better, gaining praise for a fine chase over twelve miles and seventy fences.[46] Ellis's kennel expanded as he searched for the perfect genetic combination for Meadow Brook. He developed an English drag pack that went out Tuesday, Thursday, and Saturday afternoons, and his own private American pack that hunted foxes on Monday, Wednesday, and Friday mornings.[47]

In the mid-1890s, Meadow Brook country expanded. During the fall of 1895, William C. Whitney used real estate brokers to quietly purchase fifteen separate pieces of land. By the end of the year, he had acquired ten thousand acres in Wheatley Hills, sprawling out across the backbone of the island, extending from the town of Oyster Bay and to North Hempstead. Whitney's land lay roughly between the estates of E. D. Morgan and J. Stanley Mortimer.[48] Fortunately, everyone hunted with Meadow Brook.

When, in 1894, a nonhunter purchased a large section of prime hunting country, he had to be taught the unwritten rules of the colony. General Joseph T. Torrence, a steel and railroad tycoon from Chicago, who enjoyed bragging that his fur coat cost ten thousand dollars, bought many acres and built a large house for his daughter, Jessie. It was a present when she wed Meadow Brook's Kinsley Magoun. The young couple left the design and construction up to General Torrence, while they went away on a long honeymoon. When they returned, they were horrified by the general's six-foot-high wire fence encircling the property. This was simply not done in hunting country. The young couple feared "social extinction." The contractor refused to remove the fence, because there were some outstanding bills, so General Torrence hopped on an eastbound train and took care of the matter. The expensive fence was removed almost as fast as it had gone up.[49]

A few years later, in 1898, the United States became concerned about its neighbors, in particular the Spanish occupation of Cuba. Theodore Roosevelt had a national position by then; he was assistant secretary of the Navy. When the sinking of the *Maine* in the Havana Harbor triggered America's declaration of war against Spain on April 25, Roosevelt resigned. He announced the formation of a cavalry unit—the Rough Riders.

This volunteer troop was characterized by "cowboys" from states such as Montana and Wyoming; "society boys" from Harvard, Yale, and Princeton; and "clubmen" from the Somerset in Boston, Knickerbocker in New York, and Meadow Brook on Long Island. Meadow Brook's Woodbury "Woody" Kane, at age thirty-nine, was one of the most senior volunteers. Two years behind Roosevelt at Harvard, Woodbury had been "a close friend" and someone with whom Roosevelt rode when foxhunting.[50] Two Meadow Brook Bulldags also joined: William "Willie" Tiffany and Henry W. Bull. The Kane and Tiffany families independently funded some expensive guns Roosevelt wanted for the expedition. The twin machine guns, costing ten thousand dollars apiece, were known as the "Tiffany guns." Each of the Meadow Brook members survived the battles, but Willie Tiffany died soon after in Boston from diseases contracted in Cuba. His death was widely covered in the press, and two Bulldags, Rawlins Cottenet and Henry Bull, were pallbearers at the funeral.

That autumn, Theodore Roosevelt parlayed his Rough Rider fame into political currency and was elected governor of New York. Meadow Brook Hunt Club cheered their neighbor and fellow clubman as he readied to move to Albany. Other changes were occurring on the Hempstead Plains. As of January

1, 1899, the Meadow Brook Club and all the neighboring land were no longer in Queens County, but in the brand new Nassau County.

MEADOW BROOK MEMBERS IN THE NEWS

Henry Worthington Bull

Henry Worthington Bull was the son of Mr. and Mrs. William Lanman Bull of New York City. His father was president of the New York Stock Exchange from 1888 to 1890, and later he invested in railroads, including the light rail on Staten Island. Henry graduated from Columbia University in 1896 and fox-hunted at Meadow Brook, where he was one of the Bulldags. He joined the Rough Riders and fought alongside Willie Tiffany in Company K. Henry rose from the rank of private to sergeant during the war, but his name was spelled incorrectly as *Buel* in the mustered-out rolls. His military record is correct in the National Archives, and contemporary reports verified his position. As reported previously, he and Rawlins Cottenet, another Meadow Brook Bulldag, served as pallbearers at Willie Tiffany's funeral.

Henry Bull's parents attended Grace Christ Episcopal Church in Manhattan, which sponsored a home for mothers and children in Far Rockaway. By 1899, the church had decided that the facilities were inadequate, so they moved the home to Stanford, Connecticut. The Bulls donated an adjoining Chapel of Peace as thanksgiving for their Henry's safe return from the battles in Cuba.

Henry Bull remained an active member in Meadow Brook. He served as acting Master, steward, and officer of the club. He stayed in touch with his fellow Rough Riders, and in 1910 he was selected to sail and hand deliver a reunion invitation to Teddy Roosevelt, who was in London following an African safari. Surprised and pleased to see an old friend, Roosevelt accepted and returned home in time to make the June 23 banquet.[51]

Professionally, Bull worked as a stockbroker, forming a partnership with Milton Holden. He was also president of the National Steeplechase and Hunt Association for ten years, and the Turf and Field Club for twenty-five.[52]

In 1904, he married Maud Livingston, who had been Willie Tiffany's fiancée. The Bulls were a popular couple and joined the Meadow Brook "annex" in Aiken, South Carolina. They

Figure 3.6. Henry Bull. William Patten, ed. *Book of Sport* (New York: Taylor, 1901), 208.

never had any children of their own, and when Maud's sister left her husband, they took in her two children as their legal wards. One of the children, Phyllis Livingston Baker, grew up and married the dancer and actor Fred Astaire. Fred Astaire and Henry Bull shared an interest in horses. In his autobiography, Astaire chronicled his first official racehorse: "Triplicate picked up his first race at Jamaica, New York, in my colors. These colors, incidentally, were formerly carried by Phyllis' Uncle Henry Bull, as a gentleman steeplechase jockey some years back. He turned them over to me, for which I was deeply grateful."[53] Henry died in 1958 and Maud in 1962. They were buried in Oakwood Memorial Park, outside Los Angeles, next to Phyllis and Fred Astaire.

Charles, Rawlins, and Fannie Cottenet

Edward Laight Cottenet was of French descent and the son of Francis Cottenet, a New York importer and merchant. He married Mary Huger Lowndes from Charleston, South Carolina, and his sister married William C. Schermerhorn of New York. Edward and Mary had three children: Charles Laight was born in 1861, Rawlins in 1866, and Fannie five years later.[54] Their grandfather, Francis Cottenet, and their father both died in 1884. With patronage from her well-connected sister-in-law, Mary Cottenet and the children remained in New York's high society. Charles was a popular and talented designer. Just before his death in the hunting field, he completed his work on the James Kernochans' house in Hempstead, The Meadows.[55] Afterward, his siblings, Fannie and Rawlins Cottenet, continued to hunt with Meadow Brook for many years.[56]

In 1893, Rawlins's inherited finances dwindled, and he had to find work. He opened a florist shop called The Rosary in

New York City, which was successful largely due to the patronage of Meadow Brook members.[57] Before joining the Rough Riders, Willie Tiffany became a business partner. The Rosary received much attention after it provided floral arrangements for two Vanderbilt weddings: Consuelo Vanderbilt's to the Duke of Marlborough, and Gertrude Vanderbilt's to Harry Payne Whitney. The fact that Rawlins was an usher at the latter wedding amused some.

> One of Harry Payne Whitney's ushers at his wedding will be Rawlins Loundes [*sic*] Cottenet. That is to say, one of young Mr. Whitney's most intimate friends, his supporter at the most important event of his life, is his florist, Rawlins Lowndes Cottenet.
>
> Mr. Cottenet, as usher, will wear at the wedding a boutonniere of lilies of the valley raised in the greenhouses of R. L. Cottenet, the florist. . . . He is an estimable young man who was not afraid to go to work and make his own living. This is, indeed, written for the benefit of those young men who have what is called "good blood" and a hatred for work, who have the ridiculous idea that men who work cannot be called gentlemen. . . . A very few years ago this fine young man of a fine family found that he had not as much money as he wanted. So he went to work. He opened a small florist's shop not far out of the shadow of the Knickerbocker Club, of which he is a member. Cholly and Reggy, without brains, sat in the club smoking-room and whispered, "Dweadful, eh? Rawley Cottenet's gone into the twade."
>
> They spoke in sorrow as if they said: "Rawley Cottenet was buried yesterday." But Mr. Cottenet had friends with brains as well as money. They stood by him. They sent orders for flowers to him. He flourished like his own fragrant buds and blossoms.[58]

When Samuel Sands's widow returned to New York in 1905 on the arm of her third husband, William K. Vanderbilt, she employed Rawlins Cottenet to arrange more than flowers. She hired the former "Bard of the Bulldags" to create evening musicales for the reopening celebration of the Vanderbilt mansion on Fifty-Second Street and Fifth Avenue.[59]

Rawlins went on to compose pieces that were performed by well-known artists, and he wrote articles on music and musical performances. In 1906, he sold his thriving flower shop and accepted a directorship on the board of the Metropolitan Opera.[60] Rawlins maintained homes on Long Island and in the city, but he, his mother, and sister frequently traveled abroad. In Italy, Rawlins heard an operatic tenor named Enrico Caruso, whom he convinced to travel to New York and join the Met.[61] Caruso stayed for eighteen seasons.

The youngest Cottenet, Fannie, was a charter member of the Colony Club and devoted much of her time to volunteer activities, including veterans of World War I and the National Orchestral Association.[62] Neither she nor her brother married, but together they hosted some of the most important musicians and music lovers of the period. Their apartment was featured in the September 1922 issue of *House and Garden*, and they donated art and heirlooms to the Museum of the City of New York and to the Gibbes Museum in Charleston, South Carolina.

Ralph N. Ellis

Ralph N. Ellis's father, John W. Ellis, had made his fortune as founder of the First National Bank in Cincinnati and as the director of the Northern Pacific Railroad. The family summered in Newport, where John built Stoneacre, a mansion famous for its grounds designed by Frederick Law Olmsted.[63]

Ralph Ellis had graduated from Harvard with his close friend, Teddy Roosevelt.[64] In the twenty-fifth reunion report, Ellis wrote that he attended law school at Harvard for two years and graduated from Columbia Law. He practiced as an attorney in Manhattan for several years, but then he turned all his attention to his estate, Bunga Fields, on Cedar Swamp Road, Jericho.[65] In 1906, he married Elizabeth Warder of Washington, District of Columbia, and they lived on Long Island, with additional homes in Maine and South Carolina. In addition to foxhunting, Ellis was a superior yachtsman. He died in 1930 while visiting his son, Ralph Jr., in Berkeley, California. Ralph Jr. was a naturalist and book collector. He donated his vast library (filling two railroad boxcars) to the University of Kansas. Many of his father's personal papers are also housed in the collection.

Frank Gray Griswold

After Frank Gray Griswold left his position at Meadow Brook, he traveled to England, where he managed Pierre Lorillard's racehorses for several years. In his spare time, he wrote more than twenty books on art, food, wine, cigars, opera, fishing, and riding. He returned to Long Island and served as a director of the Metropolitan Opera and a steward for the Jockey Club.[66]

Most considered him a confirmed bachelor, but in 1907, when he was fifty-three, he married a widow, Mrs. A. Cass Canfield (Josephine Houghteling), originally from Chicago. They lived at her estate, Cassleigh, in Roslyn. Her son, Cass Canfield, grew up to be president of Harper & Bros., the publisher of several of Griswold's books.[67] Frank and Josephine Griswold were married for thirty years, dying within months of each other in 1937.

Thomas and Louise "Loulie" Hitchcock

Thomas Hitchcock had mastered riding while in England—first during a college preparatory year and then while a student at Oxford University. His parents, Marie Louise Center and Thomas Hitchcock, had homes in New York City, the Rockaways, and Newport. His father was an attorney, author, journalist (under the nom de plume Matthew Marshall), and business partner of Charles Dana, owner of the *New York Sun* newspaper.[68] Both his older brothers, Center and Francis, grew up to become dedicated horsemen, and years later his son, "Tommy" Hitchcock Jr. (1900–1944), became the greatest polo player of all time and the inspiration for F. Scott Fitzgerald's Tom Buchanan in *The Great Gatsby* and Tommy Barban in *Tender Is the Night*.[69]

In *The Story of American Foxhunting*, Jan Blan Van Urk related an oft-repeated tale of Thomas and Loulie Hitchcock's foxhunt while honeymooning in Southampton in 1890. Supposedly, the Hitchcocks had a grand day during which the Meadow Brook hounds killed a fox "just below the eighteenth hole of the present National Golf Course."[70] This is probably a myth. The couple was not married until 1891, and the land for the National Golf Links was not purchased until 1908. Until the course was laid out, the land was covered in briars and bramble and was nothing more than a mosquito-infested swamp.[71]

The next year, 1891, Meadow Brook was invited to hunt the Shinnecock country by the recently disbanded Hampton Hunt. The field was large and included Loulie Hitchcock, but not her husband, whose absence was noted. Also, no fox was killed. One of the few complaints that day was the number of fence panels topped with barbed wire, but this danger was avoided, because the hounds were following a dragline.[72]

Thomas and Loulie Hitchcock are as renowned today in the equine world as they were a hundred years ago. Their love of steeplechase, polo, and riding to hounds created much of what is treasured in Aiken, South Carolina. Thomas was the premier trainer of steeplechase horses and such a venerated M.F.H. that he was elected president of the Master of Foxhounds Association four times.

Loulie Hitchcock was a champion of all riders, but many women owe her a special debt of gratitude. An injury forced her to ride astride, and her stature in the riding world made this seat acceptable. She encouraged women to play polo and became the first well-known female M.F.H. in the United States. When she died in 1934, following an accident on the hunting field in Aiken, her friend, polo student, and humorist, Will Rogers, wrote:

> She won't go to heaven in a chariot. She will go on horseback, and she won't holler for St. Peter to open the gate. I don't care how high the gate is, she will give that horse his head and kick him, and she will sail right over that gate, and old Peter will phone up to the Lord's Main House and say, "Look out, Lord, there's two thoroughbreds coming."[73]

Thomas Hitchcock died in September 1941.

Woodbury Kane

Captain Woodbury Kane was a descendant of John Jacob Astor and brother of Colonel Delancey Kane, the coaching friend of William Jay who was the first vice president of Meadow Brook. In his personal account of the Rough Riders, Theodore Roosevelt praised Woodbury for enlisting without

> seeking any position of distinction. All he desired was the chance to do whatever work he was put to do well, and to get

to the front; and he enlisted as a trooper. When I went down to the camp at San Antonio he was on kitchen duty, and was cooking and washing dishes for one of the New Mexican troops; and he was doing it so well that I had no further doubt as to how he would get on.[74]

Kane was promoted to captain of Troop K and, according to Roosevelt, became "perhaps the most useful soldier in the regiment."[75] Two of Kane's subordinates were the other Meadow Brook members, Willie Tiffany and Henry Bull.

After the short war, the U.S. government provided no financial assistance for the mustered out Rough Riders. Some had lost their jobs, others were sick, and there were dependents of the deceased. Woodbury Kane, Stanley and Richard Mortimer, and Belmont Tiffany gave a large sum of money to Roosevelt for those in need. Roosevelt persuaded anyone resisting the generosity by stating that the gift was part of a memorial for William Tiffany.[76]

When he returned home, Kane resumed his social life in Aiken, New York, and Newport, where he was a competitive yachtsman. A longtime bachelor, he surprised his friends with his marriage to the divorcee Sallie Hargous-Elliot in March 1905. Unfortunately, Woodbury caught a cold out duck hunting a few months later and died "from paralysis of the heart" in Manhattan on December 5 at age forty-seven.[77]

Woodbury left behind no children, but there was a favorite polo pony named Punch. Punch had been retired to a farm near Hyde Park, New York, where Woodbury had frequently visited him. Punch died May 22, 1910, at the record-breaking age of forty-five. The death was noted on the front page on *The New York Times*, and many attended Punch's burial on A. T. Jones's farm.[78]

Emily Stevens Ladenburg

Emily "Nellie" Stevens and her husband, Moritz Adolf Emil "Adolf" Ladenburg, were the young couple who had married before a hunt meet in 1884. He was a millionaire banker and a founder of Ladenburg and Thalmann. Emily had grown up in nearby Lawrence, and her brother, Eben Stevens, became a Master with the Rockaway Hunt. The Ladenburgs were popular with the polo, golf, and foxhunting sets as they traveled among homes in Newport, New York City, and on Long Island. In 1895, they had a daughter, Eugenie Mary "May."

The following winter, forty-two-year-old Adolf felt unwell, and his doctors advised him to seek a warmer climate. He traveled to Florida and on to Nassau, where he boarded the steamship *Niagara* for the voyage home. The seas were rough, and sometime during the night of February 14 he vanished. Eventually, it was agreed that he must have gone above deck for some reason and been washed overboard.[79] For years after, sightings of Adolf Ladenburg were reported around the world and discounted by friends and family.[80]

As a widow, Emily Ladenburg inherited a fortune and attracted a lot of gossip. She was immediately crowned the "loveliest widow," with "jet black hair, dark eyes, and a madonna-like, oval face . . . a beautiful forehead, which is never hidden by the hair and her features are clear cut."[81] Her only flaw was that she was too slender, because a plump woman looked better on a horse.[82]

The traditional period of mourning was two years, but a mere eight months after her husband vanished, the gossip columnists began matchmaking. Emily was reported engaged many times: to Meadow Brook's M.F.H. Ralph N. Ellis; to Alfred Beit, a diamond merchant and thought to be the richest man in

Figure 3.7. Emily Stevens Ladenburg jumping sidesaddle. Casper Whitney, ed. *Outing* magazine, April–September 1905, 65.

the world; to a recent college graduate, twenty-two-year-old Jay Phipps Jr. (Emily was forty years old at the time); and to John Jacob Astor. Several weeks after each announcement, a sentence would appear in the paper noting that the engagement had not materialized. Emily Ladenburg never remarried.

Emily made the news in 1906 when her daughter escaped an attempted kidnapping. From that time on, she told a reporter at least half the women who rode with the Meadow Brook

Hunt carried pistols.[83] Perhaps Emily's perceived need for self-protection led to her appreciation of boxing. She hosted several formal dinner parties, after which the guests adjourned to the coach house where a boxing ring had been set up. For several hours, a half-dozen fighters from a New York boxing club duked it out while an announcer explained the finer points of prize-fighting.[84]

Emily and May Ladenburg became women of the world. While May attended schools in Europe and the United States, her mother traveled and foxhunted around the world. Once, Emily testified that she had hunted with more than twenty different packs of hounds.[85] Her riding was gradually curtailed by age and from injuries in two accidents: one occurred in 1914, when she fell from a horse-drawn cart, and the other in an automobile crash in 1925. She continued to be involved in New York society until becoming ill in her seventy-fifth year. She died a few weeks later at her daughter's home in Westbury on August 9, 1937.[86]

Mrs. Ladenburg and the Sidesaddle

During the 1890s, one of the burning issues among the horsey-set was whether women had to ride sidesaddle. "Society" women were growing weary of the restrictions and danger of the sidesaddle. Women had always ridden astride in the more rugged and rural parts of the United States, and by the 1880s, many women in Europe, particularly in England and Germany, had adopted the "cross-saddle" or "man's saddle." America was behind the times. In 1895, the police arrested an English lady for riding astride in New York's fashionable Central Park, but the commissioner of police at that time, Meadow Brook's Theodore Roosevelt, intervened on the lady's behalf and declared it proper for a woman to ride a horse astride. Why, he said, it was no different from a woman wearing a split skirt when pedaling a bicycle.[87]

The first large horse shows to permit women to use the cross-saddle were in Chicago in 1897 and Boston in 1901. Meadow Brook ex-M.F.H. Belmont Purdy urged others to follow suit in an article in *Outing* magazine in 1905. He wrote that the "antagonism to the seat astride at the horse-show" was from the riding school element, "the last place where an innovation of any kind finds favor." Purdy said that the astride position was safer for women and more comfortable for the horse. He thought a suitable riding habit could be developed with the use of bloomers covered by a long coat.[88]

Author Roger Williams preferred women to use the cross-saddle, because otherwise they needed so much assistance. He wrote: "Nothing so thoroughly disgusts or angers a man as to be called upon in the field, especially during a run, 'to please tighten my girths.' Were a man engaged to a woman he would be justified in breaking the engagement under this great provocation."[89]

Many uncited sources credit Meadow Brook's Emily Stevens Ladenburg (often misspelled Landenburg) as the first woman to ride astride, and they cite the following news item about her appearance in Saratoga Springs, New York, dated September 1902:

MRS. LADENBURG CREATES COMMENT.
While the millionaires' piazza at the United States hotel, in Saratoga, was crowded a few days ago Mrs. Adolf Ladenburg of New York, caused a sensation by walking across to the livery stable in one of the most startling riding habits ever seen in that gay place. Later she took a trap and drove out to Ballston

stables for a horse. The habit was made of brown cloth. The skirt was a divided one, under which was worn skin-tight trousers. Mrs. Ladenburg walked up Division Street. Her appearance caused much comment.[90]

Emily Ladenburg was one of the great horsewomen of her time, and she did ride both sidesaddle and astride during her lifetime. But the story of her shocking society in Saratoga Springs probably was due to her visible "skin-tight trousers," rather than her choice of saddle.

Samuel Stevens Sands Jr.

Samuel Stevens Sands Jr. was the first casualty for Meadow Brook. At the time he was thirty-three years old, the son of a wealthy stockbroker, and the husband of the heiress Anne Harriman. They had two young sons when he died. His funeral service was held at Grace Church in New York, and honorary pallbearers were Lewis M. Rutherford, James P. Kernochan, Egerton Winthrop, and Thomas Hitchcock from Meadow Brook. Other club members were listed as attendees.[91]

After Sands's death, his relatives, including his sisters and a brother-in-law, Theodore A. Havemeyer, continued to hunt. Within a year, his widow married Lewis M. Rutherford, one of Samuel's pallbearers. The couple moved to France, where Lewis died after a long illness in January 1901. Two years later, in April 1903, Anne Harriman Sands Rutherford married her third and final husband, William Kissam Vanderbilt, another Meadow Brook member. She was Vanderbilt's second wife. By then his first wife, Alva, had already remarried August Belmont Jr.'s brother, Oliver H. P. Belmont, who was active with the Meadow Brook polo team.

William "Willie" Tiffany

William "Willie" Tiffany was the son of Isabella Bolton Perry and George Tiffany. When his father died in Newport on June 15, 1886, several obituaries stated that he was from Baltimore and, more recently, New York; a Newport mill owner; and "a gentleman of education and culture and immensely wealthy." His mother was the daughter of Commodore Matthew Calbraith Perry, who opened trade with Japan and was the younger brother of Commodore Oliver Hazard Perry, the hero of Lake Erie during the War of 1812. Her sister was Mrs. August Belmont Sr.[92]

As a young man, Tiffany had spent time in Montana, possibly meeting Theodore Roosevelt there. He certainly knew Roosevelt at Meadow Brook. Tiffany was a popular young man in Newport and New York society, where he was teased for changing his clothes "four or five times a day."[93] He may have been a dandy but he was the only one of his crowd who became a business partner in Rawlins Cottenet's florist shop. Tiffany's engagement to fellow Meadow Brook hunter, Maud Livingston from Islip, Long Island, was announced in May 1897, and the couple had not yet married when he enlisted in the Rough Riders the next spring.[94]

Tiffany was commended for his service in Cuba and rose from private to second lieutenant. On the way home, he and many of his comrades developed fevers. The troops were quarantined when they arrived at Montauk, Long Island. By that time, Tiffany was desperately ill, and, as soon as his mother and fiancée were permitted, they took him to Boston. Tiffany seemed to improve, and they nursed him in their suite at the Parker House. But then his condition suddenly worsened, and he died on August 25, 1898. His doctor released a statement that one of the causes of his death was "starvation," and this created an uproar among the relatives of other returning soldiers. The doctor attempted to explain that the diagnosis reflected the inability of his body, due to illness, to absorb food.[95]

Tiffany was buried with honors in the Perry Circle at the Island Cemetery in Newport, Rhode Island. Two of the pallbearers were Meadow Brook Bulldags: his business partner, Rawlins Cottenet, and fellow soldier, Henry W. Bull, who six years later would marry Tiffany's fiancée.

FOUR

$\mathcal{M}any$ $\mathcal{M}asters$

Moving off: term used when huntsman, hounds, Master, and field head off for a day's hunting.

The first days of the new century were unseasonably warm, and Meadow Brook members were able to hunt through January. On Tuesday, the twenty-third, they reelected Ralph Ellis Master of the Foxhounds (M.F.H.). The future of the hunt seemed secure, and Ellis continued to hunt both English and American foxhounds on alternating days. The drag hunts were short and fast, but the exploding population of foxes in the area was beginning to also provide good, fast runs.[1] Riders were happy to stay out for three hours when they raced across ten to fifteen miles of rolling country, jumping forty to seventy fences.[2]

However, changes were coming to the Hempstead Plains. Announcements for automobile shows appeared in the newspapers, dwarfing the advertisements for livestock and bicycles. Meadow Brook member James Kernochan banned horseless carriages from his property, but many of his fellow hunters flocked to the machines. Sidney Dillon Ripley bragged that his "gasolene surrey" could cover the twenty-two and a half miles from Flushing to the Meadow Brook Hunt Club in a record-breaking fifty minutes.[3] Eager to test their speedometers, members of the hunt pressured the Village of Hempstead into raising the automobile speed limit from six to ten miles per hour.[4]

During the fall of 1900, Ralph Ellis brought up a pack of American foxhounds from Tennessee and engaged their huntsman, John Lieper, to hunt them. In addition to Lieper, there were several whippers-in during Ellis's mastership. The names most often listed were, in chronological order, Harry Hewett, William Davy or Davey, Joseph Murphy, and Patrick Hannon.

In the late spring of 1901, Ellis underwent surgery for appendicitis, and his doctors recommended that he stop hunting for some time.[5] While he continued to buy hounds, Ellis was not riding that fall, and he told the stewards that he would resign at the end of the season. Henry W. Bull filled as acting Master, and with the help of John Lieper, the hunt carried on with the two packs of hounds as usual until November 16.[6] That Saturday, Lieper was riding a big black horse that he had ridden all season. The hunt was just outside Roslyn, where they came to a double jump. Lieper's horse "blundered at the jump, and fell at the five-rail fence, there being a drop of several feet on the other side. The hunter rolled over, and fell squarely on his rider, who was unconscious when picked up." Lieper was taken by ambulance to Nassau Hospital at Mineola.[7] At first, the injuries were thought to be fatal, but the tough huntsman surprised everyone by recovering with only a badly fractured jaw.[8]

Meadow Brook was now without its M.F.H. and its huntsman. By the end of November, even with the whippers-in and Henry Bull, the hounds struggled to provide good sport, and interest lagged.[9] The club stewards decided not to wait to secure a new M.F.H. Several men were considered: Henry Bull, W. Scott Cameron, Robert Stevens, Peter F. Collier, and Foxhall Keene. In addition, there were two women candidates: Emily Ladenburg and Eloise Kernochan. The choice of either would not have been unprecedented. A Denver hunt club already had a mistress of the hunt, and there were many "mistresses of the fox-hounds" in England.[10] However, club membership would have

Figure 4.1.   Eloise Stevenson Kernochan (Mrs. James Lorillard Kernochan and later, Mrs. Alexander Duncan) on Rebel. William Patten, ed. *Book of Sport* (New York: Taylor, 1901), 178.

been the sticking point. Up to this time, any women who hunted with Meadow Brook did so under the club membership of their husbands, fathers, or brothers. A few widows were specifically invited to subscribe to the hunt, but a woman could not be a full member of the Meadow Brook Club, and that was a requirement for the position of M.F.H.

In the end, the hunt announced that Foxhall Keene would be the next Master.[11] "Foxie" Keene was an athletic phenomenon of the time and one of the best-known riders on both sides of the Atlantic. Having him accept the position of M.F.H. was a coup for the club.

> Before [Foxie] was seventeen he played for America against England in the first international polo match. That same year his name led the list of jockeys over the sticks (amateur or professional). In 1887 he set a record never beaten by riding in 101 races and winning 79 of them. In every other sport in which he participated he was either at, or very near, the top, as when he was told by his doctor to lay off polo for two years, and, to solace himself, took up golf. In the course of the second year he played in the final of the National Championship.
>
> Mr. James R. Keene [Foxhall's father] offered to bet a hundred thousand dollars on his son against any man in the world at ten different sports. No one took the bet.[12]

Keene had prior commitments to attend to before spring hunting commenced. He departed late December for England, which was abuzz with anticipation for the upcoming coronation of Edward VII. As usual, Keene and his wife passed the winter months hunting in Leicestershire, but this year his additional objective was to set up an international polo match to coordinate with the royal festivities scheduled for that summer. Keene also planned to purchase hounds for Meadow Brook. While Keene

Figure 4.2. Foxhall Keene. Library of Congress, Prints & Photographs Division, LC-DIG-ggbain-03297.

was away, Harry Page, Frank Appleton, and Samuel Willets were appointed to attend to the daily hunt matters.[13]

All seemed decided, but then at the annual club meeting on January 28, 1902, the stewards changed their minds for some reason and persuaded Ralph Ellis to withdraw his resignation. Ellis agreed, and his reelection as Master was unanimous. Ellis announced that he would travel to England in the spring and return with a superior pack of hounds. John Lieper was now fully recovered and would be in charge of the American foxhounds during the spring season. Hunting foxes had begun to attract

more riders, especially from Manhattan, who found drag hunting too fast and dangerous. As an afterthought, the stewards
ended the meeting by voting to maintain the golf links near the
clubhouse, but they were concerned, because the course had
been in so little use the past year.[14]

Members of the hunt took turns as acting Masters during the
spring. Neither of the ladies was ever given the chance to lead the
field, so perhaps their election as Master had never been taken
seriously.

In the fall, Ellis was in the saddle to observe a historic set
of hound trials held on Long Island, but he did not participate
as M.F.H. He gave that assignment to Lieper. The competition was to determine which variety of foxhounds, American or
English, was the superior hunter. To do this, selected packs of
hounds assembled in Westbury for five days of testing. The foxhounds were to be judged for speed, endurance, drive, and pack
work. The prizewinner was awarded one thousand dollars. The
competitors came from Green Spring Valley Hunt (American),
Richmond C. Stewart, M.F.H.; Meadow Brook (English), John
Lieper, acting M.F.H.; Aiken (American), Thomas Hitchcock,
M.F.H.; and two packs from Hickory Valley (American), J.
M. Avent, M.F.H. Each day, two or three packs of seven and
one-half couples each hunted side by side. The hounds were
distinguished by colored collars. The judges then scored the
merits of each group. On Monday, November 3, the Meadow
Brook hounds followed a fox for fifteen miles and killed. Long
Island sportsmen hoped that would ensure the "home team" a
victory.[15] However, the judges—Dorsey M. Williams, M.F.H.,
Patapsco Hunt, and Harry Worcester Smith, expert huntsman—were not using that as the only objective. Five days later,
the judges declared a tie between two American packs—Green
Spring and Aiken. The prize money was split accordingly.[16]

Ellis reiterated his commitment to retire at the end of the fall season, and at the annual meeting on January 27, 1903, Foxhall Keene was elected the new M.F.H. At about the same time, Meadow Brook joined the newly formed governing body the National Steeplechase and Hunt Association, which was the precursor of the Masters of Foxhounds Association.[17] Keene felt he was ready for the task of molding Meadow Brook into a great hunt. He wrote of the time in his memoirs:

> All of my experience in Leicester served me in good stead when I was asked to become Master of Meadow Brook. I consented on condition that I be allowed a furlough each year to go to Melton [in Leicestershire, England], and immediately set to work bringing the famous old hunt back to its former high standard.
>
> The Master who preceded me, while a fine fellow, was not sufficiently enthusiastic to make a success of his job. To be a good M.F.H. requires a fanatic devotion to the sport. The religious zeal of a saint for his faith is hardly stronger than that of a great Master for his hunt.
>
> When I took over, the Meadow Brook Hunt had run downhill a long way from the time of Tommy Hitchcock.[18]

To illustrate his point, Keene related a story about how the Meadow Brook hounds had hunted down and killed a pet Pekingese dog instead of a fox.[19] He said that the hounds were not a first-rate pack; they were poorly matched "draft hounds" or "seconds."[20] Keene intended to rectify this and fix the "trick rails" that had recently been observed on the fences in Meadow Brook country. These rails were top bars that would easily fall when struck by a horse. The first whipper-in, Joe Murphy, was instructed to replace each one with a strong piece of timber that could be removed if it must. There would be no more fakes.[21]

Keene departed for England soon after his election, leaving W. "Scott" Cameron as acting Master for the Meadow Brook drag hounds. For the other days, ex-Master Ellis had a new private pack of English foxhounds, and he invited Meadow Brook members to hunt with him. In mid-March, just as the season got underway, Ellis's new hounds became ill. Veterinarians were called in and determined the pack had been accidently poisoned by eating tainted meat. Ellis lost all twenty-seven couples.[22]

Scott Cameron assured the worried hunters that all would be well in the autumn under new mastership. In an interview with

Figure 4.3. W. Scott Cameron.
Courtesy of Sarah F. Hunnewell.

a reporter from the *Brooklyn Daily Eagle*, Cameron outlined just
what Keene would provide:

> A radical change in the hunting methods so long in vogue
> in this section of Long Island, and that drag hunting will be
> secondary. . . .
>
> When Mr. Keene returns he will bring over a very fine pack
> of fox hounds of the very best blood obtainable in England
> and will seriously undertake what has never before been really
> attempted on Long Island. I mean fox hunting. There will be
> no more "American hounds" barking and yelping about the
> country, no more Buffalo Bill Wild West hunting, but Mr.
> Keene will turn out everything in good form, stop the earths[23]
> and carry on the sport properly.
>
> Of course the drag will be in no sense subordinated to fox
> hunting, but, on the contrary, will be carried on better than
> it ever has been before. The draghounds will meet three and
> sometimes four days a week, and the fox hounds two or three
> days a week.
>
> Owing to the fact that America, generally, and Long Island
> in particular, is bad scenting country, and that we have such
> enormous stretches of woodland from which it is hard to get
> a fox away, fox hunting can never furnish the same good gal-
> lops as it does over the highly scented pastures and among the
> small coverts of England, and so for our best sport we shall
> have to rely upon the drag.[24]

In England, Keene was not faring as well as he'd hoped.
He struggled to find good hounds and often had to settle for
"drafts." Then he heard of an "opportunity of a lifetime." Mr.
Salkeld in Leicestershire decided to quit hunting and wished to
sell his entire pack of prize-winning hounds. Keene purchased
all forty and a half couples. He hired the Englishman E. Robert

"Ned" Cotesworth (also spelled Cotsworth or Coatsworth) to become the new Meadow Brook huntsman and his son, Thomas, to serve as a whipper-in.[25] Pausing in Ireland to acquire several new hunting horses, Keene returned to Long Island on June 3.

First off, Keene wanted to show everyone the new fox-hounds. He gathered up the hunt staff, three matched chestnut horses with white markings, and five couples of hounds, and they embarked on a tour of the east coast horse shows. In a couple of weeks, they had "won everywhere including the National in Madison Square Garden."[26]

That autumn, several Meadow Brook members suggested that they hunt at night because of the nocturnal nature of foxes. Keene said there was no need for that. There were plenty of foxes in the morning, and he altered the meeting time to 10 a.m. Six mornings a week, the hunt met at Keene's estate, Rosemary Hall. These morning hunts became "the great feature of the season"[27] and perhaps, according to some, marked the "golden era of foxhunting on Long Island."[28]

The tragedy of the season was the death of Jimmie Kernochan on October 5. He had fallen off a horse during the summer, and he never recovered his health. No one was sure what was wrong. The obituary in the *Brooklyn Daily Eagle* said that Kernochan had been ill with stomach pain related to heart disease, and *The New York Times* stated that the cause was due to riding injuries and meningitis. At age thirty-five, Kernochan had been one of Meadow Brook's most promising polo players, steeplechasers, and hunters. Keene canceled all meets for a week, and the rest of the season was subdued, with fewer parties and hunt breakfasts.

In January 1904, the stewards reelected Keene unanimously, and everyone expected a great year. Members began to consider moving the clubhouse "to the neighborhood of Locust Valley or

Figure 4.4. James Lorillard Kernochan. Charles S. Pelham-Clinton, "Fox-hunting Near The Metropolis," *Cosmopolitan* magazine, vol. VII, May–October 1889, 90.

of establishing a hunt club in that vicinity. The original Meadow Brook colony has spread to the north part of the island, and the region around Hempstead is so thickly settled . . . and already the clang of the trolley is heard in the land."[29]

Before those matters were settled, the stewards heard whispers about Keene's financial problems. Much of his money was tied to a partnership with his sister's husband, Talbot J. Taylor.

Figure 4.5. Meadow Brook Clubhouse around 1904. From the Collection of the Meadow Brook Club.

By July, articles appeared in the newspapers. In a swift downturn, Taylor and Keene had lost several million dollars. Lawsuits ensued, and Keene was in serious money trouble by August.

Keene went on with his daily schedule, playing polo and accompanying his wife to luncheons and dinner parties. There had often been an ebb and flow to the Keenes' money. Keene's father had made, lost, and remade his fortune several times. The Meadow Brook colony was surprised when, on August 23, Keene resigned as M.F.H. and announced he would auction off his carriage horses, polo ponies, hunters, and the whole pack of foxhounds. He said that he and his wife had decided to travel abroad.[30]

Meadow Brook Hunt Club stewards suspected that Keene's resignation was due to the five-thousand-dollar discrepancy in their account books.[31] However, the cubbing season was about to commence, and while they could perhaps hunt with an acting Master, there was no such thing as an "acting" pack of hounds.

The situation grew worse when the English huntsman Ned Cotesworth announced that he and his son were departing after filing an eight-hundred-dollar suit against Keene. Cotesworth claimed he had paid all the travel and board expenses related to the horse shows the prior fall. Keene had never reimbursed him, as promised. In addition, for the past several months they had received no salaries for maintaining the kennels and stables.

The club stewards determined that the only way the hunt could continue was to purchase the hounds and install a new Master. Van Tassell & Kearney held the auction in their New York City show rooms on September 29.

> Nearly all the prominent clubs in this city, Boston and Philadelphia were represented, while the women, who out-numbered the men by two to one, in the reserved seats in the balcony overlooking the tan bark, were attired in dainty evening costumes and their escorts were in the regulation eve-ning dress. With the exception of the horses, as they were led up to the auctioneer's block and the knot of the horsey men grouped around the selling ring, one might easily have imag-ined he was at some fashionable entertainment. Mr. and Mrs. Foxhall Keene occupied seats in the front row of the balcony, where they had an unobstructed view of the sale below. . . . Seventeen hunters were sold, all of which have been used in this country and abroad. They brought $27,525, an average of nearly $1,620, and the price was considered excellent. It is the first time in America that a regular sale has ever been held of hunters. After the sale of horses Mr. Keene's pack of im-ported foxhounds, including thirty-seven and a half couples, was brought into the ring, making another notable feature of the sale, as it was the first time that a pack of hounds had ever been sold here at auction. The hounds were offered as a pack, and after some spirited bidding between representatives of the various hunting clubs, James H. Hyde got the pack for $6,150. He was acting for the Meadow Brook Club.[32]

As it turned out, purchasing the pack of hounds was just the first step; finding someone to accept the mastership was much harder. Henry Bull refused the office, so the club approached Mrs. Thomas Hitchcock's brother, William Corcoran Eustis.[33] Eustis often spent part of the season on Long Island. But he had recently purchased a new property, Oatlands, outside Leesburg, Virginia, for foxhunting, so he declined.

The Meadow Brook Hunt needed rescuing by a white knight who was, literally, on horseback. Help arrived in the person of Peter Fenelon Collier. Collier was the publisher of *Collier's Weekly*, a popular magazine, and the new *Collier's Encyclopedia*.

Figure 4.6.   Peter F. Collier, M.F.H. From the Collection of the Meadow Brook Club.

More important, he was an experienced fox and deer hunter, with his packs in Monmouth, New Jersey.

By mid-December, Collier stated that Meadow Brook had two hundred foxhounds and estimated it to be the largest pack in existence. He divided them into three packs: "The English foxhounds are nearly all late importations. The American fox-hounds are of old Virginia stock. The drag hounds, though of American breeding, came originally from English stock, which has been carefully kept from contamination."[34] Occasionally, Collier took out all three packs on a single day, leading three hunts

> with the English foxhounds at 10 o'clock, with the American foxhounds at 1 o'clock, and with the drag hounds at 3. He was in the saddle almost continuously eight or nine hours. He rode about forty miles, for each of the runs was at least ten miles long, and he rode the five miles from the first to the second meeting place and the three miles from the second to the third. He bestrode at least six separate horses that day, making a change whenever his mount was tired, and at the end he seemed remarkably fresh and unwearied, considering the ground he had covered and the stiff barriers he had taken.[35]

M.F.H. Collier attracted a field of about fifty riders, one hundred followers in traps and carriages, and about twenty automobiles. These "hilltoppers" in cars were an innovation to foxhunting in 1904.[36]

As a new Master, Collier wanted to be on good terms with the local farmers, so in November he determined that the hunt should host a "squires' dinner for the tenantry." His fellow huntsmen suggested that he hold a "tea" first to discuss the matter with the locals. Sixty farmers were invited to tea, caterers and waiters engaged, and the hosts dressed in their best hunting finery. Long after the appointed time, one couple, Mr. and Mrs. John Willets from Roslyn, drove up in a buckboard. Mr. Willets explained to Collier that no one else was coming to the tea.

> "It's jest this," he explained, "and it don't apply to me, though. These farmers around here are afraid of the waiters up at the clubhouse, and more'n that, they're scared stiff on account of them slippery floors. They say you've got to hev special shoes to walk right on them floors."
>
> Mr. Collier, the same man explained, was in fact very popular with the Long Island natives on account of the promptness and generosity with which he repaid damages done by the Hunt Club, but the farmers were content to reach across the table and help themselves when they needed anything, and they wanted to feel that the floor was not going to give way under them.
>
> Mr. Collier assured them that the squires' dinner was still being considered, but it would be held on the lawn.[37]

The following January, Collier was again elected Master, and the next month his new huntsman, John Foster (also spelled Forster) from the Quorn Hunt in England, arrived. The spring season went well, with Foster often acting as Master and another Englishman, William Scarrett, as first whipper-in. On alternate days, Collier hunted with an American pack of hounds supplied by H. I. Varner of Arkansas.[38] When Foster was injured racing a polo pony and unable to ride most of the fall season, Edgar Caffyn was brought in as huntsman for the English drag hounds.

Collier strived to provide good sport. On November 12, he released an ambitious schedule for the upcoming meets.

> Monday, a visiting pack of American hounds from Mississippi would go out from Woodbury at 9:00 a.m.

Tuesday, English foxhounds at Woodbury at 11:00 a.m. and drag hounds at New Cassel at 3:30 p.m.

Wednesday, a Georgia pack of American foxhounds at East Norwich at 9:00 a.m.

Thursday, the Mississippi pack at Roslyn railway station at 9:00 a.m. and drag hounds at Woodbury at 3:00 p.m.

Friday, English foxhounds at Kurby Hill at 11:00 a.m.

Saturday, the Georgia pack of American foxhounds at Jericho at 9:00 a.m. and drag hounds at the kennels at 3:30 p.m.[39]

In December 1905, the Meadow Brook stewards announced that, after reviewing the foxhound trials in Virginia, they decided that Meadow Brook would only hunt with American foxhounds. The English hounds were all to be sold, and John Foster would return to England. Advocates for the English foxhounds may have been upset, but those concerns were minimal in comparison to the gossip that erupted when the widow Eloise Kernochan announced her engagement to Foster. Some speculated that this was the real reason for Foster's departure.

In 1906, Collier brought down James Blaxland from the Canadian Hunt Club. Blaxland was a well-known huntsman, and it was hoped that he and the whipper-in, Harvey Bemus, would provide much sport on Long Island.[40] The fall season did not produce the large fields that Collier desired. Worried, the stewards sent out subscription notices, but they did not receive the response they had desired. On December 23, Collier tendered his resignation. No reason was given, but it was unusual to make a public announcement before informing the stewards.[41] Once again, Meadow Brook floundered without a clear successor.

On January 23, 1907, the stewards met at the Waldorf-Astoria and suspended the office of M.F.H. They appointed a

Committee on Hunts, comprising Robert F. Potter and Robert
L. Stevens, who both occasionally followed the hounds, but
they were most often on the polo field. They were given the
task of securing a Field Master for individual meets. No monies would be allotted to the position due to the lack of hunt
subscriptions.[42]

A few weeks later, *The New York Times* reported that the
Meadow Brook stewards had changed their minds, and, at a
special meeting held on March 8, elected Samuel Willets as their
M.F.H. His huntsmen were Michael Hanlon and William Davy
and first whipper-in, William Hayden.[43]

Willets was from an established Long Island Quaker family.
At the time of his mastership, he was described as one of several
fashionable Meadow Brook colony bachelors who, as gentleman
farmers, raised prize-winning poultry, cattle, and horses.[44] In
the fall of 1907, Willets invited Paul J. Rainey to bring up a pack
of his American foxhounds from Tippah, Mississippi.[45] Rainey
had a reputation for training top-notch hounds, and Meadow
Brook enjoyed good sport throughout the fall.

After providing such fine hunting, Willets was elected the official M.F.H. of Meadow Brook at the annual meeting on January
28, 1908. Hunting that spring was good, but during the summer
Willets's personal life created a distraction.

In July, a former stage actress who performed as Amber
Lawlor checked into a hotel in Larchmont, New York, and
signed the register "Mrs. Samuel Willets." The woman was well
known, and word of Willets's wife spread quickly. *The New York
Times* covered it on the front page.[46] Willets's parents, Mr. and
Mrs. Edward Willets, gave statements denying the marriage, but
then Samuel was seen in Larchmont with the lady.[47] Recriminations, denials, and more recriminations provided rich fodder
for the columnists.[48] Finally, after visiting the Willets's home on

Figure 4.7. Malcolm Stevenson, M.F.H. on polo pony. Courtesy of the Polo Museum & Hall of Fame.

Long Island, the young woman and her two daughters headed off to Europe and were not heard from again.[49]

Samuel Willets was able to turn his attention to foxhunting again, and that fall he brought up a new pack of Cortland Smith's hounds from Virginia. The Long Island season began late that year, because there was a rabid dog wandering in the area. All dogs, including foxhounds, were quarantined for several weeks.[50]

On Election Day, November 3, Willets tried to create more interest by adding a much anticipated innovation for Meadow Brook—the point-to-point. At 10:00 a.m., eleven Meadow Brook hunters gathered at Jericho Toll Gate. The course was only revealed at the start of the race, and it proved too much for three of them, who had "croppers." Harry Page's injury, a broken collarbone, was the most serious. In the end, Malcolm Stevenson on his big mare, Diana, finished first in the lightweight division, and Henry V. Pell won the heavyweight class on Pinkum.[51]

That afternoon, President Roosevelt's assistant secretary of state, Robert Bacon, joined thirty-seven other Meadow Brook riders on a drag hunt. So many people followed in automobiles that one reporter described the scene as "a combination automobile show and drag hunt."[52]

In January, Willets resigned, and Malcolm "Mike" Stevenson was elected the next M.F.H. Stevenson hunted regularly, but he was a polo player at heart. He announced that he would act as his own huntsman, which presumably meant he would appoint others to act as Field Master.[53] Stevenson imported some English foxhounds in the fall, but otherwise the hunt seemed to have no noticeable changes. He resigned at the end of the season.

MEADOW BROOK MEMBERS IN THE NEWS

Walter "Scott" Cameron

Walter "Scott" Cameron was acting M.F.H. when Foxhall Keene was in England. His father, Adam Scott Cameron, had invented a direct-acting steam pump, which became a necessary component in steamships. Adam died young, and his wife,

Figure 4.8.   Samuel Willets, M.F.H. Library of Congress, Prints & Photographs Division, LC-DIG-ggbain-00463.

Julia, ran the family pump company in New York for many years. Scott Cameron graduated from Yale in 1897 and settled down to life as a gentleman farmer on Long Island. In 1902, he married Rosalie Wall De Goicouria, whose sister was married to August Perry Belmont III. Cameron was closely tied to the Southampton area of Long Island, and in 1906, he joined Richard Newton, Charles Coster, and H. P. Robbins in founding the Suffolk Hunt. Cameron later divorced and married for a second time, spending much of his time in Scotland. He died there in 1932. In the 1960s, his daughter donated some of his property to the town of Southampton to form the W. Scott Cameron Beach.[54]

Peter Fenelon Collier

Peter Fenelon Collier was born in Ireland, immigrated to Ohio when he was seventeen, and attended college at St. Mary's Seminary. He then turned to publishing religious books, later expanding to encyclopedias, nonfiction texts, popular literature, and magazines, such as *Collier's Weekly*. He married Catherine Dunne, and their son, Robert J., eventually took over the publishing company.

Peter Collier's main home was his estate, Rest Hill, in Wickatunk, New Jersey, where he hunted with the Monmouth County hounds. When he accepted the position as M.F.H. at Meadow Brook, his son, Robert, hunted the New Jersey pack. Peter Collier died suddenly from apoplexy (a stroke) after watching a horse show in New York City in 1909.[55]

Foxhall Parker Keene

Foxhall Parker "Foxie" Keene was born in San Francisco, the son of James R. Keene, "who was known as the Silver Fox of Wall Street, was 'probably the greatest manipulator of stock'" in his time.[56] When the family moved to New York, the senior Keene became a particular target of Jay Gould, the railroad developer and speculator, who said that "Keene came east in a private [railroad] car. I'll send him back in a boxcar."[57] The Keenes' finances did ebb and flow dramatically. Years later, when Foxie wrote his memoir, *Full Tilt*, he categorized periods of his life as "when we had money" and "when we were broke."

Foxie spent two years at Harvard, where he developed friendships with William Randolph Hearst and Marshall Field. Much of his college life revolved around sports, and when a ruptured kidney ended football and a case of the measles suspended boxing, he packed his bags. He returned to his father's world of high finance and fast horses. The Keene Castleton Farm in Kentucky bred some superior horses, including one his father named Foxhall, after his son. The Keenes became entrenched in the sporting world on both sides of the Atlantic. They were seen in the best hotels and restaurants. Cookbooks credited Claridges in London or Delmonico's in New York for the creation of the Keenes' favorite dish, "Chicken a la Keene," which later evolved into the more regal name of "Chicken a la King."[58]

The Keenes lived in Newport and on Long Island, where Foxie became a star polo player and steeplechase rider for Rockaway Hunting Club. In Madison Square Garden, he broke the high jumping record, riding H. L. Herbert's Transport. At every horse show, Foxie was a favorite with the spectators.

> Keene, you'll know him partly from his snuff-colored hunting breeches and leggings and dark coat, but more by the little boost he gives the horse just at the jump. He does it with his feet, somehow, rising in the saddle and fair lifting the horse with him. He has had some terrible mounts this year and lots of bad luck all round, but it is just a picture and a poem when he does get a horse that has good sense, and isn't full of sin and Satan.[59]

In December 1892, Foxie married Mary Lawrence White, the daughter of Frederick Lawrence from Bayside and the widow of Frank Worth White. The couple built their home in Old Westbury in 1904 and named it Rosemary Hall. They had just settled in when Foxie accepted the mastership at Meadow Brook. All might have been well, but Foxie and his sister's husband, Talbot R. Taylor, who managed Keene's fortunes through his brokerage house, lost a great deal of money. Foxie sold most of his horses and hounds in America and went abroad. His wife,

Mary, did not go with him. She returned to her father's home and filed for divorce.

Eventually, Foxie regained some of his money and most of his stature. He moved from horses to automobile racing, but collected more speeding tickets than trophies. Still playing polo and foxhunting with Meadow Brook, he began to feel his age.

> In 1936, when [sixty-six] years old, he totaled his hurts at one broken leg; one compound fracture of the ankle; nose broken twice; one ruptured kidney; one nearly fatal internal hemorrhage; brain concussion three times, lying senseless for periods of [seventeen] minutes, [thirty] minutes, and [sixteen] days; one broken neck, collarbone broken three times; one dislocated shoulder; three broken ribs; and six stitches in his eyelid after being hit by a polo ball.[60]

On September 25, 1941, Foxie died quietly, and penniless, at age seventy-one in his sister's home outside of Quebec, Canada. His memoir ended with this:

> So I have participated in nearly all the sports that men have invented to harden their bodies and temper their spirits. In each of them I found pleasure and an incalculable profit to the soul. All but one of them were competitive and in all those I ranked well, while in some I reached the top. But my favorite always remained foxhunting, where there was no ranking and the highest award that might be gained was the simple phrase, "He was a good man over Leicestershire." Let that be my epitaph.
>
> Now I ride no more. My strength and skill, and even the fortune that enabled me to live so royally, are spent. But if I had it all to do again, I would follow exactly the same way. It was a life of pure delight.[61]

Mr. and Mrs. James L. Kernochan

Eloise Stevenson and James Lorillard "Jimmie" Kernochan married in a small ceremony at her mother's Manhattan home on January 28, 1892, and settled into the Meadow Brook colony.[62] Eloise was the daughter of Anna Louise Eve and Vernon King Stevenson. Vernon Stevenson, from Nashville, was known as "the father of Tennessee Railroads," and after the Civil War, he moved to New York City and invested in real estate. When he died in 1884, his body was returned to Nashville and buried beneath a replica of Napoleon Bonaparte's tomb. This curiosity became a local tourist attraction.[63] Jimmie was the son of James P. Kernochan, whose family had made a fortune in sugar in Louisiana, and Katherine Lorillard, a tobacco heiress. With such ancestors, the newlywed Kernochans became the darlings of newspaper readers.

Reporters covered the arrest of Jimmie Kernochan and Sidney Dillon Ripley for playing golf at Meadow Brook on a Sunday in May 1895. Sheriff Smith "compelled Mr. Kernochan to dismount from his drag and go with him across Hempstead Plains for seven miles in a dirty wagon" for arraignment. Infuriated, the Meadow Brook members pushed back, stating that Smith had been "twice removed from office, the last time on a charge of stealing honey from the premises of Mrs. G. Remsen of Hempstead."[64] The case vanished, but not before articles in the local papers mocked the incident, saying that Smith's arrest of Kernochan and Ripley might have been valid if the charges included swearing on the golf course or for wearing offensively loud "plaid knickerbockers and stockings."[65]

Then there was a newspaper story about Kernochan and his French bulldog. The Kernochans had many hunting and show dogs. Jimmie kept a kennel of beagles, and Eloise, a founder of the Ladies Kennel Club, had many breeds, but mostly smooth-coated collies and Irish terriers.

On February 23, 1896, Jimmie and several of his employees were returning from a dog show in Manhattan. They and their dogs were onboard an eastbound Long Island Rail Road train. Margot, a French bulldog who had just won second place at the show, sat on the seat next to her master. A group of inebriated firemen made several nasty remarks about the dog's appearance. When one of the firemen shoved Margot off the seat, Kernochan ignored them and handed the dog over to his groom for safe-keeping. More rude remarks were made, and finally Kernochan suggested that the firemen mind their own business.

Seeking a confrontation, a fireman punched young Kerno-chan, who fought back, and other firemen jumped in. Soon the Kernochan grooms came to help, but that encouraged twenty more firemen to join the fracas. Firemen blocked the doors, pre-venting train conductors from entering the car. The ferocity es-calated. Kernochan's youngest groom was propelled the length of the train car, and his head foreman, Harry Hewlett, was flung through a window, but somehow managed to scramble back onboard.[66] When the train pulled into the firemen's destination, Jamaica, several conductors rushed the car, and the firemen attacked them as well. Eventually sanity prevailed, and the fire-men, seeing they were at their destination, disembarked.[67] The event was reported and retold in newspapers across the country.

Young Kernochan caused a milder frenzy when he appeared in his new fur coat in Hempstead. The coat was made from the hide of a grizzly bear. The head and neck had been fashioned into a hood, and the paws covered the hands like gloves. To complete the look, the bear's tail dangled off the backside. When Kernochan passed a school, students poured outside and sur-rounded him, tugging at the fur and hooting with laughter. The situation began to get out of hand, and Kernochan sought refuge in the Hempstead post office, where the postmaster telephoned Mrs. Kernochan to rescue her husband. Eloise soon arrived in a trap and, "laughing merrily," drove "the bear" home.[68]

The young couple's good times ended abruptly in 1903. That July, Jimmie had a bad fall from a horse that he was training to be a hunter. Although he never lost consciousness, Kernochan did not recover his full health. He died at age thirty-five on October 5, and the cause of death was stated as due to injuries from a fall from the horse several months earlier and from meningitis.[69]

Years before Teddy Roosevelt's men charged up San Juan Hill, Eloise Stevenson Kernochan had been crowned "Queen of the Rough Riders"[70] for her daring feats in the hunting field.[71] After the death of her husband, Eloise remained at her home, The Meadows, except for summer visits to her mother-in-law's home in Newport. During one visit, Eloise was in a severe automobile accident in which the driver, Vinson Walsh, was killed. Eloise's injuries curtailed much of her riding for several months, and eventually, they would force her to cease hunting completely.

In December 1905, Eloise announced her engagement to John Foster, the English huntsman brought over by M.F.H. Peter Collier. Foster was described as coming from a good family, but penniless. He soon departed for England, supposedly to make arrangements for the marriage. But then, Eloise's mother-in-law, Mrs. James P. Kernochan, denied empathetically that there was any engagement.[72] Gossipy articles claimed that the elder Mrs. Kernochan controlled a vast amount of Eloise's income, and it would be reduced from sixty-five thousand dollars to ten thousand dollars per year if the marriage to the huntsman proceeded.[73] A year later, there was still no marriage, and the young widow received a generous gift of $150,000 from her mother-in-law.[74] In 1907, Eloise Kernochan became the bride of a longtime and socially acceptable friend, A. Butler Duncan.[75] Eloise gave a lengthy interview stating that her engagement to Foster had been "a mistake," and when Duncan began to court her, she forgot that the huntsman had ever existed.[76] Duncan was more of a sailor and steeplechaser than a foxhunter, but he occasionally followed the hounds. He did go on safari with Theodore Roosevelt. The couple remained married until his death in 1920; Eloise died at her home, The Meadows, in 1951. She never had any children.

Paul J. Rainey

Paul J. Rainey grew up in Cleveland, Ohio, heir to a coal fortune. He devoted his life to hunting game, big and small, photography, and philanthropy. He frequented Newport and New York society, but settled in Mississippi, where he established his Tippah Lodge. William Faulkner mentioned him in his novel, *The Reivers*.[77]

Rainey trained hounds to hunt all sorts of game, including bear and lions. He brought home not only skins and mounted animal heads, but also captured animals. He gave a walrus and two polar bears, Silver King and Silver Queen, to the New York Zoological Park in the Bronx, New York. At age forty-six in 1923, Rainey died onboard a steamship bound for Africa.[78] He was buried at sea, and as his memorial, his sister, Grace Rainey Rogers, commissioned the elaborate gates at the north entrance to the Bronx Zoo.[79]

Samuel Willets

Samuel Willets served as M.F.H. for a short period, and he gave no reason when he resigned. There must have been a good deal of speculation that it was caused by the scandal of his possible marriage to Amber Lawlor. That gossip should have passed long before the annual meeting in January 1909. But in November, Samuel's father, Edwin, died, and news quickly spread how Samuel had been cut out of the recently signed will. This fueled new chatter about the prior romance or marriage or both.

Samuel continued to live on the family's Brighthome estate with his mother in Old Westbury and ride with Meadow Brook. In the autumn of 1910, he surprised his friends by announcing that he had married Marie Holsington Holmes Arnold in Hartford, Connecticut, several months earlier. It was her third marriage; her first husband had died, and she had divorced the second. The Willets marriage lasted only a few years. Shortly after the divorce, the ex-Mrs. Willets gave an interview from her newly leased house in Flushing. Her comments on life in the Meadow Brook colony were published in *The New York Times*:

> Of course, I should like to have Mr. Willets with me at Flushing, but as long as his mother wants him with her at Old Westbury I have no objection. There certainly cannot be two bosses in one house, and to avoid any trouble I decided to live in Flushing. . . . The main thing that is interesting about me is not marriage, but the New York dog show. . . . I love my dogs too. I've got thirty-four here in Flushing, and twice as many in Virginia. . . . One thing is certain. I don't intend to bury myself in Old Westbury, L.I., where my husband wanted me to stay. I'm young and ambitious. I couldn't stand the life there.[80]

Samuel Willets married again in 1917 to another divorcee, Ida McKinney from Washington, District of Columbia. He was still living at home with his mother at the time.[81]

MEADOW BROOK ON THE STAGE

Gallops, a Play

Gallops was performed from February to April 1906 at the Garrick Theater in New York. The setting was a fictitious foxhunting colony on Long Island called the Oakdale Hunt. Theater reviewers said the location was Meadow Brook, but the author, David Gray, said at least several hunting stories included in the play were from the Genesee Valley Hunt. The play was a farce in which the hero is mistaken for a famous cross-country rider. Wanting to impress the ingénue, he pretends that he can ride and, after several twists and turns, ends up winning the girl through his valor, rather than by equestrian skills. The play included a musical hunting theme written by George M. Cohen, and the whole production received positive reviews.

However, there was a problem. One night, Kingston, the large, chestnut horse who was part of the cast, tried to throw his rider (the hero) and kicked down the set. The floor gave way, and Kingston landed on the musicians, who were playing cards in a lower room. No one was hurt, but getting Kingston up the narrow basement stairs later proved to be quite a feat. The requirement of having a live horse on stage may have prevented further productions.[82]

Meadow Brook Hunt at the *Ziegfeld Follies*

In January 1908, Florenz Ziegfeld introduced Adiline Genee to the American audience. Genee was a classically trained Danish ballerina, who often danced in London musicales.

> Among the novelties introduced by F. Ziegfeld, jr. in his big success "The Soul Kisses" now being presented at the New

York Theater is a pack of trained fox hounds in full cry. They appear in the elaborate scene called "The Meadowbrook Hunt," and dash across the stage, over rocks and stream ahead of the hunting party. This is the scene in which Mlle. Genee does her famous hunting dance. These dogs were secured from the pick of numerous kennels and represent a cost of [one thousand dollars].[83]

After returning to England, Genee founded a ballet school that became the Royal Academy of Ballet, and she was made a dame of the British Empire in 1950, the first dancer to be so honored. Genee died in 1970.[84]

FIVE

The Huntsman

Huntsman: The person who hunts hounds and is responsible for the care, breeding, and training of the hounds. He or she may be a paid professional or an amateur.

With Malcolm Stevenson's resignation, Ralph Ellis and Henry Godfrey served as acting Masters in the form of a committee. Ellis had been the backbone of the hunt for years, and Godfrey hunted regularly. During the spring season, they took turns taking out the hounds and occasionally appointed someone else to take the field.

At a special meeting on April 25, 1910, the stewards elected Joseph E. Davis as the new Master of Foxhounds (M.F.H.). At thirty-two years old, Davis was considered young for the position; however, the stewards voiced confidence in him, saying he was "a Southerner and took a great interest in both fox and drag hunting. With Mr. Davis in charge a big season in cross-country

Figure 5.1. Joseph E. Davis, M.F.H. Collection of the author.

hunting is assured to devotees of that sport."[1] The new Master and his wife, Mary "Mollie" Carleton Maxwell Davis, also a skilled rider and regular foxhunter, lived in Heyday House on Wheatley Road in Brookville.[2]

Davis traveled down to New Baltimore, Virginia,[3] to purchase some horses.[4] The seller was Dave Waller, who employed part time a young carpenter named Thomas Allison. Years later, Allison described the meeting:

> One day, Mr. Joe Davis comes down from New York to buy hosses. Dave Waller had two, Sawdust and Driftwood, that

Mr. Davis liked, and though the groun' was deep in snow, he wanted to see 'em jump big fences. There was a cattle-gate, a big one, and I jumped the hosses over that, but Mr. Davis weren't satisfied, so Dave Waller took it off its hinges and set it on two feet of snow and I jumped 'em over that. Mr. Davis bought 'em both and asked me to come no'th as huntsman to the Meadow Brook Houn's. I'd always heard the Yankees had no use for the likes of us, and I tol' Dave Waller, "I never could please them people," but he says, "Go along and try and if you don't, come on home again."[5]

Fortunately for Meadow Brook, Allison did not go home again—except each summer, when he took the hounds down to Virginia, because "Mr. Davis said he couldn't have no smelly ol' houn's serenadin' him summer nights."[6] Allison always used a cow horn with the hounds, so perhaps Davis was happy to see that migrate south as well.

Allison tried hunting the hounds he found at Meadow Brook, but he said the first season was hard, discouraging work, and he couldn't teach those old hounds anything. It was so bad that one day, when he was trotting along with them on the way to a meet, a butcher's wagon came by, and every hound climbed in. The huntsman and the whipper-ins had "a devil of a time" getting them out.[7]

That summer, Allison carted the whole pack down to his home in Virginia, where he planned to teach them to hunt properly. After his neighbors "pretty near died laughin'" at "these long-eared homely Pennsylvania houn's," he started teaching them the basics. He took them out each day with his father's five and one half couples, so that the Meadow Brook hounds could learn from the best. By the time they returned to Long Island in the late summer, Allison was pleased with the old hounds, who hunted pretty well without any young hounds to hurry them.[8]

The huntsman wanted to create a great pack of hounds, and he knew no one ever sold off their best hounds. He would have to get the best he could for breeding and then raise and train the puppies. He persuaded the hunt to purchase several hounds from Colonel Bywater's pack in Culpeper, Virginia, including one of his favorites named Teddy. These hounds formed the foundation for the Meadow Brook pack.[9]

Figure 5.2. Thomas Allison, Huntsman. Courtesy of Russell G. Corey.

Over the next few years, Joe and Mollie Davis began spending more time in Aiken, South Carolina.[10] In 1913, Davis resigned as Master, and James "Jamie" Park and Harry I. Nicholas were elected joint Masters on April 18, 1913. Park took over the drag pack.

> This world-renowned drag, under the Mastership at that time of the race rider, Jamie Park, was nothing short of a steeplechase with hounds, participated in by a group of bruisers such as Ambrose Clark, Mike Stevenson, Al Davis, Harry Page, and one or two women such as Mrs. J. A. Burden and Mrs.

Figure 5.3. James Park, M.F.H. on Clonee. Courtesy of the Elkridge-Harford Hounds.

Butler Duncan, who raced each other over the biggest and stiffest timber fences in the country—which means, perhaps, the stiffest timber in the world. The type of animal required was a Grand National—or, perhaps, more correctly, a Maryland Cup horse.[11]

Park only remained joint Master for one year, leaving Nicholas to serve alone.

For more than a decade, the hunt meets had been inching toward the North Shore, pushed along by southern housing developments and new macadam roads. In 1914, Nicholas rented land in East Norwich for six hundred dollars per year and built new kennels for one thousand dollars. The hunt had twenty-six couples of American hounds, four couples of English, six hunters, and one workhorse. The foxhounds went out three days a week, and the drag hounds two. In addition, they boarded fifteen horses for members.[12] The old stalls at the Meadow Brook Club were put to use by stabling polo ponies, and the kennels were filled with Oliver Iselin's pack of Wolver beagles.[13]

In 1916, Robert E. Tod made an offer to the hunt that was almost too good to be true. He offered a rent-free, ten-year lease on twenty acres in Syosset. He would construct stables, kennels, a huntsman's house, and a small clubhouse. The stewards offered to pay, but Tod rejected the money. The next year, Allison purchased several additional couples from Harry Worcester Smith's Grafton Hounds.[14] The hounds and horses of Meadow Brook moved into their new quarters in 1918. Tod's generosity enabled the hunt to stay afloat financially for a while longer.[15]

All seemed to be going along smoothly, but then August Belmont wrote to club secretary Frank Appleton questioning the official Meadow Brook colors. After reviewing the available notes from old meetings, Appleton realized that the color had

Figure 5.4.   Harry I. Nicholas, M.F.H. on The Tartar. From the Collection of the Meadow Brook Club.

never been written down. Even worse, the design of the hunt button was not recorded. The matter was taken up at the stewards' meeting in 1917.

Devereux Milburn said that the polo team had always thought sky blue was the correct color. The Master said he thought it was pale blue. Others stated that

> some members had given up wearing blue altogether and were in the habit of wearing a hunt evening dress coat with

buff satin in body and sleeves, red satin in skirts, maroon velvet collar, and scarlet silk facings. In fact, Samuel Willets, a former Master, had in 1911 gone so far as to ask John Patterson & Co., tailors, on 33rd Street, New York City, to register such a lurid combination as the official evening dress of the club. (The secretary recorded that Mr. Patterson's dismay was only equaled by that of the stewards present.)[16]

Henry Godfrey argued that the correct color was not pale blue, but robin's egg blue. He brought out a dictionary and specified the composition of the color: "thirty-eight parts white and forty-one and twenty-one parts, respectively of the primary colors green and blue."[17]

More discussion ensued, including a close examination of August Belmont's Gustav Muss-Arnolt oil painting of "The Meadow Brook Hounds at Westbury Pond" from 1885. Old order books showing hunt coats made for Francis Appleton and Edwin Morgan on September 13, 1882, were tracked down. The color was described as light blue. Two meetings later, light blue was voted down, and the official color was to be "robin's egg blue." The evening dress would be a scarlet coat with robin's egg blue facing, and white waistcoat. The hunt button was declared to be a circular button with the letters M-B-H in the center, the huntsman's horn above, and the date 1881 below. No one but members who had been awarded their hunt colors were entitled to wear Meadow Brook colors or hunt buttons. They voted unanimously and recorded the information in the by-laws, article IX.[18]

The stewards meeting for April took place a few days after the United States declared war on Germany on April 6, 1917. Secretary Francis R. Appleton Jr. read a letter that had arrived on March 27 from A. J. Tweed. Tweed begged the club to take

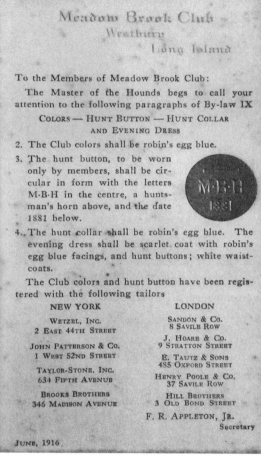

Figure 5.5. Meadow Brook Hounds official color card, 1916. Courtesy of Lee Bradley Mackay.

twenty couples of the Pytchley hounds, which were "the very best and wonders at killing foxes." If the hounds remained in England, they would "be destroyed on account of the shortage of food in England." The stewards and M.F.H. agreed to take the "ten best couples" and arranged for the balance to go to Shelburne and Myopia Hounds. Secretary Appleton then resigned his office, stating that as captain of the infantry in the Officers' Reserve Corps of the U.S. Army, he expected to be called to duty at any moment.[19]

The Pytchley hounds were not mentioned in later minutes, but the records were not as well kept during World War I, and it can only be hoped that they arrived. Van Urk wrote that Meadow Brook added "eleven couples of bitches from Warwickshire, North Warwickshire, and Flint and Denbigh." These were crossed with the best American hounds to produce the Meadow Brook half-breeds.[20]

Eighty Meadow Brook members enlisted shortly after the declaration of war. Their initial postings varied from training camps throughout the United States to "somewhere in France."[21] Some English hunts managed to survive the war. After the armistice, Colonel Frank Appleton Jr. and Captain Devereux Milburn were stationed in France for several weeks. Always seeking a day out with the hounds, Appleton and Milburn wrote B. Balding in Market-Harborough, England, about hunting. A telegram came back inviting them to join the Fernie Hunt in Leicestershire.[22]

Not only did the men of Long Island go to war in 1917, but the island itself also seemed to have been recruited. Since 1910, Glenn Curtiss and other aviation enthusiasts had filled the once quiet Hempstead Plains with hangars, runways, and air shows. When World War I started, the New York National Guard set out military barracks and airfields, the largest of which was Hazelhurst Field. Rows of large white tents sprang up overnight like mushrooms. Quentin Roosevelt, former President Theodore Roosevelt's son, trained there. He was also the fiancé of Flora Whitney, who often hunted with Meadow Brook.

Quentin was killed in action in 1918, and Hazelhurst Field was renamed Roosevelt Field in his honor. Nearby, Camp Albert L. Mills was renamed Mitchel Field for New York City Mayor John Purroy Mitchel, who was killed during training in Louisiana. After the war ended on November 11, 1918, the airline industry continued to flourish on Long Island under the guidance of Leroy Grumman and Alexander P. Seversky.[23] With all the noise and traffic, the Meadow Brook Hounds realized they had made a prescient choice when they'd moved north to Syosset.

On January 6, 1919, Meadow Brook lost one of its most famous members, former President Theodore Roosevelt. The Colonel, which was the sobriquet Roosevelt preferred and his foxhunting friends at Meadow Brook always used, died at Sagamore Hill, Oyster Bay. The country and, especially, the North Shore of Long Island mourned. They felt he was one of their own. The funeral service was held at Christ Episcopal Church, with limited seating. Members of Congress, military leaders, and heads of state clamored to receive invitations. Only a partial list of attendees was published, but among those listed were Meadow Brook's Edwin D. Morgan, August Belmont, and Francis R. Appleton.[24]

Roosevelt's death was a bleak beginning to a year that should have been celebratory after the war's end. But fewer people were riding to hounds, so the hunt created a subscription committee to drum up members. Committee members Egerton L. Winthrop Jr., J. Watson Webb, and Douglas Campbell sent out a letter on October 31, 1919. It was addressed to people who might be interested in foxhunting. They explained that the Meadow Brook Club provided the hunt with a stipend of five thousand dollars per year, but the actual expenses needed to maintain the horses and hounds were closer to fifteen thousand dollars per year. To provide the additional funds, the committee raised the subscription fees to $150 per individual, and $300 per family or individual with guests or grooms.[25]

The following year, 1920, the Masters of Foxhounds Association (MFHA), which had been formed in 1907 to act as the governing body of fox and drag hunting, registered the Meadow

Brook Hunt territory. In Meadow Brook's 1920 annual report, M.F.H. Nicholas listed twenty-nine couples of hounds, of which sixteen couples were homebred, and thirteen couples of puppies that were being walked. The foxhounds went out three days a week, and drag hounds one day a week.[26] The drag hounds were hunted by Meadow Brook member McPherson Kennedy.[27] Harry Nicholas was more interesting in developing a foxhunt.

> Harry Nicholas had hunted Long Island foxes with his long-eared hounds in snow, wind and rain. He had gone through scrub oak up to his knee on the saddle for hours on end to drive his fox into the open. With Harry Nicholas and Allison came a new era of fox hunting on Long Island. We were again building up a leisure class, a few were getting just a little too brittle for the drag, they wanted another form of hunting, so really our beginnings as an organized fox-hunting pack at Meadow Brook [were] just turning the first quarter century.[28]

Fox hunting did revive under Nicholas's leadership. Some days there were eighty-five to one hundred riders out. In November, M.F.H. Nicholas took several enthusiastic members, subscribers, and eight and one half couples of hounds to hunt with the Harford Hunt Club in Maryland.[29] They hunted the country for two weeks and had "splendid sport." The trip was such a success that Nicholas repeated it several more times over the next five years. Harry T. Peters served as Field Master while Nicholas was away.[30]

With the hunt attracting more attention and the robin's egg blue color decided, the stewards were horrified to realize the hunt's name was wrong. At its founding, the foxhunt was simply called the Meadow Brook Club, but when the club added other sports, the foxhunting branch transformed into the Meadow Brook Hunt. Some members felt that the term *hunt* implied

Figure 5.6. Map showing approximate territories of major foxhunts on Long Island in the mid-twentieth century.

that they only pursued live quarry and never the anise-seed bag. But the term *hounds* could refer to both kinds of hunting. In the April 20, 1922, meeting, "the Secretary submitted copies of correspondence with Frank J. Bryan, Secretary of the Hunts Committee of the National Steeplechase & Hunt Association, in regard to the registration of the Meadow Brook Club's pack of foxhounds as 'Meadow Brook Hounds,' instead of 'Meadow Brook Hunt,' as incorrectly registered at present."[31] Henceforth, the foxhunt at Meadow Brook should be called the Meadow Brook Hounds.

When the Meadow Brook Hounds entered the Roaring Twenties, McPherson Kennedy and two other "hunting kids of Rockaway" sought to revive the drag hunt to its old glory.[32] The hunting kids were Franklin B. "Frank" and Edward S. "Ned" Voss. The latter served as honorary whipper-in for the Meadow Brook Drag and would eventually become the Master for Elkridge-Harford Hunt. The former, Frank, went on to become the famous equine painter.

Kennedy kept a hunting diary, which revealed his desire to re-create the days of Frank Griswold, Thomas Hitchcock, Foxhall Keene, Harry Page, and Jimmie Kernochan. He wrote that those old drag hunters' names were like those of Greek heroes or supermen with superhorses. The Kennedy drag hunts attracted only the heartiest of riders in the 1920s. But this did not mean the ladies didn't join in. On October 18, 1924, Ethel Norton on a horse called Merry-go-Round made Meadow Brook history. It was a special Ladies' Day hunt, and Ethel was selected to be the "Master." According to Kennedy, she was the first woman ever to officially hunt the Meadow Brook Hounds.[33]

The newspapers took no notice of such an earthshaking event; their readers were no longer interesting in foxhunting. Polo was all the rage. The sports and, occasionally, front pages detailed the exploits of polo players on and off the field. Movie stars and world leaders flocked to play and watch polo players swing away at the white ball. Huge crowds attended the matches at Meadow Brook, and the Long Island Rail Road scheduled special trains to ferry the spectators in and out of New York City. In 1923, when Charles Wilbur Fisk, aged forty-one, suffered a heart attack and died on a hunt with Meadow Brook, only one newspaper columnist mentioned it.[34] However, when Malcolm Stevenson, former Master of Foxhounds (M.F.H.), fell off his polo pony, the newspapers carried minute details about his injury and recovery for days.[35]

An avid polo fan, Edward, Prince of Wales, scheduled his visit to the United States to coincide with the international polo match at the Meadow Brook Club. The celebrity status of this unmarried prince was enormous. When his ship sailed into New York harbor, hundreds of smaller vessels surrounded it, blowing their horns in welcome. He was given a ticker tape parade, and crowds mobbed his every move in Manhattan. He might have thought he'd find sanctuary on Long Island at the home of James A. Burden, but there were still many official functions. The first thing he did was place a wreath at President Theodore Roosevelt's grave, and then meet with local groups.

Figure 5.7. *Thanksgiving Day Meet in 1923 of the Meadow Brook Hunt* by Franklin B. Voss, 1923. Private Collection, Photograph Courtesy of Red Fox Fine Art, Middleburg, VA.

On Thursday, September 11, the prince did not need to rise early to go foxhunting before dawn. There had been no time for sleep; he simply changed out of his evening clothes, and, after a swim, put on his riding outfit.

Then the prince was motored over to the Robert Tod estate, where he inspected the Meadow Brook hounds and met the officials of the hunt. At 6:30 a.m., he mounted The Ghost, a big, gray horse lent by Harvey Ladew, and headed off with the Meadow Brook Hounds. It was cubbing season, so the dress was informal, a disappointment to reporters in search of scarlet coats. Harry Peters was in the field, and he recorded his thoughts:

> As usual on such occasions, nothing seemed to work, so H. R. H. started on a larking expedition, over the Jackson fences— five feet of solid post and rail. . . . And very ghostlike it seemed

Figure 5.8. "Meadowbrook Fox Trot," by Arthur M. Kraus. Popular dance music in the 1920s. Collection of the author.

to see one of the most important gentlemen in the world bouncing, which he literally was, over those terrific fences in the cold gray dawn. Harry Nicholas, the Master, sent me after him to try and deter him, but I found there was no use trying to make suggestions to royalty on the rampage at dawn.[36]

The prince later "remarked that the course over which he had ridden was rougher than those to which he was accustomed in England. He took all the jumps, however, and one which the others in the hunting party were forced to go around."[37]

Harvey Ladew, The Ghost's owner, was delighted when the hunt was over. The Ghost was a good jumper, but he was a strong horse, and Harvey always rode him with a curb bit. The prince's equerry had informed Harvey the prince only used a snaffle bit.

This threw Ladew into paroxysms of terror, for he felt that the horse wouldn't cooperate if he had an unusual type of bit

Figure 5.9.   Fixtures of the Meadow Brook Hounds, 1926. 1. The Kennels, 2. Sir Ashley Sparks's Farm Barns, 3. Columbia Stock Farm, 4. Mrs. Senff's Gate, 5. Mr. J. S. Stevens's Gate, 6. Piping Rock Show Grounds, 7. Mr. H. P. Whitney's Stables, 8. Mr. Ralph Ellis's Gate, 9. Mr. J. A. Burden's, 10. Mr. J. E. Davis's Stables, 11. Mr. David Dows's Stables, 12. Mr. Frederick Thomas's Stable, 13. The Blue Hotel, 14. Woodbury Church, 15. Mr. Watson Webb's Farm, 16. Mr. Otto Kahn's, 17. East Norwich Hotel, 18. Mr. Victor Morawetz's, 19. Mr. Walter Jennings's. Collection of the author.

in his mouth: "It was the worst morning I ever remember. I was a nervous wreck." He recalled, "We were hunting on one of Meadow Brook's biggest countries. The fences were exceptionally high and solid. . . . But every jump he made was perfect. We had a good fast run and the prince was delighted with the morning's sport." After the hunt, Ladew recovered his nerves with "a breakfast which consisted mostly of several stiff drinks of scotch."[38]

(It might be noted that in 1924, Prohibition was in full force.) After the foxhunt, the prince played polo, and, although there was talk of another foxhunt the following morning, the prince slept in. He had been up for twenty-eight hours.[39] For about a week, he remained on Long Island, where he attended parties given by the Burdens, Morgans, Vanderbilts, Clarks, and Mackays, and dined at the Meadow Brook and Piping Rock Clubs. The visit was considered a great success, especially by the victorious Meadow Brook polo team.

At the end of 1924, Harry I. Nicholas decided that his November trips to Harford County were not long enough, and he announced that he was moving to Maryland. Meadow Brook hosted a dinner in his honor. Glasses were raised, and Francis R. Appleton Sr., the only living founding member of the hunt, toasted Nicholas:

> A Master of Hounds is one of the most difficult characters to fill. That Mr. Nicholas has filled it so well is evidence of his peculiar fitness for the place. A Master of Hounds, so we read, must in the first place have a keen love of sport for sport's sake. He must be bold as a lion and cunning as a fox, with the calculation of a general, the decision of a judge, the politeness of a diplomatist, the generosity of a sailor or the patience of a Job. To these should be added a slight touch of the eloquence

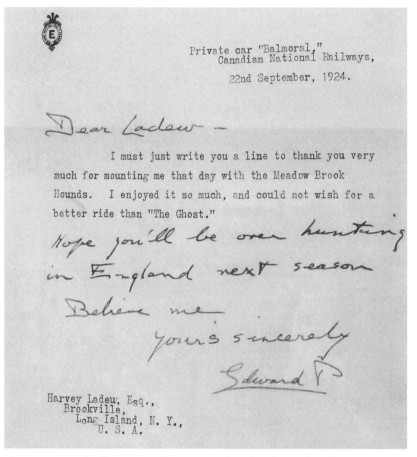

Private car "Balmoral,"
Canadian National Railways,

22nd September, 1924.

Dear Ladew —

I must just write you a line to thank you very
much for mounting me that day with the Meadow Brook
Hounds. I enjoyed it so much, and could not wish for a
better ride than "The Ghost."

Hope you'll be over hunting
in England next season
Believe me
yours sincerely
Edward P

Harvey Ladew, Esq.,
Brookville,
Long Island, N. Y.,
U. S. A.

Figure 5.10.   Thank-you note from HRH Edward, Prince of Wales. Courtesy of the Ladew Topiary Gardens Archives.

of Cicero, with a temper as even as the lines in a copy book. To all these qualities Mr. Nicholas has added his own personal character commanding the respect of men and the love of animals. He has possessed the vision of his opportunities, and in his conduct has ever been mindful of the vision."[40]

The seventy-four members gave the retiring Master an inscribed George II silver bowl in appreciation for his service.

Figure 5.11. *Meadow Brook Hunt*, presentation portrait, Harry I. Nicholas, M.F.H. on The Tartar with Huntsman, Thomas Allison on Sawdust, painted by Franklin B. Voss, 1916. From the Collection of the Meadow Brook Club.

MEMBERS OF MEADOW BROOK

Mr. and Mrs. James A. Burden Jr.

James Abercrombie and Florence Adele Sloane Burden lived on their estate, Woodside, in Syosset. James was president of the family business, Burden Iron Works, vice president of Eastern Steel, and served as a director for the American Iron and Steel Institute and the United National Bank of Troy, New York.

Florence often foxhunted with Meadow Brook, but her husband's name only appeared a few times in extant reports. The descriptions of the Burdens' hosting of the Prince of Wales in 1924 imply that "hosting" meant essentially turning the house over to the prince and his staff.

James died in 1932 at age sixty-one. Florence then married Richard Tobin, the former U.S. minister to the Netherlands. The Tobins continued to reside at Woodside, raising cattle and prize-winning roses. Florence lived to be eighty-seven, dying in 1960. The house became the Woodcrest Country Club, which was later reorganized as the Woodside Acres Golf and Country Club.

Frederick Ambrose Clark

Frederick Ambrose "Brose" or "Brosie" Clark was heir to the Singer sewing machine fortune. He had a large horse farm in Cooperstown, New York, and Broad Hollow House on six hundred acres in Old Westbury, Long Island. As a young man, he often hunted with Meadow Brook. Harvey Ladew liked to tease him for being too focused on the task at hand when out hunting. When M.F.H. Joe Davis's wife, Mollie, fell at a jump and lay there, dazed, Clark galloped up and asked if she were hurt. Mollie, still trying to assess any damage, replied that she didn't think so. "Well, then," shouted Clark, "roll out of the way so I can jump that fence."[41]

Clark foxhunted, played polo, steeplechased, and drove coaches. Injuries eventually curtailed his riding; he bragged that he had probably broken every bone in his body at one time or another. Horses were his life. After World War II broke out in Europe, Clark mentioned to his wife Florence that they should bring their horses back to the United States. Florence replied that she was surprised he even knew there was a war going on. He said, of course, he did. It had been mentioned in a horse racing magazine.[42]

In the 1950s, Ambrose sometimes arrived in one of his grand, yellow and black coaches to see the Meadow Brook Hounds off. One of his coaches is on display at the Long Island Museum of American Art, History, and Carriages in Stony Brook, New York. Ambrose Clark died in 1964 and was buried, according to his instructions, in a small family cemetery in Cooperstown, New York. Next to him are the graves of his horse Kellsboro' Jack and Button, a beloved dog. Ambrose Clark's headstone is the smallest of the three, and only shows his name, dates, and the inscription, "lover of animals."[43]

The Clark Long Island estate, Broad Hollow House, became the property of the State University of New York College at Old Westbury in 1967. While undergoing renovations the following April, the house caught fire and burned. Only the one-story south wing survived, and it was known as the Prince of Wales ballroom, because it had been built for the prince's 1924 visit.[44]

Joseph E. Davis

Joseph E. Davis came from Piedmont, West Virginia. He was a director of Island Creek Coal Company and Pond Creek Pocahontas Company and, at one time, head of the Blaine Coal Mining Company. He served as secretary-treasurer and steward of the Jockey Club. During World War I, he was an Army captain and was posted to France.[45]

Before he went overseas, Davis inspected a remount station, a location where horses, donkeys, and dogs were held before being shipped overseas for military duty. Afterward, a local newspaper reported on Davis's visit.

RICHEST MAN IN THE ARMY

Des Moines, Ia., Nov. 27, 1918—To be the richest man in the army is a distinction which would make any man proud, yet Capt. Joe Davis, Q.M.C., West Virginia, who bears that distinction, is one of the most democratic men wearing the uniform.

In fact, he was so democratic that after he had visited the remount station at Camp Dodge yesterday and had dinner at the officers' mess, Lieut. E. W. Stanley remarked to Capt. Brooks P. Sparks, "Davis certainly is one good scout. I wish he was with us here."

When Captain Sparks explained that Captain Davis was worth some [ninety million dollars], controlled the coal fields of West Virginia, and was the son of Gassaway Davis, Lieutenant Stanley nearly fainted.

"Good night," another lieutenant exclaimed. "Here I thought he was kidding when he said he was living at the Blackstone [Hotel] in Chicago and had closed his Long Island home. Anyway, I didn't make a mistake when I said he didn't know any more about horses than I did. He didn't look like a horseman and I shouldn't imagine him a millionaire."

"That is where you made another mistake," Captain Sparks interrupted. "He is the Master of Hounds at the Meadowbrook Hunt club of New York and an expert polo player."

To tell further of the dismay of the two lieutenants would not be proper, but with all his wealth they have all voted Capt. Joe Davis a good scout, and are only waiting to apologize for their under-estimation of his horse knowledge.[46]

Elise and Harvey Ladew

Siblings Elise and Harvey Ladew grew up on the large estate called Elsinore in Glen Cove. Their father, Edward R. Ladew, was involved in the leather business that became the United States Leather Company, a conglomerate of smaller tanneries and leather goods firms. After Edward's death in 1905, their mother, Louise Wall Ladew, took over the company, which she expanded and made exceedingly profitable. Louise died in 1912 and left her children, Elise (age twenty-two) and Harvey (twenty-five), independently wealthy.

The young Ladews thrived in the colony of Meadow Brook and embraced foxhunting. Harvey credited Mrs. Emily Ladenburg for her kindness to him not only in the hunting world, but also for introducing him to great literature, music, and art. He attended one of Ladenburg's famous after-dinner prizefight exhibitions and enjoyed how the women "in low-necked evening

Figure 5.12. *Finest View in America*, watercolor by Harvey Ladew, 1924. Courtesy of the Ladew Topiary Gardens Archives.

gowns and jewels" became "rather startled" when blood and teeth landed near them.[47]

Never fond of the overly large and ornate Elsinore, Harvey soon moved to Brookville and settled in his own residence, which he called The Box. He set out to study foxhunting from the best instructors in the world: M.F.H. Thomas Hitchcock, Loulie, and daughters Titine and Helen; M.F.H. Joe Davis and Mollie; M.F.H. Harry Nicholas and Dotsie; Emily Ladenburg and her daughter, May; Ambrose "Brose" Clark; and Harry S. Page. Under their tutelage, Harvey graduated from his pony, Fireworks, to the Davis's high jumper, Nimrod.

By September 1924, Harvey had a stable of horses, but his big gray one called The Ghost reached celebrity status when Edward, Prince of Wales, visited. The Ghost was selected to carry the visiting royal on a Meadow Brook hunt. Afterward, all sorts of people wanted to buy the big gray horse. Harvey resisted for a while, but then sold him for ten thousand dollars, an exorbitant price at that time. Harvey thought The Ghost should have a big send-off, so he hosted a lavish "Ghost party" at which his guests were instructed to dress appropriately—as ghosts. His more creative friends embraced the challenge and arrived in some elaborate and spooky costumes. Over the ensuing years, Ladew became friends with the Prince of Wales, who was demoted to the Duke of Windsor with his abdication in 1936. The duke teased Harvey claiming he owed him a sales commission for the Ghost transaction.[48]

In 1929, Harvey Ladew departed Long Island to settle in Monkton, Maryland. There, he bought the Scarff farmhouse

Figure 5.13. *Harvey Ladew on The Ghost,* painted by James Earl c.1922. Courtesy of the Ladew Topiary Gardens Archives.

and extensive grounds, which became his life's work. He opened the gardens to the public in 1971, five years before his death in 1976. The topiary of the foxhunt is one of the best-known garden images in the United States. The scene, originally in Brookville, was transplanted to Monkton, so although visitors today think that the rider represents a local hunt, Meadow Brook people know that the bushy, green fellow once wore a robin's egg blue collar on his hunt coat.[49]

Harvey's sister, Elise, married William Russell Grace in April 1914 in what was called the "wedding of the year." The groom's late father had founded the firm W. R. Grace, and most important for the newspaper coverage of the time, he had been the mayor of New York City. After the couple returned from a yearlong honeymoon, they settled in Westbury, living on the estate Crossroads.[50] The Graces continued to hunt with Meadow Brook and were so impressed by the huntsman, Thomas Allison, that they named the middle of their three daughters Alison after him.[51] The Grace's youngest daughter, Pat, married Alan Corey, a keen polo player, and their children foxhunted with Meadow Brook in the 1950s and 1960s.

Figure 5.14. *Fox Hunt*, Ladew Topiary Gardens, view of hounds and riders. Courtesy of the Ladew Topiary Gardens.

Harry I. Nicholas

Harry Ingersoll Nicholas was a foxhunter who happened to be a stockbroker. He and his wife lived on Rolling Hill Farm near East Norwich, Long Island. Nicholas and huntsman Thomas Allison directed and shaped the Meadow Brook Hounds together until the mid-1920s. The two men bonded over the love of foxhunting and, like golfers, enjoyed rehashing the day's events on the nineteenth hole. Allison said, "When we'd get through huntin', Mr. Nicholas he'd come into the house and we'd sit about and talk and talk. 'Bout two hours later, telephone would ring. That'd be Mrs. Nicholas. All she'd say was, 'Allison, send Mr. Nicholas on home.' She knew where he was at."[52]

In 1925, Nicholas surrendered to the roads, shops, and housing developments of Long Island and retreated to Harford, Maryland, outside Baltimore. From 1928 to 1933, Nicholas served as M.F.H. for the Harford Hunt (later this became the Elkridge–Harford Hunt) and as an officer in the MFHA.

Dorothy Snow "Dotsie" Nicholas and Harvey Ladew were good friends. Harvey loved telling and retelling a humorous story about her. They were all out hunting one day, when a Broadway actor who had a reputation as a lothario joined the Meadow Brook field. Dotsie had a fall, and the actor helped her remount. Later, she gushed about how kind the fellow had been. One of her crowd quipped that it was no surprise. After all, the actor had a reputation "for picking up fallen women."[53]

Harry and Dotsie's family contained several more foxhunters. Their son, Harry I. Nicholas Jr., married Josephine Auchincloss, and they became joint Masters of the Pickering Hunt and officers in the MFHA. Dotsie's brother, George Palen Snow, rode with Meadow Brook. His wife, Carmel White, had little time for dashing around the countryside in hunting togs. She was busy with jumping hurdles in the male-dominated world of publishing and women's fashion. Carmel rose from fashion editor at *Vogue* magazine to the editor-in-chief at *Harper's Bazaar*, a position she held from 1933 to 1957.

Ethel Roosevelt and Dr. Richard Derby

Ethel Roosevelt was the fourth child and youngest daughter of Edith and Theodore Roosevelt. She and her husband, Dr. Richard Derby, a surgeon, rode regularly with the Meadow Brook Hounds. On more than one occasion, Derby was called upon to be the "hunt doctor" out in the field. He was the first on the scene when Charles W. Fisk suffered a heart attack.[54]

The Derbys' son and the late President Roosevelt's first grandson, Richard Jr., died at age eight from blood poisoning in 1922. The Derby family donated the flagpole and the Richard Derby Jr. Medal to Green Vale School in honor of their son. The recipient of the Derby Medal is awarded to the member of the graduating class who most personifies the school spirit of honor and courage.[55] It is inscribed with "What is excellent, as God lives, is permanent."[56]

SIX

The Meadow Brooks

Foxhounds: When used in a foxhunt, they are never called dogs, and they don't bark—they give voice. Their tails are called sterns. Foxhounds are counted in couples; three and a half couples would be seven hounds. Meadow Brook Hounds used several types of foxhounds: American, English, and crossbred.

Harry T. Peters succeeded his lifelong friend Harry Nicholas as Master of Foxhounds (M.F.H.) for Meadow Brook on January 27, 1925. The "two Harrys" had known each other since childhood and shared their first foxhunting experience when they "were very young." They'd selected a cold, snowy day and assembled a few hounds (not foxhounds) and a purebred Dalmatian called Ten Spot. His name reflected his price rather than his markings. Mounted on ponies, the duo headed into the woods, where they found many foxes, and Ten Spot killed one.

We decided for home, icicles were hanging from the ponies' noses, we were numb with cold, also, we were lost. Harry [Nicholas], as usual, had ideas so off we started. At last, after an hour of plodding through, we suddenly found we were back in our tracks again. We had made the usual snow circle. Hopelessly lost, no sun to go by, temperature about zero, we were thoroughly frightened, and well disgusted with winter fox hunting. We pounded each other to keep clear-headed and decided to take the bits out of the ponies' mouths and see if they would take us out [of the woods] if we gave them their heads. It was our only hope. We also shouted "Home!" to old Ten Spot and he would prance out in front occasionally and show some signs of interest in getting there. Hounds, as everyone knows who has been out with them in a heavy snow storm, are at that time the dumbest creatures on earth.

The strategy succeeded. After another weary hour of plodding we found ourselves back in civilization, colder but wiser boys. This first fox of two boys, who were subsequently to become Masters, was nearly the end of the road.[1]

Losing those two boys in the woods would have changed Meadow Brook. Their successive Masterships (Nicholas 1913–1925 and Peters 1925–1946) spanned thirty-three years.

Born in 1881, Peters grew up on the family estate in Islip. His grandfather and father had been successful coal merchants with offices in New York City. Harry joined the business after he graduated from Columbia in 1903. One of his contemporaries, Marjorie McDonald, said Peters "was a fabulous gentleman and a figurehead for Meadow Brook. He was also the handsomest thing in his hunting clothes."[2]

Peters wrote a treatise on foxhunting, *Just Hunting*, and described his time as M.F.H. at Meadow Brook Hounds. He addressed many of his complaints about the hunt, including his dislike for the competition element that was most evident in drag hunting. Nor did he like the obsession with jumping. He was irritated when the "Saturday hunters" proclaimed the day "wonderful" because they'd "jumped every available fence, whether necessary or not, flying at them for no reason but the love of jumping."[3] Then these same people discounted one of the best hunting days Meadow Brook ever had because they had only gone over two small jumps.[4] His huntsman, Thomas Allison, agreed with him: "You got it right, boss; what they want is a circus."[5] Peters longed for a day when people understood the finer points of the sport.

> Now if you do get a good hunt at Meadow Brook, and one sometimes does, it is almost sure to require a really good post and rail horse to stay with the hounds. Yet one of our staunchest supporters and best sportsmen, the late Mr. Egerton Winthrop, who never missed a hunt or failed to be well up at the end, never jumped a fence worthy of the name. How did he do it? He was a fox hunter—he knew his country and his foxes, and rode with his head and avoided fences.[6]

Like the Englishman Brooksby, who had hunted with Meadow Brook in the 1890s, Peters noted the dominance of youth in the hunting field. "In America, hunting has no tradition connected with it, the young and rich hunt for the thrill of it. No fence is too high, no run too fast, nothing is unjumpable, and no one too reckless. A fierce competitive spirit is injected into it all."[7] Begrudgingly, Peters admitted that he had drag hunted with Meadow Brook for eleven years. But that had been during a time in his life when he suffered "from the American malady— lack of time to hunt—and this was the only possible hunting [he] could get."[8]

Some of the Long Island farmers hadn't changed much since the 1890s either. M.F.H. Peters received angry notes, letters, and the occasional threats from landowners. One read: "Please, hereafter see to it that your abominable hunt gives my acres a wide berth. Should you appear here again I will see the sheriff does his full duty. I may further add you are a disgrace to your family."[9] The Master said he called on the lady and tried to calm her, but to no avail. Other farmers welcomed the hunt when it flushed the fox out into the open, where they shot the varmint. In Dix Hill one day, a woman stepped out of her house, raised a blunderbuss, and fired off a round of buckshot into the nearest hound. When riders yelled in protest, the woman simply went inside and shut the door.[10] Peters said that his strategy in dealing with landowners was "first cigars, then whiskey, and if all else fails, try hard cash. If that fails, leave as fast as you can with dignity."[11]

He and Allison worked together studying the hounds to see which worked best in Meadow Brook's environment. Peters had seen Sir Edward Curre's pack hunt in Wales, and he imported several of those hounds. Each of the hounds was listed in the English Stud Book, so he didn't consider them really Welsh.[12] Peters thought Factor a "smooth Welsh hound, mostly white, with hare pie markings," the best hound he ever knew.[13] Factor was a proficient hunter and a winner in both Welsh and American hound shows.

Allison liked the new blood in the kennel: "Those good English houn's when they're good, can't be beat nowheres. They've been bred for hundreds of years to kill foxes, while our American houn's just hunts 'em."[14]

Peters described the differences a little differently:

The American hound will find scent with head down when others will not; as it gets better the half-bred will do his full share; seldom until a fox is actually afoot will a good English hound acknowledge the line here with us.

On most days the English hounds on Long Island will stay well in the middle of the pack, not taking the lead. Let a day come with breast-high scent, heavy damp air, and those same English hounds, with heads up, will come galloping out right into the lead.

Welsh hounds gallop with heads down and do far better on average days in America than English hounds. They are not at all the same in their work.[15]

Allison interbred the lines, and Peters claimed that hound show officials created the crossbred class specifically for Meadow Brook. Personally, he didn't use the term. He called them "Meadow Brooks." And after years of breeding, he finally had a pack that would, on the best days, hunt as one, as if covered by a blanket.[16]

The members of the hunt may not have known all the work involved, but they appreciated the good foxhunting. In 1925–1926, the hunt secretary recorded eighteen cub hunts and fifty-four foxhunts. David Dows, in charge of the drag hounds, reported only eight outings, and the fields were small, sometimes consisting of only three people. The stewards decided that Meadow Brook would no longer maintain a drag pack.[17]

During the summer of 1926, John Iselin, president of the Suffolk County Taxpayers Association, released a report stating that the Long Island State Park Commission "desires to annex Long Island to New York City as a playground for the masses, without regard to the rights and interest of the present owners." Iselin pointed out that the North Shore and Wheatley Hills were central targets for roads and developments.[18] He was correct— Robert Moses's park report was soon being hailed by park planners all over the United States.

New York Governor Al Smith wanted to win votes, especially among the urban poor. What could be more illustrative of his desire to alleviate their burdens than parks? Smith encouraged Moses and appointed him president of the Long Island State Park Commission. Moses's ambitions swelled.

> He wanted forty thousand acres of parks. He wanted not just a parkway along the South Shore and one along the North Shore but a parkway connecting them far out on Long Island so that families from New York could drive out on one, loop around and drive home on the other without retracing their path. He wanted another parkway—he wanted two more parkways— linking both the northern and southern parkways with two causeways running to Jones Beach. He wanted still another parkway linking them with Fire Island. He wanted more than 124 miles of parkways. And he wanted the parkways to be broader and more beautiful than any roads the world had ever seen, landscaped as private parks are landscaped so that they would be in themselves parks, "ribbon parks," so that even as people drove to parks, they would be driving through parks.[19]

The foxhunters were well aware of the encroaching roads. In just one year, automobiles had killed three and one half couples. Other hounds had been the victims of trains.[20]

Northern Boulevard ran along the north edge of Fairleigh, the George S. Brewster estate. Meadow Brook was hunting there on November 2, 1926, and both ex-Master Nicholas and current Master Peters were out. The hounds picked up the scent and took off. Allison galloped across the fenced fields, and the horsemen and -women were right behind. At the first post and rail, Allison's horse jumped big, landing clear of a pile of wood stacked dangerously on the far side of the jump. Allison pulled up and turned, shouting, "Don't jump."

It was too late. Gladys Dick's horse was at the fence, and she leaned forward in her sidesaddle, ready for the jump. But then something happened. Dick may have heard the warning and tugged on the reins, or the horse may have tried to stop on its own. Whatever the reason, the horse hesitated, and Dick slid up and over his head. The horse slid into the fence, and he tried to jump. His legs tangled in the cross bars, and he somersaulted on top of Dick.

Everyone ran over to help, and someone hailed a car to transport Dick to the nearest house. Doctors were called frantically, and nine arrived, but nothing could be done.[21] Gladys's husband, also a foxhunter, was inconsolable.

Gladys Dick's father was Theodore Roosevelt's cousin, and she was buried with other Roosevelts in Green-Wood Cemetery in Brooklyn, New York. Her tombstone bears the inscription: "Killed in the hunting field. A gallant life and a gallant death."

Peters made no notation of the accident when he summarized the year's hunting activities the next spring. He recorded it as a good season. The hounds had been shown as usual and were "very successful in their classes." The hunt had imported a few more English hounds, but he did not say from where.[22] The hunt had gone out sixty-seven times.

The next spring, Harry Peters sailed off to England, presumably to do some foxhunting, so he appointed Jackson Dykman and Colonel Francis R. Appleton to serve as joint acting Masters. The first meet of the spring season took place at the clubhouse, where they had not met for many years, and that attracted a large field. The entire season went well, and the club's annual report next spring showed an excess of income. This was partly due to the sale of a horse, but Meadow Brook Hounds had also added twenty-six subscribers who were not members of the club.[23]

Figure 6.1. Jackson A. Dykman, M.F.H. Courtesy of the New York State Bar Association.

Some people grumbled that there were too many riders now. On September 1, 1928, Master Peters sent a letter to members and subscribers of the Meadow Brook Hounds. He explained that the hunt would be limited to those who (1) were members of the Meadow Brook Club and (2) had subscribed in the past. Anyone wishing to join the hunt now had to contact the subscription committee first. The prices rose: $200 for a member of the Meadow Brook Club and each of his family, per person; all others were $250 per person.

The letter stated that Jackson Dykman would act as assistant to the Master in the field, and Thomas Allison would hunt the hounds for the upcoming season. The whippers-in were James Reynolds, Wesley Heflin, and Charles Plumb. The patrolmen

Figure 6.2.   *Francis R. Appleton Jr. M.F.H. on Orme's Head*, painted by Franklin B. Voss, 1928. Courtesy of the Trustees of Reservations, Appleton Farms Collection.

and wardens were Henry Devine, Charles Bailey, and Tom Smith. The missive concluded with instructions about automobiles, which were not to follow or precede the hunt, as that spoiled the sport.[24]

In the fall of 1928, Meadow Brook welcomed another royal visitor. On Thanksgiving, the club hunted with Prince Gustaf Adolph of Sweden, who was in the area for a family wedding. The prince had a passion for all equine sports and could not pass up the opportunity of an outing with Meadow Brook. Marjorie McDonald recalled the day: "Anyone who could find a pair of riding pants, jacket, and some sort of horse to ride came out that day. There were hundreds of people."[25]

Figure 6.3.   Harry T. Peters, M.F.H. and HRH Prince Gustaf Adolph of Sweden, Thanksgiving Day, 1928. From the Collection of the Meadow Brook Club.

Frank Appleton Jr. was a little more precise; he wrote his father the next day and said that he'd counted 193 in the field. The prince had a great day, enjoying a good long run and jumping some big fences. Appleton said it was one of the best hunts he had ever been on. In fact, it was so good that he wondered if there hadn't been a drag laid. Regardless, the prince said that he was "very anxious to come hunting with us again only he would have to come incognito" to avoid all the crowds.[26] The next day, Harry and Natalie Peters and several other members of the field motored to Pleasantville, New York, for the wedding.[27]

Automobiles went everywhere those days, and the champion of roads, Robert Moses, was waging a fierce battle with landowners about the proposed Northern State Parkway. "The barons of the Dix Hill in the western portion of Suffolk County—Otto

Kahn, Stimson, Mills, Winthrop and DeForest—had thrown back with contemptuous ease [Moses's] attempt to penetrate the fastnesses they controlled." Kahn, Moses's relative, had handed over ten thousand dollars to convince Moses to run the road over farmland rather than the Kahn property.[28]

Once that stretch was settled, Moses turned his sights on Wheatley Hills and the estates of Morgan, Whitney, Winthrop, Grace, Garvan, and Phipps. These land barons hired Grenville Clark to defend their interests. Clark was a friend of the newly elected governor, Franklin D. Roosevelt, and on October 23, 1929, Clark notified Roosevelt that he was prepared to show how Moses had accepted money to bypass Kahn's estate and throw farmers off their land.

> Less than two weeks after Clark issued the barons' ultimatum to Roosevelt, Moses agreed to a "compromise." Under the "compromise," the Northern State suddenly altered its eastward course at Glen Cove Road, the western border of the Wheatley Hill, just as it was about to plunge into the estate area, and instead swung south for two full miles, far enough so that when it resumed its course, it would never come near the Wheatley Hills.[29]

Six days later, on October 29, the stock market crashed, and the United States entered the Great Depression.

Meadow Brook was no longer worried about too large a hunt field. Marjorie McDonald (later a Meadow Brook M.F.H.) said the foxhunting was wonderful in the 1930s with smaller fields. Her theory was that Meadow Brook people reduced the number of horses they owned from three to two and kept on hunting.[30] Elizabeth Thompson "Betty" Babcock, wife of Richard F. Babcock, was the hunt secretary during the Depression. She observed that many families with houses in Aiken, South Carolina, or Harford, Maryland, closed up their Long Island residences and moved further south permanently.[31]

In 1932, thirty-eight members resigned from the Meadow Brook Club, including faithful foxhunters such as Harvey Ladew and George Rose Jr.

Despite all the worries about the hunt's impending extinction, Meadow Brook members carried on. They were rewarded on January 21, 1933, with a run that hunt secretary Betty Babcock called "Meadow Brook's Great Day." Babcock was a talented writer and artist, and she employed both her skills when describing that outing—a hunt that became a legend among Long Island foxhunters.

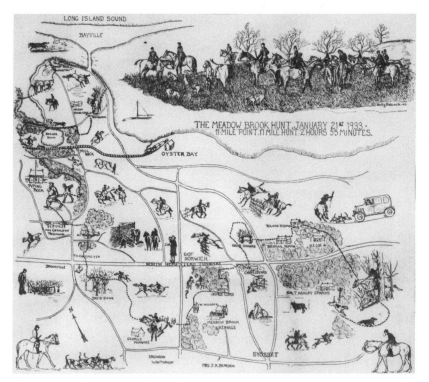

Figure 6.4. *Illustration of Meadow Brook's Great Day, January 21, 1933*, by Betty Babcock. From the Collection of the Meadow Brook Club.

Meadow Brook's Great Day

Despite the Encroachments of Civilization, 1933 Adds to Sporting History

The Meadow Brook hunting country is restricted in size, over-burdened with houses, intersected by highways. That fox hunting is carried on with pleasure to a large and enthusiastic field is extraordinary, but that a truly great hunt can be had amidst such overwhelming difficulties is amazing. It happened January 21 last.

The day was overcast, the wind light and from the southwest, the footing soft and damp. Hounds met at the kennels at 10 a.m. Thomas Allison, the huntsman, with Charles Plumb, Wesley Heflin and James Reynolds, moved off at a nod from Harry Peters and Jackson Dykman, joint M.F.H.s, with a field of eighty crowding after.

We first drew Mrs. [James A.] Burden's western cover, hounds finding in the first few minutes. Scent was catchy and the fox unwilling to extend himself, but after some twenty minutes, the relentless bitches finally forced the lazy varmint to move about a mile, where he went to ground. We went on and drew both the Jackson and Bruce covers blank, proceeding to Sir Ashley Sparks'.

Hounds were no sooner cast here than they found and were away before most of the field had completed the conversations started en route. Through the thick woods and on down to the sixty foot wide North Hempstead Turnpike [25A] the fox flew, crossing it and vanishing up the wooded hill on the other side. Hounds hesitated momentarily on the pike, as well they might with motor traffic surrounding them and late members of the field barging into their midst, but leading hounds crossed the road, picked up the scent and away they all went, through H. E. Coe, Jr.'s woods, over the vegetable garden, down the front drive of Beekman Hoppin, across the Syosset-Oyster Bay road, and so onto Edgar Leonard's lawn.

Before us lay those big Chilton farm meadows divided by the best line of indestructible fences on Long Island. Horses were refusing right and left, while furious or grateful riders either whacked their animals with rage or accepted gratefully the excuse to pull out. Hounds bore left-handed, re-crossed the turnpike and sped into the Cass Ledyard place, then bearing right crossed another concrete road, and disappeared in the woodland north of the kennels.

Allison, in anguished pursuit, turned turtle at the next fence and though he emerged [covered in mud], he was up and galloping again before ladies' last gasps of delighted horror had expired. The field came roaring after him and came to a panting standstill in the field south of the wood. Nary a hound in sight, nor a sound of any either. For a few seconds it appeared that nobody but the pack was going to enjoy this hunt, but this distressing thought vanished as hounds suddenly poured out of the wood, scampered beneath our horses, and proceeded towards the Willocks' new terraces. They checked here, while the masters shepherded their unruly flock from themselves fruitlessly for a moment, called them over to a tool shed where they found the line, and we were off again.

We crossed another road by Police Headquarters and entered the old Hudson farm, where we bumped and crushed each other as we wound around the buildings, cantered down the back road, meandered about the greenhouses and sunken gardens, and went on into the large fields to the north. Here hounds were away once more, burst into the woods, went right-handed back of George Murnane's stables, on to David Dows', then bearing right across the turnpike once again, sped into Theodore Havemeyer's famous nursery at Brookville, squeezed under a stout wire fence, and raced toward the Oliver Iselin fields.

Here the fox changed his mind, crossed another artery of traffic, and fled back of the Geraldyn Redmond farm, then right-handed through a mass of sumac and brambles to a grass lane, over another road, where two interested but inaccurate motorists had viewed him. Hounds needed no assistance as they travelled tirelessly on through more woods, eventually emerging by the fourteenth hole on the Piping Rock golf course. Here they checked a minute, while the Masters made it known that the hunt could not finance even a mangled bunker. Being a golfing widow, as well as an opportunist, I joyfully disobeyed orders and perpetuated some slight damage with infinite satisfaction. Into the woods again, endless miles of woods which stretched to the shore road by Beaver Dam.

The fox left the road for the swamp and headed for Connecticut, then wisely changed his course, came back to the road, took the turn for the Mill Neck Station, but bore left before reaching it, up a front drive, left again over fields, into woods, then back to open country and across the shore road into the Nelson Doubledays'. Hounds lost the line here, but Mrs. Rathborne had viewed our gallant fox and her halloa brought the pack to the edge (if you can believe it) of another impregnable forest. This one grew on the side of a precipitous hill, and was negotiated with heads buried in arms at a good gallop. Breasting our way through the last lashing branch, we opened our eyes to behold the bay at our feet. A wide concrete road divided us from the beach, and hounds had checked by a drain on the road side. The drain led to the beach, and an enterprising bitch leaped down the ten-foot embankment and investigated the other end with gratifying results to the pack, and questionable ones to the few weary members left.

Down the beach towards Bayville these amazing hounds flew, while we clattered down the road behind them. Under the new bridge they raced as we left the road and joined them. It seemed that even clam shells and streamers of seaweed could not puzzle these lovely ladies. Another mile, fetlock deep in sand and shells, then to solid ground again, over Robert

Huntington's sweep into paddocks, where the dividing fences were fortunately brittle, and on down to the beach once more. By the shores of the inlet we reined, for an ebbing tide had left a glittering stretch of flats and across its glassy surface the tracks of our stout-hearted fox were imprinted, vanishing on the far bank where a wood kindly hid him.

Mr. Peters looked at his mud-caked panting pack, at the sixteen gasping survivors of his field. The fox was to be spared.

The hunt had lasted two hours and fifty-five minutes. It had been an eleven-mile point with a conservative six added by our circuitous journey. It was a memorable day and the chief honors belong to the dean of American huntsmen, Thomas Allison, whose twenty-five years with the Meadow Brook hounds lie lightly on his capable shoulders and add year by year to his excellence and renown. The laurels go to that fourteen and one half couples of bitches for all but one and one half couples went the entire hunt.[32]

The end-of-year stewards' report mentioned that during the past season they had experimented by hunting the dog and bitch packs separately, and they felt that this innovation had been a great success.

At the 1933 spring meeting, Jackson Dykman stepped down as joint Master, and Harvey Dow Gibson accepted the vacancy. The hunt subscription committee, concerned with the dwindling membership, courted the ladies and sent out invitations to Mrs. Robert Bacon, Mrs. A. Butler Duncan (awaiting response), Mrs. Elbert H. Gary, Mrs. Thomas Hastings, Mrs. C. Oliver Iselin (declined), Mrs. Walter B. James, Mrs. H. Van R. Kennedy (declined), Mrs. Alice T. McLean, Mrs. John T. Pratt, Mrs. J. C. Rathborne (declined), Mrs. Geraldyn L. Redmond (awaiting response), and Mrs. James A. Burden (declined).[33]

Figure 6.5. *Harvey D. Gibson, M.F.H. on Justice*, painting by Edward Margaree, 1935. Courtesy of the Gibson/Woodbury Foundation.

In neighboring Suffolk County, Thomas S. Durant and Edward S. Voss, joint Masters of the Smithtown Hunt, faced the same problems. On May 23, 1933, the two hunts agreed to form a joint operation for five years (1933–1938). Meadow Brook would hunt foxes, and Smithtown would be a drag hunt. Meadow Brook defined its territory running along the north shore from Little Neck to the Suffolk County line, and Smithtown hunted around the towns of Smithtown, Deer Park, Manorville, Commack, and neighboring communities. The two hunt territories would be hunted by both clubs, and they would register jointly "additional country east of and bordering on the existing Smithtown country." Two fixtures would be set each week: one foxhunt and one drag hunt. Members would wear their own hunt colors, and subscribers, of whom there were estimated to be one hundred, were entitled to hunt with both hunts. Harry Peters, Meadow Brook M.F.H., was named as Master of the combined clubs, and Thomas S. Durant, Smithtown M.F.H., as assistant Master.[34]

That summer and early fall, much attention was given to the newer country, east of Smithtown. It had to be cleared of dense underbrush and hanging vines. The clubs also constructed numerous panel jumps throughout the area. The opening meet that season was held at the Harry Payne Whitney stables, and one hundred riders showed up. The riders had a short, but fast run. After the hunt, Mr. and Mrs. George Murnane gave a hunt breakfast, after which many rode over to Mr. and Mrs. E. F. Hutton's estate, Hillwood, to attend a large party before the United Hunts Association race meet.[35]

The merged hunts prospered, and soon they met three days a week, sometimes twice on Saturdays, with a foxhunt in the morning and a drag in the afternoon. There were a total of 48 foxhunts, with 105 riders in the largest field of the season, and 18 drag hunts, with 40 riders in the largest field. The members also hunted in Southampton several times at the invitation of Richard Newton, M.F.H. of the Suffolk Hunt. Meadow Brook Hounds subscriptions for 1933–1934 included thirty-three Meadow Brook Club members and sixty non-club members.[36]

In the spring of 1934, Meadow Brook decided not to hold its point-to-point due to lack of entries, but in the fall the club inaugurated hunter trials, which were held at the Middleton S. Burrill estate in Jericho. These were a great success and something they vowed to continue.

In December, Meadow Brook and Smithtown decided to exercise the option in their agreement stating that either party could dissolve their joint venture with a six-month notification. There was no official reason stated for the change. The only hint given was a letter from Harry Peters to the Masters of Foxhounds of Association, in which he stated that Meadow Brook did not want to revert to drag hunting. He commented that scheduling three hunts a week had been difficult to coordinate with Smithtown, and in some weeks riders were expected to go out three days in a row (twice in Meadow Brook and once in Smithtown country). He felt this was unreasonable. He was disappointed that more Smithtown people did not attend more of the Meadow Brook meets. He also reiterated that the additional country east of Smithtown had originally been recorded as Meadow Brook and should remain so.

As part of the dissolution, the hunts agreed to attempt to coordinate their fixtures. In addition, anyone who was a member of either hunt as of February 14, 1933, when the agreement had been signed, could continue to hunt in both organizations for the next season. Finally, Smithtown refunded 20 percent of its subscription income that was due to Meadow Brook, and Meadow Brook relinquished five couples of drag hounds that had migrated to its kennel.[37]

In 1935, Commander David C. Patterson resigned as Meadow Brook's secretary, and Betty Babcock accepted the honorary position as well as Field Master.[38] Many foxhunters at the time kept hunting diaries in which they recorded the horse they rode on a hunt, the location of the meet, the weather, the names of huntsman and whippers-in, how many were in the field, and details of the actual hunt. However, Babcock also drew maps, images, and recorded her impressions of the day.

Her diary described the opening day meet at C. V. Whitneys', October 5, 1935:

> The great dust storm of the middle west had little on what Long Island provided this morning. Into eyes, noses, ears

and mouths it flung itself and settled like a blanket over faces, horses and hounds. And all of us dressed to kill! Once the photographers were satisfied we moved off, but drew the Whitney woods without success and so proceeded in a cloud of dust to Broad Hollow. In the Elk pen, hounds jumped a fox who was instantly lost in his own dust screen. Ditto with the following three foxes found. In orderly formation we then trotted and coughed our way to the [Piping Rock] show grounds, where breaking into a smart stampede we leapt into the ring amidst the applause of loyal friends and intelligent employees.[39]

The New York Times reported that the spectators were thrilled when the hounds and one hundred huntsmen suddenly swept into the ring and galloped over the course of brush jumps.[40]

From 1937–1942, Harry Peters Jr. and Anthony N. B. Garvan served as assistant Field Masters to Betty Babcock.[41] The hunt struggled to reduce its persistent deficit. Meadow Brook raised the subscriptions for club members to two hundred dollars and three hundred dollars for nonmembers. The combined memberships averaged around eighty people per year.

Meadow Brook recorded forty-five couples of English hounds, five couples of American, and twelve couples of cross-bred with the Masters of Foxhounds Association (MFHA) in 1937. Over the next few years, the club purchased hounds from the Pytchley Hunt in England, but in an October 4, 1939, letter a month after World War II started in Europe, Pytchley said there would be no more shipments of hounds from England.

The war was coming closer, and the airfields on Long Island were operating at full throttle. In July 1940, U.S. government officials considered buying the Meadow Brook Club grounds. If nearby Mitchel Field were to be converted from a bomber station to a headquarters for pursuit planes, the government would need longer airstrips. Experts quoted in the local papers said that the spacious club property would be a valuable acquisition.[42] Around the same time, the Infantry School Hunt, Fort Benning, Georgia, and the First Cavalry Division Hunt, Fort Bliss, Texas, purchased several couples of hounds from Meadow Brook. Perhaps the soldiers had time to foxhunt.

Real change occurred after the United States entered the war on December 8, 1941. Harry Peters wrote Joseph J. Jones, clerk of the MFHA, on March 3, 1942:

> For your information, hunting is not going too well with us. People apparently are very rapidly losing their enthusiasm, and two other factors are becoming very serious with us, namely, the fact that we are in the heart of war work, airplane factories and Coast Guard, and it is almost impossible with the prices they are paying to get any men to take care of horses or hounds. We are down from fourteen full-time men in the hunt to just four, and many stables that usually keep five and six men have just got their old coachman and a groom. I thought that you might like to know this as I am quite sure our conditions are a great deal more difficult because of our location right in the heart of things than a lot of these other hunts that are in outlying districts. I hope to try and keep this group of hounds together, certainly for the present, and have made all the reductions that I contemplate at the moment.[43]

Jones responded:

> I have some idea of how hard the going is for your hunting on Long Island. Other hunts have some difficulties these days— but none have the war industries, shore patrols and coast artillery which I know you must contend with. You deserve a

lot of credit for saying that you are going to carry on in a small way—and I hope things work out all right, though it is going to be a lot of work for you.[44]

In July, Peters wrote again to update Jones, telling him that Meadow Brook had reduced the hounds to fifty couples. Hunt secretary Betty Babcock had resigned to perform "war work," and there would be no replacement. Most whippers-in were in the service then, but several devoted leave time to the kennels. Peters felt that the prospect of hunting was extremely slim, since most of the field was involved in wartime activities. Airplane factories were springing up right in the field where Meadow Brook hunted. He ended, saying that the war seemed very close, because his neighborhood farmers had lost thirteen sons at Pearl Harbor.[45]

Jones wrote back from the Naval Training School, informing Peters that his sister was now running the MFHA office. But he believed that "even a small pack will mean a lot to any fellows who get (lucky enough) furloughs or leaves and can go out with you—or even watch others go out."[46]

On Long Island, horse people were getting ready for gas rationing. Charles D. "Charlie" Plumb, whipper-in at Meadow Brook, said he was breaking in some of his trotters to pull two-wheeled jog carts. Betty Babcock was getting Peter, one of her hunters, used to the harness, and Gertrude Whitney reported that she'd dusted off the ancient rigs stored on the estate. Marian Shotter had thirty small pony carts at the ready for her Shetland ponies. Ambrose Clark and Frederic Pratt reminded everyone that they had used carts for years on short market runs.[47]

Horses might be well advised then to learn to pull carts, because horse traders were making the rounds. They were looking for "killers"—horses fit for dog food—and draught and riding horses. The Army wanted horses for artillery ($150–$207 a head) and cavalry ($160 a head), but the animals had to be shades of brown. No grays, whites, dapples, pintos, or light roans need apply.[48]

In September, as hunting season approached, Masters Peters and Gibson wrote a long letter to members and subscribers of the Meadow Brook Hounds. They hoped to continue the hunt in some small fashion because they believed that if the hunt stopped, it would never come back. They had reduced the foxhounds and horses to a minimum, and Robert E. Tod continued to house the kennel, stables, and huntsman's house free of charge. In that spirit of generosity, Meadow Brook had agreed to house the nucleus of Buckram Beagles at its kennel.

Thomas Allison, the huntsman; Wesley Heflin, the second whipper-in; and Henry Devine were taking care of the animals. Charlie Plumb was doing war work, but he attempted to help on Saturdays and holidays if the hunt decided to go out.

If they were to keep the hunt, the Masters thought they would need one thousand dollars per month or twelve thousand dollars per year to cover minimal expenses. However, it was difficult to estimate, because prices for feed and labor altered during wartime. In the interest of reducing the cost for riders, they suggested that all hunt livery should be reduced to dark clothes.

M.F.H. Peters was a lieutenant in the Navy and M.F.H. Gibson was engaged in war work, so they would not be leading the field. Mrs. Harvey Gibson and Mrs. James Hewlett agreed to act as Field Masters if people wanted to keep going. The Masters ended their letter with this: "Your cooperation and your comment is earnestly asked for and desired because we are facing a situation where together Meadow Brook will stand and certainly divided it will fall, perhaps never to be returned to the place in the sun it has occupied in American sport."[49]

Evidently, the response was positive for foxhunting, because the women were soon seen at the front of the field.

MEMBERS OF THE MEADOW BROOK HOUNDS

Thomas Allison

Thomas Allison might have remained in Virginia had Joe Davis not found him. One of his favorite jokes was when someone asked him his profession before becoming a huntsman, he would quip, "The same as the Lord's." It usually took a few seconds

Figure 6.6. *Thomas Allison on Pickles*, painting by Franklin B. Voss, 1937. Courtesy of Barbara H. Conolly.

for people to figure he meant carpentry instead of creating the world.[50] Allison, with his southern accent and love of swapping yarns, built a pack of foxhounds who, with their descendants, endured far longer than many Gold Coast mansions. Allison was one of the lucky ones who found his calling.

Foxhunting expert Jan Blan Van Urk hunted all over the country, and he thought Allison was a master huntsman.

> Having hunted behind this extraordinary man, I should say he could find a fox, put his pack on the line and show good sport on a crowded metropolitan subway. In fact, I'm surprised the City of New York hasn't tried to get him to revive the Chase in Central Park; for in spite of baby-carriages, keep-off-the-grass signs, run-of-the-bridle-path horsemen, lovers on park benches, band concerts, and a zoo, Allison could make a foxhunting shire out of what is now only a bit of scenery. The man is really terrific! And it is certainly a joy to the eye and a delight to the senses to see him work a pack under the conditions existing in Meadow Brook. As a hunting country, it has little to recommend it, but Allison turns in one good day after another.[51]

Peters told a story in *Just Hunting* to illustrate Allison's ability to improvise. The hounds were hot on the trail of a fox who raced down an embankment and took off down some railroad tracks. The hounds tore after him, but the riders had to halt. The train tracks were cut into the terrain, with steep slopes on either side. The only way to follow was on the track, but that would endanger their horses' legs. Nearby, a group of men were mending the track, and Allison spied their handcar. Without hesitation, he abandoned his horse, hopped on the handcar, and feverishly pumped the handle up and down. Soon he was whizzing along the rails behind his hounds. In about ten minutes,

Figure 6.7.   Allison on handcar following hounds, by Betty Babcock. Harry T. Peters, *Just Hunting*, 199.

"he came pumping back more leisurely, waving his fox, with the pack trotting behind."[52]

Age and poor eyesight finally forced Thomas Allison's retirement from Meadow Brook in 1951, but many Meadow Brook friends continued to stop by his home and talk with him about their favorite subject—foxhunting.

Elizabeth Thompson "Betty" Babcock

Betty grew up foxhunting with the Monmouth County Hunt in New Jersey. At age twenty, she married a stockbroker, Richard S. Babcock, and moved to Woodbury, Long Island, where she began hunting with Meadow Brook. When she accepted the position of honorary secretary in the 1930s, she was required to keep track of who was riding each day and to accept "capping fees" from nonsubscribers.[53] She found a blank English hunting diary in a bookshop and decided to use it. Each page had lines for the date, weather, location, names of staff, and number of people in the field. Then there were large rectangles for a map, observation, and illustration.

A talented artist with an eye for fun, Babcock drew detailed maps and wrote funny comments and humorous sketches. She was masterful with her portraits of riders in their hanging-on-for-dear-life moments and in catching a hound's "What is going on?" expression. She completed two diaries covering 1935–1936 and 1936–1937. The Masters then had copies made and distributed them to hunt members.

Betty's work can be seen in several published books, her own for children called *An Expandable Pig* and Harry Peters's *Just Hunting*. She also illustrated place cards for dinner parties and calendars that she gave to friends. Her art showed up in Meadow

Figure 6.8. Frank Voss by Betty Babcock. Betty Babcock's Diary, December 14, 1935, author's collection.

Brook Club records too. Her secretary notes often became re-
buses. Why write the word *hound* when you can draw one?

Jackson A. "Jack" Dykman

Jackson A. "Jack" Dykman was born in 1887 and grew up in
Brooklyn, where his attorney father, William N. Dykman, was
also head of the Brooklyn Riding and Driving Academy. Jack
started riding young, and he competed in many horse shows. In
October 1908, Jack was hunting with Meadow Brook when he
had a terrible fall from a runaway horse. He was unconscious for
hours and not expected to live. When he recovered, he had lost
all hearing in one ear.[54]

Jack graduated from Yale in 1909 and Harvard Law School
in 1912. He joined his father's law firm, Cullen and Dykman,
and in 1915, he married Susan Merrick of New Orleans. Jack
served in World War I, achieving the rank of colonel. In the
1920s, the family moved to Duck Pond Road, Glen Cove, and
Jack continued to practice law. He became president of the New
York State Bar Association and also served on the National
Council of the Episcopal Church.

Marjorie McDonald knew him all her life and described
him as

> a dear little man, but not really very adept at the fox hunt-
> ing deal. He came in as sort of a substitute every once and a
> while. When Mr. Peters went hunting in England one season,
> we inherited Dykman. We were not very happy. He was the
> cautious type. Nice little man, but you'd find people standing
> around. Hounds and fox were running, and he wouldn't let
> you move. You'd see people sneaking away from the back and
> going around him. Pretty soon, he'd be standing there all by
> himself.[55]

Anthony N. B. Garvan

Anthony Garvan was assistant Field Master from 1937–1942, and then he went to Yale University, where he received his bachelor's, master's, and doctorate degrees. He served in the Navy at the end of World War II. After the war, he became a popular professor of American Civilization at the University of Pennsylvania. His son said that his father "had a sharp Irish wit and could take on a group of any size and delight them. He was really funny on his feet and could do it for hour after hour."[56]

Dr. Garvan's obituary stated that "as much as he loved teaching he loved hunting more." For forty years, he had his own pack of beagles, Little Prospect Foot Beagles, which he hunted on his thirty-six-acre estate in Spring House, outside Philadelphia. He said it had been more than twenty years since the pack had killed anything, and that wasn't the point anyway. He liked hunting because "it was always different"; he "never knew what the beagles would do next. It got you completely away from normal cares and concerns like nothing else could."[57]

Harvey Dow Gibson

Harvey Dow Gibson was born in North Conway, New Hampshire, in 1882 and settled at Land's End, his eighty-two-acre estate in Locust Valley. Both he and his wife, Helen Whitney Bourne Gibson, hunted with Meadow Brook.

Harvey had graduated from Bowdoin College in 1902, supporting himself by banjo playing at college parties and local theaters. His next job was with American Express, but he soon went into banking. In World War I, he went to work for the Red Cross, directing its work in France. After the armistice, he returned to banking and during the Great Depression rose to

Figure 6.9. Harvey D.
Gibson, M.F.H. Courtesy
of North Conway Public
Library, NH.

the head position of Manufacturer's Trust. In 1939, he was appointed chairman of the New York's World's Fair.

When World War II started, Gibson served as the commissioner for England and Western Europe, service for which Dwight Eisenhower presented him with the United States' highest civilian award, the President's Medal for Merit. In 1947, he and his wife retired to North Conway, where in 1938 he had opened one of the first modern ski resorts. Gibson died on September 11, 1950. His legacy includes the Harvey Dow Gibson Playground in North Conway and the Harvey Dow Gibson Hall of Music at Bowdoin College.[58]

Marguerite Kirmse

Marguerite Kirmse was not a member of the hunt; she was an artist whom Harry Peters encouraged. English born, Kirmse

Figure 6.10. *The Fox*, hand colored dry point, by Marguerite Kirmse, 1931. Courtesy of Red Fox Fine Art, Middleburg, VA.

moved to America and soon became well-known for her dog portraits. She was particularly fond of Scotties, and her husband was president of the Scottish Terrier Club of America.

In the 1930s, her work attracted Meadow Brook M.F.H. Harry Peters, an important collector of sporting art. Peters

Figure 6.11. *The Hound*, hand colored dry point, by Marguerite Kirmse, 1933. Courtesy of Red Fox Fine Art, Middleburg, VA.

convinced Eugene Connett of Derrydale Press to publish Kirmse's work as illustrations in books. They were successful, so Derrydale commissioned several foxhunting scenes and two prized dry points, *The Fox* and *The Hound*. The panel behind each of these was painted robin's egg blue, a color closely tied the Meadow Brook Hounds.[59]

Harry Twyford Peters

Harry Twyford Peters worked in the family coal business, but much of his legacy relates to his life as a sportsman and connoisseur of sporting art. He loved horses, raised cattle, showed many breeds of dogs, and judged at the Westminster Dog Show. His interest in art led him to "rediscover" the prints of Currier and Ives. During his lifetime, he amassed a huge collection of early American prints. He donated them to the Smithsonian Institution, but they are now housed in the Museum of the City of New York. The Curator of Prints and Photographs described the collection:

> The collection of Currier & Ives at the Museum of the City of New York is largely built around the collecting and research done by Harry T. Peters. When the 1920s brought an upsurge of interest in artifacts of the American past, the modern collecting of Currier & Ives prints began in earnest. Peters led the way by amassing a collection of more than 2,800 prints and subsequently published the first history of the firm. In 1956, the Museum of the City of New York organized a major exhibition of Peters' unique collection, which resulted in its donation to the Museum. Today, the collection affords the opportunity to examine original Currier & Ives prints and to consider their place in history as a way of understanding how nineteenth-century Americans perceived and idealized themselves.[60]

Harry Peters died at age sixty-six in 1948, but he is remembered through several awards. For example, riders between ages fourteen and twenty-one still compete for the Harry T. Peters Trophy given by the U.S. Equestrian Federation.

Harry and Natalie Wells Peters had two children to whom they passed on a love of the outdoors. Their daughter Natalie Peters Webster lived on the family estate, Twyford, in Islip, Long Island, for many years. She was an avid gardener, and the National Garden Club of America gives a medal in her honor. She left her land as a preserve for future generations to enjoy.

Harry Jr. foxhunted with Meadow Brook before moving down to Windholme Farm in Orange, Virginia. There, he bred Angus cattle and had a kennel for his show dogs, especially whippets and greyhounds. Upon his death in 1981, his estate funded the Harry T. Peters Jr. Large Animal Clinic, which specializes in caring for horses, cattle, llamas, and alpacas under the direction of the Veterinary Teaching Hospital at the Virginia-Maryland Regional College of Veterinary Medicine in Blacksburg, Virginia.

The Vosses

William H. and Caroline Kane Neilson Voss and their five children were a founding family of the Rockaway Hunting Club, which ceased foxhunting in 1898.[61] Several of the children then hunted with Meadow Brook. Franklin B. "Frank" and Edward S. "Ned" were particularly fond of drag hunting. Ned went on to serve as M.F.H. for the Smithtown Hunt in the early 1930s, but he and his wife, Elsa, soon led the family exodus to Monkton, Maryland.

The Voss family seemed to have two dominant genes: one made them horse lovers, and the other gave them artistic talents. Ned was a watercolorist, and some of his illustrations appear in *Over the Open* and *Between the Flags* written by Meadow Brook's Harry S. Page. As a horseman, Ned served as the M.F.H. at the Elkridge-Harford Hunt for almost thirty years. Frank B. Voss

Figure 6.12. *The Meadow Brook Grays,* painting by Franklin B. Voss, 1930. Collection of the author.

foxhunted throughout his life, and his paintings reveal his understanding of that world. Frank is considered by many to be "the finest equine painter in America in the twentieth century."[62] Several of his best works are of Meadow Brook subjects: the *Thanksgiving Day Meet in 1923 of the Meadow Brook Hunt,* 1923; *The Meadow Brook Grays,* 1930; and *Thomas Allison on Pickles,* 1937.

SEVEN

$\mathcal{L}osing\ \mathcal{G}round$

Ware: Short for "beware." Riders call this out to
whomever is following them to warn them of danger:
"Ware wire!" or "Ware hole!" or "Ware car!" or
"Ware truck!"

Less than a month after the United States entered World War
II, acting Master Marjorie Hewlett had the hounds out for the
children's hunt. On January 3, 1942, the field met at Charles
V. Hickox's Boxwood Farm. The hosts, Charles and Catherine
Hickox, and their four children, Katrina, Sarane, Chat, and
Bark, rode matching dapple grays, while Barbara Hewlett was
on a handsome Appaloosa. The youngest rider was six-year-old
David Schiff, accompanied by his father, John. Two visiting
English girls provided an unusual sight, because they rode one
horse and, by sitting close together, they took the jumps as one.
One girl was the daughter of Dorothy Whitney Elmhirst, and
the other was her English friend. The girls had been sent to the

United States to escape the German bombing of Great Britain.[1] In February 1942, the Masters appointed Marjorie Hewlett Field Master, and she ran the Meadow Brook Hounds and Smithtown Hunt combined horse show the following August. Gas rationing meant that only local riders competed, but they held it to raise funds. At the end of the day, they had raised enough money to purchase two air raid sirens needed for the thirty-six-mile stretch of land between Babylon and Huntington.[2]

Field Master Hewlett continued taking the hounds out once or twice a week during the hunting seasons in wartime. Few records have survived from that period, but the dedicated

Figure 7.1. Sarane Hickox on Silver Shilling and Katrina Hickox on Grey Girl at the Children's Hunt Meet, Christmas 1940. Courtesy of Sarane Hickox Ross.

staff, hunting subscribers, and continuing generosity of Robert E. Tod worked together to keep the Meadow Brook Hounds active.

By 1944, seventy-seven-year-old Tod suffered from depression and unexplained fevers, which confined him to bed. On November 9, Tod shot himself.[3]

Hewlett offered her land as a new home for the kennels and stables. Over the next few weeks, everything was packed up and moved. Her estate was close enough that some of the smaller buildings were raised up, placed on skids, and pulled over to her property.[4]

When the war ended in 1945, both Harvey Gibson and Harry Peters returned and served out one year, with much assistance from their Field Master Marjorie Hewlett. On July 1, 1946, Robert "Bob" Winthrop II became Meadow Brook's new Master of Foxhounds (M.F.H.). That December, Winthrop wrote the Masters of Foxhounds Association (MFHA) and apologized for the lack of records kept during the war.[5]

The hounds remained at the Hewlett property, and over the next decade, she and her daughter, Barbara, became well acquainted with the puppy and adult hounds. They participated in hound shows up and down the coast, winning many awards for Meadow Brook.

Bob Winthrop and the Meadow Brook stewards were aware how much Hewlett was doing for the hunt. After several months of discussion and debate, they elected her joint Master on April 27, 1948. Hewlett's qualifications had never been an issue; the problem was her gender. A lady M.F.H. was not unusual in the foxhunting world by then, but this hunt was still governed by the Meadow Brook Club. The club by-laws stated that the M.F.H. was an honorary member of the stewards' committee. How could a woman sit on the governing committee of a men-

Figure 7.2. Robert Winthrop, M.F.H. Courtsey of Shelby Bonnie.

only club? The stewards skirted the issue then by having joint Masters, one of whom was a member and could sit on the board. Several months later, the MFHA wrote Hewlett and welcomed her as a member.[6]

Meadow Brook was ready for an exciting fall. In September, the cubbing season was underway, and Hewlett was busy with both the hunt and horse shows. On September 23, 1948, she hosted the Helping Hand Charity Horse Show on her estate. She was the show secretary and participated as an exhibitor.

Figure 7.3. *Marjorie Beard Hewlett McDonald, M.F.H.*, painting by Jean Bowman. Courtesy of Barbara H. Conolly.

In the ladies hunter class, she was having a good round on the thoroughbred gray mare Oxmoor Cherry. But then after jumping a fence, the mare stumbled on the landing, and both horse and rider went down. Hewlett was rushed to the hospital, and X-rays revealed a broken vertebra in her spine. She was placed in a body cast, where she would remain for at least three months. Thus began the first season of Hewlett's full Mastership at Meadow Brook.[7]

In September 1950, she married John J. McDonald, a fellow horse person, and they took time off for a honeymoon.[8]

Over the next few years, Meadow Brook purchased some new hounds from hunt clubs in Westchester, New York; Fairfield, Connecticut; and Chester, Pennsylvania. By the end of the 1940s, the Meadow Brook Hounds enjoyed a bit of a renaissance; one hundred riders, decked out in pink coats with postman blue[9] collars, were following the hounds on some Saturdays.[10] Many of the big estates were gone, but there were still a number of meeting places that would show up on a fixture card:

Mr. Atherton's gate, Brookville
Howard Bailey's stables, Glen Head
Brookville Church
Mrs. M. S. Burrill's stable
W. R. Coe's gate
Columbia Stock Farm
J. E. Davis's stable
H. P. Davison's gate, East Norwich
Ralph Ellis's gate
Harvey Gibson's stables, Locust Valley
Guinea Woods
Mrs. James A. Hewlett's, Woodbury
Richard Howe's gate, Jericho
Hudson's gate, Jericho
Otto Kahn's east gate
Meadow Brook Club
Meadow Brook kennels (old), Syosset
Meadow Brook kennels (new), Woodbury
E. D. Morgan's, south gate
Old Westbury
H. C. Phipps's stable
Piping Rock Show Grounds
John Schiff's gate, Oyster Bay
Senff gate
Sir Ashley Sparks's farm barns
J. S. Stevens's gate
Arthur Underhill's farm

Westbury Pond
West Hill Race Course
Wheatley Pond
C. V. Whitney's stable
Bronson Winthrop's
Robert Winthrop's
Woodbury Church
Woodbury Post Office
Woodside, Syosset[11]

Island Trees, once a popular meeting place for the hunt, did not appear, because it had been purchased by Levitt and Sons Inc. for its housing development, Levittown. By 1948, the Levitts had put up 2,867 homes, but they said that due to "unprecedented demand," they had decided to triple the size of the project. The company was speeding up construction so that it could complete 150 houses a week and reach the new goal of more than 6,000 homes by the end of the year. In addition, it was building four retail buildings, sixteen bowling alleys, a bar, restaurant, and swimming pool.[12]

Three miles east of Levittown, Robert Moses's bulldozers and asphalt trucks were ready to return to work. The Meadowbrook State Parkway, stretching from the Northern State Parkway southward to Jones Beach, had never been completed. Money for it had been diverted to other projects during the Depression and World War II. Now Moses had the funding and was ready to proceed.

He recalled the defeat he had had years earlier, when wealthy landowners had forced him to reroute the Northern State Parkway. At one point during that battle, Judge Townsend Scudder had taken Moses to a meeting at the Meadow Brook Club to discuss the Northern State design. Moses said that those "fox hunters in their red coats" stood up and denounced the parkway simply because their foxhounds would lose the scent when the foxes ran across the highway. Governor Al Smith supposedly proposed the construction of a tunnel for the fox and pursuing hounds and riders to use.[13] Smith's suggestion was often repeated on Long Island to demonstrate how little the parkway supporters understood the rural life.

Moses was not going to be either deterred or detoured a second time by these Meadow Brook families. He took direct aim at the Meadow Brook Club, sending the Meadowbrook Parkway right through the club grounds. Armed with the right of eminent domain, Moses purchased the two hundred acres at

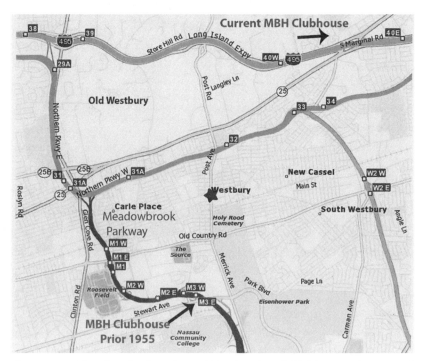

Figure 7.4. Map showing locations of Meadow Brook Clubhouses. Courtesy of the Museum of Polo & Hall of Fame (with alterations by author).

six thousand dollars per acre. There was no rescue this time, and the Meadow Brook Club started to look for a new home.[14]

In July 1950, everyone was forecasting doom for the hunt. In the local paper, the *Locust Valley Leader*, Madam Sopho speculated on its demise.

> Even in the midst of summer, with fall far away, the hunt is worrying and many of those in the know at the Meadowbrook Hunt are filled with misgivings that the coming season is the

Figure 7.5. Charles V. Hickox, M.F.H. on Keswick, 1938. Courtesy of Katrina Hickox Becker.

last one that will be run in this vicinity. New developments and the paving of many more roads are making it virtually impossible to have a good hunt without endangering the horses and riders or running across property that is injured by the horses. There is talk of transferring the hunt within a year or two to Smithtown where such things as wide open spaces still exist.[15]

The foxhunt was also in a state of flux. Bob Winthrop resigned as joint Master, and Charles V. Hickox accepted the position on April 1, 1951. Marjorie McDonald agreed to remain as joint Master. But the most radical change was that Thomas Allison put down his hunting horn at the end of the spring season. Deteriorating eyesight and other health problems made it impossible for him to continue. Whipper-in Charles "Charlie" Plumb took over the hounds for Meadow Brook. Charlie had

Figure 7.6. Charles Plumb, Wendy Plumb, and Meem Plumb near Whitney Tower. Photograph by Raymond Brown. Collection of the author.

grown up on Long Island and served as Allison's right hand for several years. He knew the hounds and territory.

That fall the cubbing season went well, but Barbara Hewlett, acting as honorary secretary, noted that the professional whippers-in had yet to be engaged. The opening meet was held at the Hickoxes' Boxwood Farm on November 10, and the weather was perfect. M.F.H. Hickox and his wife, Catherine, rose extra early to prepare not only for the hunt, but also for the traditional "hunt breakfast." The field was large and included Marshall Field with his daughters, Phyllis and Fiona. But then Hickox's big bay horse fell at a jump, sending his rider flying. It was a bad fall, and the brand new Master was whisked off to the emergency room. There, he learned he had a broken jaw, four cracked ribs, and numerous other lacerations.[16] He would be recovering for several weeks, proving that it was a good idea for Meadow Brook to have joint Masters.

Hunt breakfasts, such as the Hickoxes', were less common in the 1950s. Riders often ended their day's outing at a local restaurant instead. Ye Olde Rooster in Greenvale tried to lure the hungry crowd by creating a hunt room decorated with prints, hunting horns, and a few polo mallets.[17] However, it could never compete with Rothman's in East Norwich. That eatery had been a favorite watering hole for Meadow Brook riders since it opened in 1909.

The next year, the hunt ran more smoothly, and both joint Masters were out regularly. On Friday, October 31, 1952, the new hunt secretary, Cora Cavanagh, filed the autumn report. She listed the whippers-in as Mrs. Charles (Mary "Meem") Plumb and William F. "Billy" Dobbs; the foxhounds as sixteen couples crossbred, two couples English, and two and a half American; and the season as October to April, Wednesdays and Saturdays. The hounds went out fifty-two times that season. The Meadow

Brook country extended twenty miles or more from east to west and about twelve miles North to South. The area included pen fields with high rail fences and some panels, and a good deal of woodland traversed by riders. Through reciprocal agreement, the Meadow Brook hunts also used the Smithtown Hunt territory. The combined available area, therefore, comprised practically all of Long Island east from the New York City line to the Peconic Bay at Riverhead, an area sixty miles long and fifteen miles wide.[18]

The hunting country sounded bigger than it was. While there were still some landholdings, they were cut off from one another by roads and housing developments. Whether a large estate was sold intact or divided into just a few residences, the hunt fared no better. The new owners were of a different mindset than old Long Islanders. They circled their perimeters with chain link fences and hammered up "Keep Out" signs on bridle paths that had been cleared by the Country Lanes Committee and used by riders since the 1930s. Longtime residents complained:

> "They are killing one of the picturesque features that attracted them to the North Shore, the so-called Gold Coast. The fox hunters have a legitimate gripe and a crusade may be started. In Rome you may or may not do as the Romans, but if you settle in the horsey country and do not hunt, at least let those who have done it for generations, continue."[19]

Charles Hickox was an executive in the insurance business, and he knew about planning for the future. He recognized that Meadow Brook needed to find land if it were to survive. He decided to look at the land east of Smithtown. That section had been registered as Meadow Brook Hunt territory back in the 1920s and shared with Smithtown in the 1933–1938 agreement. That agreement had expired, and no one was hunting that country in the 1950s. Over the next months, Hickox studied the land and met with the landowners. He and Meadow Brook cleared underbrush in the country and placed panels where jumping would be necessary.[20]

The Meadow Brook Club also searched for new land for their clubhouse. The club purchased Jericho Farm, the estate of a past member, Middleton S. Burrill. The focus of the club would be a new, championship-level golf course designed by L. S. "Dick" Wilson. Perhaps those golfers owed a debt of gratitude to the stewards who, in 1902, had decided to keep the golf course even though few people were using it.[21] The stewards also cut the few remaining ties with the foxhunt at the January 27, 1953, meeting. They changed the constitution, removing the M.F.H.'s ex officio seat on the Board of Stewards and eliminating the requirement for the M.F.H. to be a member of the Meadow Brook Club. The stewards did leave in place the traditional payment of $1,500 from the club to the M.F.H. to support the hunt. Originally, this payment had been 60 percent (but not more than five thousand dollars) of the club dues, when the Meadow Brook Club had been a foxhunting organization. Many years earlier, that money had lured Frank G. Griswold to become M.F.H. for Meadow Brook.

Marjorie McDonald resigned as joint Master in the spring of 1953, but the foxhounds remained at her farm in Woodbury. Billy Dobbs accepted the vacant position and served alongside Charlie Hickox beginning in the fall of 1953. The Masters entered a few meets in the eastern country on the fixture cards, but only a few riders showed up at each.

Smithtown complained that Meadow Brook was now hunting in its land. Hickox fired back that Smithtown had more than enough land to hunt. It wasn't even using all of it. This land east of Wading River had been Meadow Brook's country long before either the Smithtown Hunt or the MFHA existed. He also argued that that Smithtown, established in 1900, had never hunted or paneled the area, as MFHA rules mandated.[22]

Hickox corresponded with the MFHA, saying there had been a July 26, 1956, agreement that permitted Meadow Brook to hunt the extended territory, and that he was approaching Joseph Krupski to discuss hunting on his land near Calverton Station.[23] He admitted that he was concerned with the growth of Grumman and the U.S. Naval Weapons Industrial Reserve Plant in the area. The MFHA clerk, Joseph J. Jones, replied that Meadow Brook might try to recruit hunters at the officers' club.[24] This comment was punctuated by a string of exclamation marks to indicate humor.[25]

Meadow Brook hunted the eastern country, but, again, the fields were small and the enthusiasm lacking. Travel should have been easier with all the new roads, but the average Meadow Brook foxhunter had a different lifestyle than one fifty or seventy years before. Then, the foxhunter often lived on a massive estate with stables of hunters, coach horses, and polo ponies. By the mid-1950s, many of those large houses had been torn down, left to fall down, or turned into universities or golf clubhouses. Some parcels had been split up, the mansion house razed, and the stables or other outbuildings renovated into smaller, but lavish, homes.

Many riders now kept their horses at the local riding stables run by the Plumbs, Patrick "Paddy" McDermott, John Brennan, Ralph Peterson, George Hudson, Mollie Harnden, Mike Roche, and J. Barney Balding. Many riders no longer had their own horse transports. They had to rent and share vans, which were provided by Walton P. Davis (shiny green ones with big lettering) or Harry Kopf (shabby chic, gray ones). In addition, the majority of the foxhunters worked in offices or took care of their own children; they were unable to devote a full day to hunting. The extra travel time to the eastern sections of Long Island discouraged participation.

Hickox did not give up easily. He noticed that the establishment of stables brought more children into the sport of riding. Maybe the hunt membership would increase if youngsters could be introduced to the sport. So in the fall of 1955, he hosted a meeting for the hunt committee, comprising joint Master Billy Dobbs, Bob Winthrop, John Schiff, Frederic Pratt, Elise "Mouse" Cavanagh, Marjorie McDonald, and the current Field Master Kathleen Merrill. Merrill recruited Deborah Robertson, and the women met with the officials of the U.S. Pony Club in Massachusetts. With enthusiastic support from members of the Meadow Brook Hounds, Merrill and Robertson applied and

Figure 7.7. Kathleen Merrill and Deborah Robertson, two proponents of the Meadow Brook Hounds Pony Club, at Hunter Trials 1960. Courtesy of Lynn Merrill Gray.

were granted a charter for Meadow Brook Hounds Pony Club (MBHPC).

The MBHPC was an immediate success. Membership grew rapidly, and there was a waiting list until enough adult mentors were found. Over the years, many hunt members offered their services. In addition to those who founded the MBHPC, they included Phyllis Field Samper, Cora Cavanagh Cushny, Dorothy Long, Sara Cavanagh Schwartz, Jane Greenleaf, and Joan Read.[26]

Members were sorted into four groups: foxes, vixens, hounds, and horses. Many pony clubbers were introduced to foxhunting, and for some it "took," but many were lured away by the more competitive world of horse shows. There were also guest speakers at meetings. Paul Brown, a local artist, came several times and showed everyone how to draw horses.

In 1958, Charlie Hickox retired, and Billy Dobbs convinced Devereux "Dev" Milburn Jr. to share the mastership. That year marked the division of Westbury, as the Long Island Expressway sliced through houses and old estates. Families held farewell parties on lawns that were soon paved over. And another change was underway. After a decade of living at the McDonalds', the Meadow Brook hounds found a new kennel. They moved to the Meadow Brook Club grounds in Jericho. The togetherness was only geographic; the two organizations operated independently from that time on.[27] The kennels were located on the west side of the clubhouse, tucked along the edge of the woods. Perhaps golfers were not so obsessed with silence in the 1950s.

The Meadow Brook Hounds still had some wonderful hunting country. A fixture card for December 1959 listed meets at H. P. Davison's, Austin H. Warner's factory, C. V. Whitney's stable, George S. Brewster's, Mrs. Marshall Field's, Piping Rock Show Grounds (followed by a hunt breakfast hosted by

Figure 7.8. *Back Home Again, Back Where He Started,* pencil drawing by Paul Brown. Collection of the author.

Mr. and Mrs. James F. Cavanagh), R. C. Leffingwell's, De-vereux Milburn's, J. B. Ault's, Robert Winthrop's, and Joseph Krupski's farm. Other months' meets were held at Sir Ashley Sparks's, John M. Schiff's, J. B. Balding's, Charles Zeh's, Alan Corey's, Edward Pulling's, Richard S. Emmet's, and Foxland. The huntsman and whippers-in tried to stay on the property,

Figure 7.9. Billy Dobbs, Joint M.F.H.; Dr. Edward Keefer; and Devereux Milburn, Joint M.F.H. Courtsey of Elizabeth Keefer.

but when a live fox became the quarry, anything could happen. Foxes dashed through basements, into partially drained swimming pools, and across highways.

The clatter of hooves on pavement had become a hunting sound as familiar as the hunting horn or hounds giving voice. In 1935, Master Peters had asked:

> Does anyone really stop to see a hunt here? On Long Island the motor traffic will not even stop long enough to let the hounds cross some of those terrible new roads, even when a fox is in front of them, let alone in the field. It's difficult hunting between motor vans loaded with potatoes, cauliflowers, or pianos. We had three and a half couple of hounds killed last season that way.[28]

Whipper-in Mike McDermott must have often thought the same, trotting out on a main thoroughfare, waving his hands, and hoping drivers would notice. McDermott stopped more cars on Northern Boulevard than the Brookville Police and earned the nickname "Mr. 25-A." Even with the best of care, hounds went missing. The notation "lost, presumed dead" appeared with heartbreaking regularity on the annual roster of Meadow Brook hounds filed with the MFHA.

Horses weren't hit by cars, but Barbara Conolly remembered a day they almost lost one on a building site. The hounds were running, and the riders were coming out of the woods. They turned a sharp corner, and Barbara said the horse in front of her seemed to disappear. He had fallen in a newly dug hole that she guessed was for a septic tank. Amazingly, both horse and rider were unhurt, but an excavator was needed to make a ramp for them to walk out.[29]

Charlie Plumb loved his hounds and knew them well. Neither he nor Allison raised them in isolation. Marjorie McDonald, her daughter, Barbara, and the Plumb and Cavanagh families spent hours interacting with the hounds, especially the puppies. Sara Cavanagh recalled a puppy named Hasty, who fell off a porch and broke her leg. Sara's sister, Cora, was young at the time, but she knew that a hound with a broken leg would not be kept. According to Sara, Cora wept and "carried on" until she persuaded her mother, Mouse Cavanagh, to let her try to rehabilitate Hasty. With only a little guidance from a local veterinarian, Cora worked like a physical therapist with her canine patient. In the end, Cora was triumphant. Hasty always had an unusual bend in one leg, but she returned to the pack and became a good foxhunter. When Jean Bowman painted Cora years later, she portrayed one hound with a leg bent a little oddly in honor of Hasty.[30]

Cora and Sara joined Plumb and whippers-in on horseback rides to train the puppies, even before the cubbing season started. They studied how individual hounds found a scent and worked a line. Both young women could soon differentiate the hounds not only by their markings, but also by their voices and mannerisms. Some hunted silently and needed encouragement to give voice, while others babbled on and on, even when they had nothing to say.[31] Plumb's puppy training rides were some of Sara's favorite experiences: "It was like a real hunt, but with just a few of us."[32]

Meadow Brook was now a hunt, not "a kill." Charlie Plumb knew that even with the best training, his hounds would probably never kill a fox on Long Island. Joint Master Milburn said that in his experience, "Meadow Brook has killed only one fox and we are pretty sure that one was dead when we got there."[33] Plumb's hounds hunted both the anise-seed bag and the fox, and he didn't need to have separate packs. He said that some hounds would be better at drag hunting, while others were more proficient on the line of a live scent, but many could do both.

Foxhunting on Long Island was always difficult because of the sandy soil, which didn't hold scent. And if one dug down very far, one likely as not would hit water. In an interview with the author on November 22, 1981, Plumb recalled a time when someone came out with a terrier, traditionally sent down a hole after the fox had gone to ground. The foxhunter rode all day with the dog in a box on his back. Plumb thought that was crazy. How could anyone enjoy a ride with a dog slobbering down his back and neck? More importantly, there would be no sense in sending a terrier down the hole in Long Island soil. More than likely, the terrier would end up in water. He thought that terrier sort of thing might work elsewhere, but on Long Island it was only done for photographers.

Another problem with hunting on Long Island was the wind. Some of the fixtures were at places like Marshall Field's Caumsett Farm, which were near the shore, and that wind could be fierce. It was hard to pick up a scent near the shore when the wind was really blowing. In addition, it could be hard to hear the horn or the hounds.

Sara Cavanagh Schwartz recalled a day when she was a whipper-in riding a mare named Night Lily, that they had purchased from the estate of Mrs. Ambrose Clark. They were on the Marshall Field estate, and Charlie Plumb told her to go bring back some hounds that had taken off on their own. Sara rode and rode, and heard nothing, except wind. Finally, she gave up and turned around. Or tried to. Night Lily would have none of that. Usually, an obedient horse, the mare refused to head back. Sara finally gave up and let the mare go in the direction she wanted. In about ten minutes, Night Lily located the wayward hounds. The mare knew the whipper-in's assignment, and she wasn't going back without them.[34]

Figure 7.10. Charlie Plumb, Huntsman; Mike McDermott and Sara Cavanagh Schwartz, Whippers-in. Photograph by Raymond Brown. Collection of the author.

Neither wind, nor rain, nor snow deterred the Meadow Brook Hounds. Plumb's hounds hunted well in snow, even when it got pretty deep, as long as it hadn't melted and refrozen a few times. If it had done that, it was hard on the hounds' paws.[35]

The weather wasn't the only problem on Long Island. The foxes were pretty darn smart too. Crowell "Cokie" Hadden, M.F.H. Billy Dobbs's stepson, related a story illustrating the wily Long Island fox. He'd left the hunt early because his horse was lame. Walking down the road, he saw a red fox ahead. Not wanting to cross the line (the scent), Cokie pulled up and waited. The hounds were a good distance away, but from the sound of their voices, he was pretty sure they were following this fox.

The fox trotted into a nearby field where a small herd of Black Angus cattle grazed. He weaved in and out of the cattle and then ran to the far side of the field along the top of the fence part way before jumping off and vanishing to the south. A minute later, he doubled back, walking on the fence for a way before he ran off to the north.

At this point, the hounds arrived. Hadden told one of the whippers-in what he'd witnessed, and the information was relayed to Plumb. The field checked, and everyone watched the hounds work it out. The cattle had moved by now, and the hounds went to the spot where they'd been, but the hounds seemed confused and milled around for a bit. A few fanned out, and one hit the line. The hounds were off, until they lost the scent where the fox had doubled back. They returned to the field and tried again. Several minutes passed before one of them picked up the fox's new line heading north. The hounds were off again, and the hunt followed over a couple of fences and a short run. But then the hounds again lost the fox, which Hadden thought had probably created some other diversionary tactic. Reynard was miles away by the time the hounds figured it out.[36]

Plumb could have cast the hounds on the correct line. They might have found the fox and even killed it, but hunting with Meadow Brook was never about killing the fox.

Some days Meadow Brook still drag hunted. Plumb said Meadow Brook often dragged the anise-seed bag on bad scent days or on special days when many people were hunting, such as Thanksgiving, which they had done for years. As the country closed up, the hunt dragged more often, sometimes to prove good sport, other times to make sure that the hounds weren't going to be exposed to chases across major highways.

Meadow Brook, like most organizations, had its share of self-inflated personalities. Plumb tolerated them with good humor. A longtime Meadow Brook member, Mollie Eckelberry, remembered a day when a guest was riding with the hunt. Her outfit looked brand new and expensive. She spoke with an English accent that Eckelberry thought was more Eliza Doolittle than House of Windsor. The hunt was on Sir Ashley Sparks's land, and they had a nice run. Afterward, the visitor went up to the huntsman and gushed excessively about the exciting gallop. She asked if they'd been chasing a red or a gray fox. Charlie hesitated before replying in a serious, thoughtful tone. "Madam, I think they were after a Labrador retriever just then. And it was probably either yellow or black."[37]

In November 1963, Meadow Brook was shocked, as was the rest of the country, when President John F. Kennedy was assassinated. The club canceled the hunt the next day, a Saturday, but it did go out the following Thursday, which was Thanksgiving. Everyone in the field wore a black armband, which contrasted dramatically on the scarlet hunting coats. At this sad time, there was something comforting in such a traditional display of mourning.

The next summer, Jacqueline Kennedy moved to New York City and boarded her horses at J. B. "Barney" Balding's stable. Balding had died suddenly the year before, and Nate Townsend, the head stableman, had stepped into Balding's shoes or, more accurately, riding boots. He took over the riding lessons and, on hunt days, led a flock of youngsters at the back of the field. Townsend was the first black man to become a regular subscriber to the Meadow Brook Hounds, something of which he was proud. Then he housed the Kennedy horses. He was even prouder. The Kennedy family bought a place in New Jersey eventually, but before then, Mrs. Kennedy rode out with the Meadow Brook Hounds at least once.[38]

Figure 7.11.   Judith Tabler, who rode out of Barney Balding's stable, on Spring Fever. Collection of the author.

Although somewhat less glamorous than the ex-first lady out in the hunting field, Edward B. "Doc" Keefer, MD, was always a welcome sight. His daughter, Elizabeth "Libby," on her roan pony, Corkie, and the doc on his big gray, Poncho, were regulars. When someone took a tumble, the calls, "Where's the doc? Get the doc," rippled down the line of riders. Then the doc, who was a top New York City surgeon, would canter up to inspect the injury. Flying by, Poncho might be mistaken for

Figure 7.12.   Libby Keefer at a meet with Meadow Brook Hounds Pony Club pin displayed on her cap. Courtesy of Elizabeth Keefer.

an ambulance. The doc clipped his horse's hindquarters artistically, leaving the outline of a medical bag on one side and a medical cross on the other.

In December 1966, the Smithtown Hunt complained to the MFHA that Meadow Brook was hunting its eastern territory. Letters flew back and forth, focusing on a line near Wading River. The correspondence became quite heated, stating that the dividing line between the two hunts was Peconic Avenue, which stretched between Old Country Road and the Peconic River. Marked-up maps were exchanged. Meetings between the Masters were set up by the MFHA. Meetings were canceled. The matter dragged on and on.

At the conclusion of the spring season 1967, Billy Dobbs resigned, and Dev Milburn welcomed Cora Cushny as a new joint Master. The lady Master wasted no time. She got in her car and drove out to inspect Peconic Avenue, which was drawn on the maps issued to both Meadow Brook and Smithtown. To her surprise, she discovered there was no road in that spot, just an old fence. Cushny fired off a letter to the MFHA informing it that the road everyone was discussing only existed in the mind of the mapmaker. The MFHA explained the error to Smithtown, and the argument ended.[39]

During the 1967–1968 season, Meadow Brook sent out an annual report to the membership. It listed one hundred subscribers on its roster. The hunt had gone out fifty-two times, with an average of twenty-six riders in the field. The kennels held twenty-two couples of hounds: thirteen couples crossbred, one and a half English, and seven and a half American.

The numbers were small, and people spoke about its being the last season. Since the 1930s, the Meadow Brook Hounds had been fending off that prophecy. It didn't seem like a good omen though when the honorary hunt secretary, Jessie Emmet,

Figure 7.13.   Cora Cavanagh Cushny, M.F.H. (Mrs. Theodorus V. W. Cushny) on Peck How, Opening Meet at Milburn's 1961. Courtesy of Cora Cavanagh Cushny.

wrote and informed everyone that Milburn had resigned as of September 23, 1968.[40] Always the gentleman, Milburn did not leave Cora Cushny without an escort. He convinced Billy Dobbs to return as joint Master.

Cushny, like Charlie Hickox, attempted to lure people to eastern Long Island, but there were few takers. To begin with, there were few foxes. The land had been farmed for years, and, therefore, there weren't woods providing coverts for fox families. However, whipper-in Sara Cavanagh remembered terrific runs if the hounds found one.

Figure 7.14. Jessie Emmet, Honorary Secretary and Richard Emmet. Courtesy of Katie Emmet Peterson.

We were hunting down in Riverhead. It was always a small field there. Hounds hit a line, and Charlie immediately said to me—don't gallop too fast—this is going to be a long run, so we need to conserve our horses. I have no idea how he knew it was going to be a long run, but it sure was. It lasted almost an hour and a half, with, as I recall, at least ninety percent of the pack on the line. At one point, two deer crossed the line not very far ahead of the hounds—where they could clearly see them—not a hound lifted his head! At the end, just Charlie, Mike McDermott and I were with hounds. Although I think the rest of the field found us eventually. It was a great run![41]

But according to M.F.H. Cushny, this was not a typical day. And even more important, there were few jumps. Cushny said that what kept the members of the field happy was, in a word, jumping.[42]

Meadow Brook members hadn't changed since Harry Peters' mastership (1925-1946); hunting was still about the jumping. The North Shore country didn't support long runs anymore, but there were plenty of fences. The fences might not be five feet high, but they were big enough, ranging from three and half to four feet. And Meadow Brook people jumped them, hardly anyone ever dropped a rail. If one couldn't jump it, one had to find a way around.

Figure 7.15. Billy Dobbs, M.F.H. and Charlie Plumb, Huntsman, confer. Photograph by Raymond Brown. Collection of the author.

Certainly, Huntsman Plumb didn't drop rails. When he wasn't hunting or training hounds and horse, Plumb was eventing. Eventing competitions span three days, during which the rider and horse exhibit in dressage, cross-country riding, and show jumping. In 1969, sixty-two-year-old Plumb was riding Johnny O, a top eventing horse, on the cross-country course in Pebble Beach, California, when the horse slipped at a turn. Marjorie McDonald said the grass on that course could become incredibly slippery when wet. She called it "ice grass." The accident paralyzed Plumb from the waist down.[43]

The loss of Charlie Plumb sent Meadow Brook reeling. He had been huntsman since 1951, and before that he had been a whipper-in. The majority of those in the field had never hunted

Figure 7.16. Mike McDermott on Tourist Encore at Piping Rock Horse Show. Photograph by Budd Studios. Courtesy of Mike and Jane McDermott.

without him. Whipper-in Mike McDermott became the new huntsman. Meadow Brook was blessed to have McDermott, who also had been with the hunt for years.

Then came another blow in what seemed to be the final element of a perfect storm. The Christie estate, approximately 550 acres in nearby Muttontown, became a preserve with no hunting allowed.

The Meadow Brook Hounds struggled to find sport for the 1970–1971 season, but then the club had to face reality. Perhaps it was time to end the hunt. Or maybe not. The club held meetings, and the membership entertained several ideas. The most viable one seemed to be that the club should become a drag hunt. Many members were horrified at the thought. They waved signs at meetings that proclaimed Meadow Brook Hounds would never be a drag hunt. Belmont Purdy would have laughed. Back in 1881, Meadow Brook's founders had regularly chased the anise-seed bag, but they had called it hunting in "the Pau form of sport."[44]

There was talk of merging with Smithtown. Or maybe the club could move to the east country. Members would have to travel in order to hunt there if there were no alternative. But there were the finances. The dwindling coffers. The members looked for other lifeboats, but then they realized they had been sitting in the last one for years.

Cora Cushny wanted the hunt to end with dignity. Her cousin and hunt secretary, Lee Bradley Duryea, said, "We just knew the time had come." Billy Dobbs and Dev Milburn agreed. So in May 1971, the Meadow Brook Hounds Hunt Committee, comprising William F. Dobbs, M.F.H.; Cora C. Cushny, M.F.H.; Lee Bradley Duryea, honorary secretary; Thomas A. Bradley Jr.; Fern T. Denney; and William M. Duryea Jr., wrote to the president of the MFHA, William Wadsworth, M.F.H., and stated that the Meadow Brook Hounds was dissolved.

The decision had been made after the hunting season closed. So there was no formal last hunt. Cushny remembered that the last meet that season had gone from the Balding stables, owned by Dorothy "Dot" Balding. Her parents, Mollie and Joe Davis, M.F.H., had lived there and called the estate Heyday Farm. It seemed fitting that the last meet had been at a Master's home. It was also easier that no one knew it was the last one at the time, so there were no tears.

The day would have ended like a thousand others. The last sounds would have been the huntsman's calls for the hounds to load in the "wagon." Paws and nails would scrape the tailgate as they scrambled in. Horse hooves would clip-clop up the ramps to trailers. Then someone would call to the Masters, huntsman, and whippers-in, "Thank you. It was a good hunt."

MEADOW BROOK MEMBERS

Cavanagh Family

James F. and Elise Burns "Mouse" Cavanagh were a Meadow Brook family. James was president of the Horre Coal Company, a division of the Burns Brothers, a coal distribution company. He also served as president of many Long Island horse shows. Mouse was a talented equestrienne and a mother of five children, but she still had energy to lead hunt activities and horse shows. She was honorary secretary of the hunt for many years.

Daughters Cora (secretary, whipper-in, and M.F.H.) and Sara (whipper-in) and granddaughter Lee Bradley (secretary) served as staff or officers for Meadow Brook Hounds. Other family members and extended family members were on the hunt committee or rode to hounds. Throughout the 1940s, 1950s, and 1960s, if someone wanted to know something about the hunt, they called the Cavanaghs at Cavcote Farms.

MEADOW BROOK HOUNDS

The Foxhounds Will Meet for Hunting

Tuesday, February 2nd (Ground Hog Day)
Mr. Charles Zeh's .... 11:00 A.M.

Thursday, February 4th
Piping Rock Club .... 12 Noon

Saturday, February 6th
Mr. John M. Schiff's (Drag) .... 12 Noon

Tuesday, February 9th
Mr. Charles Zeh's .... 11:00 A.M.

Thursday, February 11th
Meadow Brook Club .... 12 Noon

Saturday, February 13th
Mrs. Ogden Phipp's (Drag) .... 12 Noon

Monday, February 15th (Washington's Birthday
                    National Observance Date)
Mr. and Mrs. Edward Pulling's .... 12 Noon

Thursday, February 18th
Mr. Charles Zeh's .... 11:00 A.M.

Saturday, February 20th
Piping Rock Club (Drag) ....12 Noon

Tuesday, February 23rd
Mr. Charles Zeh's .... 11:00 A.M

Thursday, February 25th
Meadow Brook Club .... 12 Noon

Saturday, February 27th
Mrs. J. B. Balding's (Drag) .... 12 Noon

*All meets are Weather and Ground
Permitting*

If ground conditions are poor some carded drags
may be changed to foxhunting.

Call 671-2509 or 922-9095 or 922-4840

By direction of the Masters
Meadow Brook Club   Mrs. Wm. M. Duryea, Jr.
January 20th 1971   *Honorary Secretary*

Figure 7.17. The Last Fixture Card of the Meadow Brook Hounds. Collection of the author.

When it finally came time to end the hunt, Cora and Lee were there to make the decision. Both of them said it wasn't easy, but they knew it was time.

William F. Dobbs

When William F. "Billy" Dobbs wasn't foxhunting, he trained horses, primarily for Liz Whitney Tippet. Many of his hunters, including his big chestnut, Perennial, came from her stable. Dobbs was arguably the longest serving Master for the Meadow Brook Hounds. He held the position from 1953 to 1971, with one year off (1967–1968), for a total of seventeen years. Harry Peters served longer, from 1925 to 1946, or twenty-one years, but Peters was in the military during World War II, and he missed several seasons while traveling abroad.

Dobbs didn't go elsewhere when it was foxhunting season. His stepson, Crowell Hadden, remembered hacking alongside Dobbs on the way to a meet. It was cold and rainy, and Hadden commented on how slippery the footing might be. Dobbs thought a minute and then told Hadden to listen. All they could hear was the scrinch-scrunch noise that the horses' hooves made in the inch-deep mud.

"That sound means it's a perfect day for hunting," said Dobbs.

Hadden laughed. Dobbs would have said the same thing no matter what noise the hooves made. He thought every day was a perfect day for hunting.[45]

Charles V. Hickox

Charles V. "Charlie" Hickox was from Springfield, Illinois, and graduated from Yale in 1911. His wife, Catherine Barker, came from Michigan City, Indiana.[46] When they met, she was heiress to her family business, Haskell and Barker, which in 1907 was the largest railroad car manufacturer in Indiana. "As early as 1889, assembly lines using prefabricated assemblies were being used at the plant, predating Detroit by many years. It has been said that Henry Ford visited the Michigan City plant to study such assembly procedures."[47] Catherine's childhood home in Michigan City, the Barker Mansion, is on the National Register of Historic Places and open to the public.

On Long Island, Charlie and Catherine Hickox resided at Boxwood Farm. The stable was named Kasachabar, which combined the names of their children, Katrina, Sarane, Charles "Chat," and John "Bark." Like many Meadow Brook families, everyone learned to ride, so they could enjoy the activity together.

The family was generous to the hunt and the riding community, hosting meets, hunter trials, point-to-points, horse shows, and hunt breakfasts. Bark continued the family tradition, playing polo and serving on the board of the Polo Training Foundation for many years. Katrina Hickox Becker raised racehorses and then became involved in carriage driving. Much like her parents, she generously shared her expertise and hosted events on her farm near Aiken, South Carolina.

Catherine Hickox died in 1970, and M.F.H. Charles Hickox in 1979. Their land is now the home of the Meadowbrook (one word) Polo Club, so there are still horses cantering on the fields of Boxwood Farm.

Edward B. "Doc" Keefer, MD

Edward B. "Doc" Keefer, MD, was a surgeon at Cornell Medical College and a polo player, foxhunter, and horse lover. His passion was the Equine Preservation Society, whose goal was to save horses with injured legs. He was the first person to fit a horse with an artificial leg. He did this in 1973 for Secretariat's stablemate, Spanish Riddle, who after surgery became a sire of successful racehorses.

Keefer went on to save a dozen more horses and tried to do the same for the filly Ruffian, who broke her leg in a widely televised race in 1975. Unfortunately, her leg was too badly shattered, and the shock to her system made her difficult to treat.

Keefer hoped that his efforts would persuade all racehorse owners to consider the possibility of saving an injured horse and its breeding potential before just taking the insurance money for a dead horse. Keefer died in 2000, but veterinarians continue to study much of his work as they explore the area of artificial legs for horses.[48]

Marjorie Beard Hewlett McDonald

Marjorie Beard Hewlett McDonald, M.F.H., was the consummate horsewoman. She hunted and showed horses, judged horse shows and mentored riders, and tended and showed foxhounds. She was involved in the selection of riders for U.S. Olympic teams. She and her husband, John J. McDonald, devoted their lives to the world of horses and dogs.

Her daughter, Barbara Hewlett Conolly, continued on the same path. Much of her life was spent in support of the Meadow Brook Hounds. She married someone outside of the horse world, Dr. Joseph "Joe" Conolly, who served as Master of the Buckram Beagles from 1952 to 1962. Always resilient, Barbara soon added beagling to her résumé.

Figure 7.18. Barbara Hewlett on "Professor" at Underhill Farms, 1950. Courtesy of Barbara H. Conolly.

Devereux "Dev" Milburn

After suffering an elbow injury on the polo field, Devereux "Dev" Milburn took up foxhunting. Polo's loss was foxhunting's gain. As Master, Milburn brought a confidence and calmness to the hunting field. When he was up in front, riders knew there would be no unnecessary galloping this way and then the other. He understood how the huntsman and hounds worked, so he let them go about their business, a strategy that produced many great runs.

Perhaps Milburn's composure developed from his work experiences. During World War II, he served as a navigator on warplanes in North Africa. After the war, he practiced law, becoming a senior partner at Carter Ledyard and Milburn. In addition, he was president of the Meadow Brook Club for more than four decades.[49]

Milburn displayed a self-deprecating sense of humor in correspondence with the MFHA in 1968. He was concerned about who would be the "senior" M.F.H. when Billy Dobbs returned to the hunt after a year's retirement. Milburn asked whether Master A (Dobbs), a longtime but retired Master, would outrank Master C (Cora Cushny) when Master A returned. He explained all this confusion was caused by the retirement of Master B (Milburn), who was "an old poop and should never have been there in the first place."[50] On the last point, the Meadow Brook Hounds would have disagreed.

Charles D. Plumb

Charles D. "Charlie" and Mary "Meem" Plumb were both riders and animal lovers. Charlie rode in steeplechases and three-day events. His career spanned decades of victories, including the Maryland Gold Cup in 1929 and the National Open Three-day Event Championship in 1965. Meem served as a whipper-in for Meadow Brook, a popular horse show judge, and the mother of three children, Michael, Wendy, and Peter.

Michael Plumb became the most honored equestrian of recent times, participating in eight Olympics, more than any Olympian in the modern history of the games. He won two team gold medals, three team silvers, and one individual silver. He was the first rider elected to the U.S. Olympic Hall of Fame.

Figure 7.19. Charlie Plumb, Huntsman; Wendy Plumb and Mike Plumb. Photograph by Raymond Brown. Collection of the author.

In the 1984 Olympics, Torrance Watkins was on the same gold-winning team as Mike Plumb. As a child, Watkins and her family rode with the Meadow Brook Hounds.

After his fall and paralysis, Charlie Plumb moved down to Cochranville, Pennsylvania. There, he and Meem filled up their house with show dogs and rescued animals. Charlie died in 1985, and Meem in 1994.[51]

Sir Ashley Sparks

Sir Thomas "Ashley" Sparks's estate, Northlaw, was important Meadow Brook country. The land covered almost three hundred acres along Northern Boulevard and Berry Hill Road. For many years, Meadow Brook could have a good day hunting the Schiff estate and Northlaw. Ashley Sparks was the head of the American division, and later, deputy chairman of the board of the Cunard Steamship Company from 1917–1950, spanning two World Wars. He was knighted for his work in the shipping industry during World War II.

His wife, Mina Jane Roberts Sparks, was a New Yorker and active in local charities died in 1958, and when he died in 1964, Northlaw was bought by developers. It was a major loss for the hunt.[52]

Robert "Bob" Winthrop II

Robert "Bob" Winthrop II, M.F.H., was probably first and foremost a philanthropist, then a banker and a sportsman. His service and support of the Nassau Hospital in Mineola led the hospital to change its name to the Winthrop-University Hospital. He graduated from Harvard in 1926 and was the tenth generation of Winthrops to do so.

Winthrop's philanthropy extended to the conservation of animals, including serving as the president of Ducks Unlimited. He believed in the cause of government intervention to preserve the Mississippi flyway for migrating ducks, so he asked duck hunters to send postcards with the word *Ducks* on them to President Lyndon Johnson. Before the postcards went out, a fellow duck hunter was to alert the White House, but his letter went astray. The president was flooded with 5,460 unexplained duck postcards. Once everything was sorted out, Ducks Unlimited garnered far more publicity than it had anticipated.[53]

Bob and his first wife, Theodora Ayer, remained active horse people, as did several of his children and grandchildren.[54] He was Master at Meadow Brook from 1946 to 1951, but he continued to host the hunt on his estate, Groton Place, until the hunt ended in 1971.

EIGHT

The Competitions

Larking: When riders jump fences unnecessarily when hounds are not running.

Many of the founders of the Meadow Brook Club were gentleman riders in steeplechases. Steeplechase racing in the United States had its roots in the early nineteenth century, well before the Civil War, but the opening of Jerome Park course in the Bronx in 1866 and the addition of a steeplechase course in Saratoga in 1870 raised the sport to a new level. Many regular horse-racing spectators had no idea what a steeplechase was, but they enjoyed the new races at Jerome Park, and they soon spread the word about high jumps and close finishes. Crowds starting coming just to see those races.

Racing at top speed over jumps that simulated obstacles found in the countryside didn't seem so different to many gentleman foxhunters. Harry Page, who became a skilled steeplechase rider, wrote that the best advice he was given was to ride as if he were drag hunting.[1] However, Page recognized that not every hunting horse made a good steeplechaser. The problem was that some of the races (and horse show classes) were only open to horses that were ridden in the hunt. The rider had to obtain a certificate from the Master. Page complained about the unfairness of this practice.

> One master will give you a certificate if you will only promise never to bring the runaway, fence-destroying brute out again; another will only sign his name when he is assured that the candidate for 'chasing honors has been "regularly and fairly'" hunted; and a third must be convinced by seeing him cut out the work in a gallop that will try the old fox-catcher to the limit.[2]

Page wanted to certify a new horse named Nestor, and he wagered with his friend that he could convince Ralph Ellis, Master of Foxhounds (M.F.H.) at the time, to sign the necessary form without Ellis ever seeing Nestor jump over a fence. At the beginning of the hunt, Page showed Ellis the horse. Then he asked where the hunt would finish, because he wanted his groom to meet him there. After the hunt headed off, Page traded horses with his groom. The horse Page mounted was not the same color as Nestor, so he kept back, except for a few times when he trotted up behind Ellis and made a few remarks. He wanted Ellis to know he was still in the field. When they approached the end destination, Page found his groom, swapped horses, and trotted over to the Master. Ellis signed the paper, and Page won the bet.[3]

Most Meadow Brook members were not so devious, but many were more drawn to the excitement of steeplechasing than foxhunting. From the early days, when Frank G. Griswold took the Queen's County Hounds up to Newport, Rhode Island, the riders held informal steeplechases. By 1877, this Newport event spanned two days and attracted thousands of spectators.[4]

The Meadow Brook Club formed in May 1881 for the purpose of foxhunting and other outdoor sports. Steeplechasing was one of these other sports from the onset. On April 28, 1882, the club announced that the Meadow Brook Hunt races were scheduled for May 6 at Meadow Brook, Long Island.

> The first will be a flat race of half a mile for half bred hacks or hunters for [ten dollars]. The second will be a three mile run over the regular steeple chase course for [twenty-five dollars] and a piece of plate added. The third race will be a mile and a half dash over six hurdles for [twenty dollars]. The heavy weight hunters' race is to be over the third mile steeple chase course for [twenty dollars], horse to carry 185 pounds. There is to be a pony race and a sweepstakes for high jumpers.[5]

No results were posted in local newspapers. The minutes of the Meadow Brook stewards' meeting on August 1, 1882, made no mention of a race day in the annual summary. However, a December newspaper article discussing elderly racehorses who were still running listed two horses as winning in the Meadow Brook Hunt races earlier that year: Bombast took the Hunt Cup (three miles, no time taken), and Elmwood won the Heavy Weight Hunters Steeplechase (three miles, no time taken).[6]

The next spring, the Meadow Brook Races attracted more attention.

FIVE THOUSAND PEOPLE ON THE TURF NEAR GARDEN CITY— SEVEN EXCITING CONTESTS

The Meadow Brook Hunt inaugurated its racing season yesterday. The weather was all that could be desired, and the attendance was estimated at [five thousand]. A special train of eight crowded cars went to the ground from Long Island City, and not less than [five hundred] carriages and farm wagons were scattered over the field. The track is about a mile east of Garden City. It is a natural racing ground. On one side is a hill from which [twenty thousand] people might view the race without obstructing the view. The Meadow Brook Hunt represents the aristocracy of New York, and numbers among its members many millionaires and sons of millionaires. August Belmont, Jr., Colonel William Jay, Edwin D. Morgan, A. Belmont Purdy, Winthrop Rutherford, Frederic Beach, Stanley Mortimer and F. R. Appleton were the Committee in charge of yesterday's races.[7]

The first race was a half-mile dash on the flat for half-bred qualified hunters. Pierre Lorillard's Sinbad won, although the second-place horse, E. D. Morgan's Kathleen ridden by Belmont Purdy, had been the favorite. The second contest was an open sweepstakes steeplechase for qualified hunters, maximum weight 160 pounds, thoroughbreds carrying 15 extra pounds penalty, and over a short course of about two miles. Long Island Stable's Bombast ridden by George Work finished first.[8] The third race, titled the Kennel Purse, was a half mile over flat. There was no entry fee, and it was open only to horses used for farming on farms hunted by the Meadow Brook Hounds. This type of race was sometimes called a "farmers' race" and often provided a good deal of fun. On this day, however, there was little laughter, because the horses were exceedingly fast and the race exciting. The winner was named Puck, owned by farmer F. Horton.

Race four was a heavyweight steeplechase over the long course, about three miles, and the trophy cup was presented by E. D. Morgan. Ex-M.F.H. Samuel S. Sands rode Mercury to victory, and Henry L. Herbert rode Carmelite to finish second.

However, the third-place finisher, Elliott Zborowski, objected.[9] He said that the race steward had informed him that there was an additional lap, so when the first two horses finished Zborowski continued over the course again and then claimed his victory. When this was denied, he protested, but to no avail.

The next race was for polo ponies under 14.1 hands, half mile on the flat, and was won by Homer Richardson on Tom Boy. August Belmont Jr., riding a chestnut mare named Flirt, fell during the race when his saddle slipped, but he was not badly injured.

The sixth race, the Hunt Cup, was the "crack race of the day" over three miles.[10] Rockaway Hunting Club member Frederick Gebhard had the favorite horse, Biloxi. Gebhard would have won, but his horse was disqualified for running around the second fence. This gave Stanley Mortimer on Hobson's Choice the victory. Then came Belmont Purdy on Edwin Morgan's Kenny. The last race was the consolation run, and it was won by Adolf Ladenburg.[11]

Meadow Brook found that having a racecourse next to a hillside, where people could view the races without charge, did not enhance the club finances. The nearby Rockaway Hunting Club had formed the Rockaway Steeplechase Association with the idea of building a new racecourse in Cedarhurst. August Belmont, Stanley Mortimer, Edwin Morgan, Samuel Sands, Thomas Hitchcock, George Work, and other Meadow Brook members supported the venture. They were appointed to the race and executive committees.[12] On the inaugural race day in 1885, the second race was sponsored by Edwin D. Morgan, ex-M.F.H., and the fourth race was the Meadow Brook Cup.[13]

For the next several years, races were held at Cedarhurst in the spring and fall.[14] The spring meet in May spanned four days. Members of Meadow Brook sponsored all six races the first day, and it became known as "Meadow Brook Day."[15]

By 1891, Meadow Brook had decided to run its own race and returned to Hempstead Plains. A large tent, similar to one of P. T. Barnum's, was erected. The stated purpose was to provide a covered space from which spectators might stand and view the race. The added benefit was that the tent blocked most of the racecourse from the eyes of unpaid spectators on the hillside. There was also a small grandstand. On the opposite side, near the rail, were spots where those who arrived in carriages could, for a fee, park their vehicles. The horses were unharnessed, and men pulled the rigs up to the railing. This created a sort of miniature grandstand with spectators sitting in their own carriages or buckboards.

There were six races that day. Foxhall Keene won two, and James Kernochan the other four, including the most important trophy of the day, the Meadow Brook Cup.[16] Kernochan won on Retribution, who became a legendary steeplechaser and, later, Eloise Kernochan's favorite hunter. Another rider, Harry Page, described what the races looked like in the 1890s.

> Hempstead Farm! What pleasant recollections the name brings back, race meetings, schooling and gallops. I can't for the life of me remember riding but one winner there, but what jolly times we had. In the early [18]90s there was a grand stand with a mile flat course on turf, and a steeplechase course that went out into the country over natural fences, crossing the Hempstead-Farmingdale road. In [18]90 and [18]91 I saw Jimmy Kernochan win the Meadow Brook Cup there on that good 'chaser Retribution. W. C. Hayes, who had just come from Virginia, and who was about to make such a name for himself in the steeplechase world, was second each time. In both contests he opened up a long lead in the first two miles of the four-mile course, but was eventually caught and easily vanquished. I used to go there with my friend Jack

Wilmerding, taking from Long Island City a special train which stopped on the Garden City-Hicksville Branch of the Long Island Railroad, opposite the course. What a wonderful sight was a race meeting on the then beautiful plains. The Meadow Brook country was the center of sport and fashion: Sport was not commercialized, Fashion not scattered. If you arrived early you could see coach after coach, with the music of the pole chains and the rattle of the lead bars, cross the course to park opposite the stand, or at the upper end thereof. They came from Hempstead, Cedarhurst, Westbury, the South Shore and New York with the gayest parties on the outside and the best lunches within. Hempstead Farms, then a stock company, was run on a lavish scale, everything top from cattle to chickens. There was ample stabling for the horses that were to furnish the meeting's sport, as well as for the teams that made the journey from country or town house to the race course side, a sport in itself.[17]

Page was one of The Bulldags. The group spent their hours in the hunting field outracing one another, so it was logical that they insisted on a private Bulldag steeplechase race. In 1892, four Bulldags—Roman Baldwin, William "Billy" Hayes, Charles Cottenet, and Harry Page—entered. Hayes, the only experienced steeplechase jockey at that time, won easily.[18]

Meadow Brook Hunt members dominated the list of winners of the coveted Challenge Cup for Gentleman Riders, first awarded in 1883. Gentleman riders were amateurs, and the trophy was awarded to the owner of the horse who won the most races in various steeplechase meets.[19] Harry Page listed the Meadow Brook winners for the first decade:

1883 Stanley Mortimer's Hobson's Choice
1884 Samuel S. Sands Jr.'s Vivian ridden by George Work

1885 George Work's Mars

1886 Edwin D. Morgan M.F.H.'s Halefellow ridden by Thomas Hitchcock M.F.H.

1887 Edwin D. Morgan M.F.H.'s Schoolmaster ridden by Thomas Hitchcock M.F.H.

1890 James Kernochan's Retribution

1891 James Kernochan's Retribution[20]

Rockaway Hunting Club clubhouse burned in July 1893, and the club purchased the fourteen acres of steeplechase course for its new building and golf course. This was primarily due to finances. A steeplechase course was expensive to maintain, and the races themselves ran for only a few days, generating little profit. In addition, the New York State government and the State Racing Committee, which included August Belmont and Edwin D. Morgan, were in a struggle over gambling legislation.[21]

The Meadow Brook Steeplechase Association held its own races on the Hempstead course in 1896, but in 1896 and 1897 it abandoned the circular track. Those years, the race was more like a point-to-point, with the course stretching between the J. F. D. Lanier property and Dudley Winthrop's. Flags marking where a rider should turn around were placed on each property, and certain hacking lanes were blocked off in between, but other than that the riders picked their own courses over the four and one half miles. This did not make the journey easy; the fences were big and the pace fast. One year, fourteen horses started, but only five finished the race.[22]

In 1899, the steeplechase moved to William C. Whitney's new training track in Wheatley Hills, where it remained until 1906, when it moved to Hempstead again. But not everyone was sure exactly where in Hempstead.

Some of the spectators arrived on the special train which left Long Island City shortly after noon. In this party was John Drew, who created a deal of amusement by his by-play because of the comedy episode of the trip. This was occasioned by the engineer and conductor losing their way upon the Hempstead Plains after the train left Mineola. Three times the train was stopped while engineer, conductor, and the men of the party reconnoitered to locate the racetrack while the women picked violets by the wayside. A peculiar condition of the atmosphere and the bright sunlight seemed to obscure a definite horizon so that it was difficult to distinguish landmarks far away. By the aid of field glasses the pavilion tent and the flags marking the course were finally sighted and the train was brought as near to them as possible.[23]

In 1907, the race went back to the Meadow Brook Club grounds, and Russell Grace's horse, Willie Price, ridden by Fletcher Harper won the Hunt Cup. However, in all these moves, the original Cup vanished and was not rediscovered for many years. As a result, many winners' names were never inscribed.[24]

A few more location changes occurred before the steeplechase was back at the Meadow Brook Club. Wanting to provide the spectators with the best view of the finish, the club set the finish line on the polo field closest to the grandstands. Joe Davis, M.F.H., won the Meadow Brook Hunt Cup in 1910. But the polo committee was unhappy with the damage done to their best field, and the race was transferred to Belmont Park in 1913. There, over the next few years, the crowds began to recognize and cheer for the top Meadow Brook competitors, such as Skiddy von Stade, Joe Davis, James Park, Ambrose Clark, Thomas Hitchcock, and Harry Page. Page rode many winners and wrote much about the sport, but his race fans knew him best as the jockey who wore the monocle, which stayed in place throughout the rough and fast races.[25]

The Meadow Brook steeplechase had held a spring and fall meet for years. Then the races' locations were split: the spring one to be held at Belmont Park along with other horse races, and the fall meet held at the club and still controlled by the hunt members. Over the next decade, the meets continued bouncing from field to field, or estate to estate.

The race was scheduled for Harry Payne Whitney's homestead on May 9, 1915, but news arrived about the sinking of the *Lusitania* the day before. Alfred G. Vanderbilt, Whitney's brother-in-law, was on the ship, and the racing committee was ready to cancel. However, "when word was received from an unidentified source that Mr. Vanderbilt had been saved, it was decided to go ahead with the day's sport as outlined."[26] By the next day, everyone knew that unidentified source had been incorrect. Vanderbilt had indeed gone down with the ship.

The United States entered World War I on April 6, 1917. There was a Meadow Brook Cup race at Belmont that June, but the fall steeplechase was abandoned and replaced with a point-to-point, won by F. Ambrose Clark. Belmont Park ran a Meadow Brook steeplechase in the spring of 1918. After that, the Meadow Brook Hounds ceased hosting their steeplechase until 1926, when it finally found a home with Ambrose Clark. He hosted the race at his estate, Broad Hollow until 1941.[27]

The one drawback to selecting this location was Clark's abhorrence of motorized vehicles. They were banned from Broad Hollow. People could park their cars along the near roads, but then they had to either walk to the course or ride in one the tally-ho carts that Clark provided. When the race was broadcast over the radio in 1931, the radio engineers were forced to leave their equipment truck on a neighbor's property and convey their

Figure 8.1. *Meadow Brook Steeple Chase at Ambrose Clark Estate, Broad Hollow, Old Westbury, Long Island,* dry point etching by Paul Brown. Courtesy of Chisholm Gallery.

microphones and other instruments to the course atop a horse-drawn carriage.[28]

Ambrose Clark's greatest steeplechase achievement took place across the Atlantic when his horse Kellsboro' Jack won the Grand National in Aintree, England, on March 24, 1933. Technically, it was his wife's horse. Two years earlier, in 1931, the horse was not schooling well, and Clark suggested changes to the training. The frustrated trainer retorted that Kellsboro' Jack did indeed need a change—perhaps even a new owner. Impulsively, Ambrose sold the horse to his wife, Florence, for a British pound. When Kellsboro' Jack won the Grand National, Florence insisted that Ambrose take her place in the winner's circle.[29]

Four years earlier, in 1929, another woman, Maud Stevenson, who hunted with Meadow Brook, owned one of the great steeplechase horses of its time. The horse was Alligator, and he

Figure 8.2. Ambrose Clark. From the Collection of the Meadow Brook Club.

won the Maryland Hunt Cup. Riding him that day was Meadow Brook's whipper-in (and future huntsman) Charlie Plumb. Adding to the excitement of the race, Alligator fell at a fence, but Plumb remounted and won.[30] Alligator won all four important races that year: the Rose Tree Challenge Cup, the Maryland Hunt Cup, the Meadow Brook Hunt Cup, and the New Jersey Hunt Cup.[31] In December 1930, Plumb rode Alligator in the Grassland International Steeplechase in Tennessee. The course was wet and slippery. Alligator and Plumb went down at the last fence, but so did the next horse. Plumb remounted, as he had in the Maryland Hunt Cup, and was rewarded with the victory.[32]

Steeplechasing continued through the Great Depression, but Meadow Brook's autumn meets ended with World War II.

Figure 8.3. *The Last Fence at Meadowbrook,* pastel and ink, by Paul Brown, 1928. Courtesy of Chisholm Gallery.

Figure 8.4. Hunt team, Harvey D. Gibson on gray horse. Courtesy of the Gibson/Woodbury Foundation.

The Meadow Brook Stake race continued at Belmont, but it bore little resemblance to the hunt-sponsored races before the war.

The members of the Meadow Brook Hounds shifted their attention to showing hounds, hunter teams at horse shows, hunter trials, hunter paces, and point-to-points. For many years, the Meadow Brook Hounds and Green Spring Valley Hounds competed in the crossbred classes at Bryn Mawr.

The hunt teams Meadow Brook produced over the years were formidable, winning regularly at the Piping Rock Horse Show and the National Horse Show. Less competitive, perhaps,

Figure 8.5.   Marjorie McDonald, M.F.H. on Wings and Dorothy Long on Safety Pin crossing the Whitney Paddocks, 1950. Courtesy of Barbara H. Conolly.

Figure 8.6. Marjorie McDonald, M.F.H. showing hounds. Courtesy of
Barbara H. Conolly.

but more closely relating to hunting were the hunter trials,
paces, and point-to-points.

The winners for these events in the mid-1960s were:

Hunter Trials

1964   Mr. and Mrs. J. H. Leib's Shannon Castle

1965   Mrs. and Mrs. J. H. Leib's Broom Boss

1966   Pear Tree Farm's Sight Unseen

Figure 8.7. Keith Rehberger on Social Security, Meadow Brook Bays Hunt Team, National Horse Show, Madison Square Garden, 1961. Courtesy of Keith Rehberger.

Figure 8.8. Billy Dobbs, M.F.H. on Oxmoor Cherry, Piping Rock Horse Show. Courtesy of Barbara H. Conolly.

Figure 8.9.   Katrina Hickox on Sir Echo, Meadow Brook Hunter Trials. Courtesy of Katrina Hickox Becker.

Figure 8.10.   Lib Maloney on Flicka. Courtesy of Barbara H. Conolly.

Figure 8.11. Eben Pyne and daughter Lillian Pyne, Meadow Brook Point-to-Point. Courtesy of Lillian Pyne Corbin.

Hunter Pace

1965 Mrs. Henry Stockman and Dr. Henry A. Chase
1966 Mr. John Greenleaf and Dr. Edward Keefer
1967 Miss Alane Gaeta and Master David Perlman

Old-Fashioned Point-to-Point for the Blackout Memorial Trophy

1964 Miss Wendy Plumb on Sweet Chicle
1964 Miss Ann Clark on Ballet Master
1965 Michael McDermott on Pear Tree Farm's Peck How
Mrs. Charles D. Plumb on Ivy League (first amateur to finish)
1967 Mr. David Thomas on Miss Wendy Plumb's Sweet Chicle[33]

All these events, competitive or not, were run primarily by volunteers. They spent hours supporting and promoting the hunt. The Meadow Brook Hounds would not have existed at all without them.

Figure 8.12. Jeanne Stockman, winner of Meadow Brook Hounds Point-to-Point, receives the trophy from Richard S. Emmet. Courtesy of Jeanne Stock-

FOLLOWERS OF THE
MEADOW BROOK STEEPLECHASE

Paul Brown

Paul Brown was the Garden City artist who came to Meadow Brook Hounds Pony Club meetings in the 1950s and showed youngsters how easy it was to draw horses. He always wowed the audience by telling them he was color blind, and how that little problem didn't keep him from being what he most wanted to be—an artist. After he showed the group how he drew a horse, each pony clubber was given paper and pencil and asked to draw one. This, of course, just reminded everyone how difficult it was to draw a horse.[34]

Brown had been drawing animals for thirty years. He drew horse illustrations for magazines in the late 1920s, which caught the eye of Eugene V. Connett at Derrydale Press. Brown illustrated David Gray's work, *Gallops*, for Derrydale in 1929. Coincidently, the author dedicated the book to Mr. and Mrs. Thomas Hitchcock, Broad Hollow Farm, Westbury. In 1931, Brown produced the action-filled aquatint, the Meadow Brook. Brown also illustrated advertising materials for Brooks Brothers.[35]

Throughout the 1930s, 1940s, and 1950s, Brown was a familiar figure at foxhunts, horse shows, and steeplechases. His children's books, some co-written and all beautifully illustrated, created a generation who knew exactly what Black Beauty looked like. For many years, Long Islanders enjoyed Brown's artwork on the posters and yellow and blue catalogues for the Piping Rock Horse Show.

Henry L. Herbert

Henry Lloyd Herbert was most often associated with polo. He developed the handicap system in 1877, and, with Thomas

Figure 8.13. *Henry L. Herbert on Transport.* Foxhall Keene won the high jumping record of seven feet with this horse at Madison Square Garden. From the
Collection of the Meadow Brook Club.

Hitchcock, he formed the Polo Association in 1890. Herbert
served as chairman of the Polo Association for thirty-one years.
When he died, his obituary proclaimed Herbert "the father of
polo."[36] However, as a young man he rode in steeplechases and
was a regular foxhunter with Meadow Brook.

Maud Stevenson

Maud (also Maude) Kennedy Stevenson owned Alligator when
Charlie Plumb rode him to victory in the 1929 Maryland Hunt
Cup and in the 1930 International Cup in Tennessee. Maud had
grown up in Hempstead, and she often followed the Meadow
Brook Hounds. Her second husband, Malcolm "Mike" Steven-
son, was the polo player and Meadow Brook Master of Hounds.
After the marriage ended in divorce, she married S. Bryce Wing,

M.F.H. of Harford County Hunt, and moved to Monkton, Maryland, in 1933. Maud died at age forty-four from a heart attack in 1937.

The Whitneys

William Collins Whitney grew up in Conway, Massachusetts, and went to Yale University. At Yale, he became friends with Oliver Payne from Cleveland, Ohio. Payne was two years older and left college to join the Union army. Whitney graduated in 1863, attended Harvard Law School, and became a New York City lawyer, rising to the position of City Corporation Counsel. There, he allied himself with Samuel Tilden and the reform Democrats as they took on Boss Tweed.

Whitney was active in Democratic politics and was instrumental in the election of Grover Cleveland in 1884. President Cleveland appointed Whitney Secretary of the Navy. Whitney resigned at the end of four years, and the Democratic Party urged him to run for governor of New York or president. He declined and supported Cleveland.

After the end of the war, Oliver Payne went to work for John D. Rockefeller's Standard Oil, where he became the treasurer. Payne and Whitney renewed their friendship, and Payne introduced Whitney to his sister Flora. Flora and William Whitney married, cementing the two families.

William and Flora had four children and gave each one the same middle name: Harry Payne, William Payne, Pauline Payne, and Dorothy Payne. Flora died in 1894, and William remarried in 1896 to a widow, Edith Randolph. It was a controversial marriage and created a schism between the two brother-in-laws. This was also the same year that his son, Harry Payne Whitney, married Gertrude Vanderbilt in Newport.

In February 1898, Edith broke a vertebra in her neck while horseback riding in Aiken. She was paralyzed, and any movement was painful. Whitney bought his estate on Long Island for Edith, who loved the horses and horse racing. The steeplechase course was installed nearby so that she could watch the horses train from the house. With the aid of special railroad cars and automobiles, Edith was moved from Aiken to Long Island. That November, Whitney invited Meadow Brook to hold its steeplechase at the Whitney estate in Westbury. His wife enjoyed watching it, so he asked them to come back in the spring. Friends who saw Edith at the spring meet thought she was improving, but she fell into a coma the next week, dying on May 6, 1899.

William Whitney died following a surgery for an appendicitis in 1904. Harry Payne Whitney inherited a share of his father's estate. Harry Payne was the favorite nephew of his uncle, Oliver Payne, and when Oliver died in 1917, he left Harry Payne essentially his sole heir.

Harry Payne and Gertrude Vanderbilt Whitney were horse enthusiasts and generous supporters of the Meadow Brook Hounds. Their heirs and relatives continued to foxhunt with Meadow Brook through the 1960s.[37]

Frank Work

Frank Work was victorious in the early days of the Meadow Brook steeplechase, and both he and his daughter, Lucy, often rode with the hunt. Work was a self-made millionaire. He started in a dry goods store, and through his interest in trotting horses, became acquainted with Commodore Vanderbilt. When Work's store teetered on edge of bankruptcy, Vanderbilt rescued it. Vanderbilt then induced Work to sell his store and invest in the stock market with him. Work was good at it and made a lot of money for himself and Vanderbilt, with whom he eventually had a disagreement.[38] Work, split from Vanderbilt, began managing other people's money. It was said that he "made half a dozen fortunes and most of them he retained." He also invested in Delmonico's, a popular Manhattan restaurant at the time.[39]

Lucy Work, one of his two daughters, was a keen rider. Her name appeared on list after list of riders out in the late 1890s and early 1900s. In 1897, she married Peter Cooper Hewitt, the son of the mayor of New York at the time, and grandson of Peter Cooper, the philanthropist. While his sisters pursued their interests in the decorative arts, Peter Cooper Hewitt was an electrical engineer, who was happiest when he was working on his inventions. His most successful was the mercury vapor light.[40] The couple had no children and eventually divorced.

When Frank Work died in 1911, he left an estate of about eighteen million dollars, tied up by fifteen detailed codicils. Lucy's sister, Francis, who had married and divorced an Englishman named James Jeffrey Burke-Roche, would inherit nothing if she ever went back to England. Her twin sons only inherited if they became American citizens and remained in this country.

Figure 8.14. A Meadow Brook Fox. Photograph by Raymond Brown. Collection of the author.

One of Francis's daughters received an income only if she ceased exhibiting in horse shows or training animals for horse shows. Nor could she marry anyone engaged in these exhibitions.[41] If those provisions were not met, Lucy stood to inherit everything. The family hatched a plan; they broke each provision in the will, and then, as sole beneficiary, Lucy set up trust funds for her relatives.[42]

If Lucy had not broken the will, the course of history might have been altered. One of the twin boys did grow up in England, where he became the 4th Baron Fermoy. His daughter was the mother of Diana, Princess of Wales.[43]

Notes

PREFACE

1. Extant records show only the years of election, not the actual date.

CHAPTER ONE

1. Harry T. Peters, *Just Hunting* (London: Scribner's Sons, 1935), 168.
2. "The Hunting of Reynard," *New York Sun*, November 23, 1875.
3. August Belmont Purdy was his full name, but it appears also as A. Belmont Purdy or Belmont Purdy. Friends called him Bob.
4. "Riders Thrown at Meadow Brook Hunt," *New York Times*, November 1, 1906.
5. His name usually appears as Frank Griswold in club records.

6. "A Glorious Fox Hunt," *Boston Post*, December 2, 1876.

7. A. Henry Higginson and Julian Ingersoll Chamberlain, *The Hunts of the United States and Canada: Their Masters, Hounds, and Histories* (Boston: Frank L. Wiles, 1908), 73.

8. Frank Gray Griswold, *Horses and Hounds: Recollections of Frank Gray Griswold* (New York: Dutton's, 1926), 3–4.

9. Higginson and Chamberlain, *Hunts of the United States*, 73.

10. Griswold, *Horses and Hounds*, 4–5.

11. Spelled *Turbitt* in Jan Blan Van Urk, *The Story of American Foxhunting: From Challenge to Full Cry* (New York: Derrydale, 1941), 2:103.

12. Griswold, *Horses and Hounds*, 6.

13. Ibid., 5.

14. Richard Panchyk, *A History of Westbury, Long Island* (Charleston, SC: This History, 2007), 34.

15. Circular, Collection of Long Island Museum of American Art, History, and Carriages, Stony Brook, NY.

16. "Following the Hounds," *New York Times*, October 4, 1877; "The Chase on Long Island," *New York Sun*, October 4, 1877.

17. "Mr. Bergh's View of Fox Hunting," *New York Times*, October 10, 1877.

18. Ibid.

19. "The Sport Defended," *New-York Herald*, October 11, 1877.

20. "Hunting Animals," *New York Times*, September 28, 1880.

21. "Hunting the Anise-Seed Bag," *New York Times*, October 5, 1877.

22. "American Snobbery," *Fort Wayne (IN) Daily Sentinel*, January 9, 1877.

23. Van Urk, *Story of American Foxhunting*, 2:109.

24. "William E. Peet Dies in Paris," *New York Times*, December 26, 1912.

25. *Brentano's Aquatic Monthly*, May 1879, quoted in Van Urk, *Story of American Foxhunting*, 2:113.

26. "The Queens County Hunt Ball," *New York World*, November 24, 1878.

27. Van Urk, *Story of American Foxhunting*, 2:112.

28. "The Queens County Ball," *Brooklyn Sunday Eagle*, December 2, 1877.

29. Van Urk, *Story of American Foxhunting*, 2:116.

30. Ibid., 2:118.

31. "Fox Hunting on Long Island," *Brooklyn Sunday Eagle*, September 5, 1880.

32. Griswold, *Horses and Hounds*, 11–12.

33. "Killed on His Bicycle," *New York World*, April 18, 1895.

34. "The Late Robert Center of New York," *Illustrated American* (New York) 17, May 4, 1895, 558.

35. "Killed on the Railroad," *New York Times*, July 17, 1879. This is the obituary for Elliott's uncle, but it gives a complete background of the family.

36. "Baron de Stuers's Case," *New York Times*, January 27, 1892; "Free and Married Again," *New York Times*, March 8, 1892; "Count Zborowski Is Killed in Auto Race," *New York World*, April 8, 1903; Elliott Zborowski's son, Louis, may have been another victim of the family curse. He died in a racing car accident in Milan, Italy, on October 19, 1924. "Deaths," *New York Times*, October 21, 1924.

CHAPTER TWO

1. Meadow Brook Club, Articles of Incorporation, May 5, 1881.

2. Bill of Sale, Belmont Purdy to Meadow Brook Club, June 1, 1881, 2004.00.235, Collection of Long Island Museum of American Art, History, and Carriages.

3. Cleveland Amory, *Who Killed Society?* (New York: Harper and Brothers, 1960), 193.

4. When the inaccurate spelling of Meadow Brook appears as Meadowbrook in a quotation reproduced in this book, it is not noted. The error is simply too common.

5. Edward J. Smits, *Nassau, Suburbia, U.S.A.: The First Seventy-Five Years of Nassau County, New York, 1899 to 1974* (Syosset, NY: Friends of the Nassau County Museum, 1974), 13.

6. Ibid.

7. Meadow Brook Club, Stewards' Report, August 1, 1882.

8. J. D. Cheever to Frank Appleton, October 29, 1882, 2004.00.238, Collection of Long Island Museum of American Art, History, and Carriages.

9. Meadow Brook Club, Stewards' Report, January 29, 1929.

10. Meadow Brook Club, Letter, February 1, 1883.

11. Edwin D. Morgan, *Recollections for My Family* (New York: Charles Scribner's Sons, 1938), 133–34.

12. The groom's full name was Moritz Adolf Emil Ladenburg, and he was called Adolf. The variation "Adolph" also appears in contemporary news reports, but I am using "Adolf," because that is how it is written in the official list of members of Meadow Book Club in 1882.

13. "A Pretty Country Wedding Followed by a Fox Hunt," *New York Times*, November 12, 1884.

14. "Wedding Guests in Scarlet," *New York Sun*, November 12, 1884.

15. "Pretty Country Wedding."

16. "Wedding Guests in Scarlet."

17. Sagamore Hill wasn't finished until 1887, so a photograph of the meet in front of the house is probably from a later period. In his memoir, Edwin D. Morgan identifies himself in the image as the man standing with his back to the camera. Morgan was Master from 1883 to 1889.

18. "Mr. Roosevelt In at the Death," *New York Times*, October 27, 1885.

19. The original manuscript for this article is housed at the National Sporting Library and Museum, Middleburg, VA.

20. Theodore Roosevelt, "Riding to Hounds on Long Island," *Century Magazine*, July 1886, 335–41.

21. "The Hon. Theodore Roosevelt Followed the Meadowbrook Hounds," *Boston Post*, October 3, 1885.

22. David Black, *King of Fifth Avenue: The Fortunes of August Belmont* (New York: Dial, 1981), 707–8.

23. "Goodnight, Ladies," *Boston Post*, November 20, 1885.

24. Black, *King of Fifth Avenue*, 691–92.

25. "The Steamer Oregon Sunk," *New York Tribune*, March 15, 1886.

26. John G. Beresford was a banker and husband of Emilie Iselin, youngest daughter of Adrian and Eleanora Iselin. Beresford was a cousin of Lord Charles Beresford (1846–1919), who was a renowned (even in the United States) British admiral and a member of Parliament.

27. Meadow Brook Club, Stewards' Minutes, Special Meeting, February 10, 1886.

28. Blanche Wiesen Cook, *Eleanor Roosevelt*, vol. 1, 1884–1933 (New York: Penguin Books, 1993), 86–87.

29. Meadow Brook Club, Stewards' Report, January 25, 1887.

30. The junior and senior suffixes for the Thomas Hitchcock name can be confusing. Thomas Hitchcock Jr. (1860–1941) was the M.F.H. at Meadow Brook from 1889 to 1893. However, after the 1900 birth of his son, who is given the same name, the junior suffix is transferred to the son, Thomas Hitchcock Jr. (1900–1944). Thereafter, the father is usually identified as Thomas Hitchcock Sr.

31. "A Lively Five-Minute Race," *New York Sun*, November 29, 1889.

32. The Trustees of Reservations operates Appleton Farms today.

33. "Secret of World's Most Exclusive Club Revealed at Last," *Boston Post*, August 13, 1916.

34. "C. F. Havemeyer's Widow Is Now Mrs. F. O. Beach," *Brooklyn Eagle*, November 28, 1899; "Beach Indicted for Attack on Wife," *New York Times*, June 15, 1912; "Beach Acquitted, Charges Con-

spiracy," *New York Times*, February 18, 1913; "Frederick O. Beach," *New York Times*, November 18, 1918.

35. "Canine Aristocrats," *Pittsburgh Dispatch*, November 17, 1889.

36. "August Belmont Stricken in Office, Dies in 36 Hours," *New York Times*, December 11, 1924.

37. Harvard College, *Seventh Report of the Class Secretary of the Class of 1874* (Boston: Geo. H. Ellis, 1899), 109.

38. "The Goodwin-Swift Assignment," *Brooklyn Daily Eagle*, June 19, 1894.

39. "Players' League," *Sporting Life* (Philadelphia), December 25, 1898.

40. Harold Seymour and Dorothy Seymour Mills, *Baseball: The Early Years* (New York: Oxford University Press, 1960), 240–50.

41. "Death of Wendell Goodwin," *Brooklyn Daily Eagle*, March 5, 1898.

42. "Col. William Jay Expires Suddenly," *New York Times*, March 29, 1915.

43. Morgan, *Recollections for My Family*, 130.

44. Robert MacKay, Anthony Baker, and Carol A. Traynor, *Long Island Country Houses and Their Architects, 1860–1940* (New York: W. W. Norton, 1997), 31.

45. Ibid., 285–87.

46. Raymond E. Spinzia and Judith A. Spinzia, *Long Island's Prominent North Shore Families: Their Estates and Their County Homes* (College Station, TX: VirtualBookworm, 2006), 1:543.

47. "The Steamer Oregon Sunk," *New York Tribune*, March 15, 1886.

48. "E. D. Morgan Dies; Famed Yachtsman," *New York Times*, June 14, 1933.

49. "Necrological," *American Register* (London), September 4, 1886.

50. "Mrs. Edwin D. Morgan Dead," *New York Times*, August 19, 1886.

51. "Famous Races Recalled," *New York Sun*, April 11, 1897.

52. Black, *King of Fifth Avenue.*

53. Ibid., 43–44. Purdy's middle initial is incorrectly recorded as T. instead of F.

54. "Famous Races Recalled."

55. "Blue Blood's Fad," *Boston Sunday Globe*, July 28, 1889.

56. Ibid.

57. "A. Belmont Purdy Divorce," *New York Sun*, October 6, 1899.

58. "Wedded at Far Rockaway," *New York Times*, October 29, 1911; "Died," *New York Times*, June 29, 1912.

59. A. Belmont Purdy, "The Cross-Saddle for Women," *Outing*, July 31, 1905, 463–64.

60. "The Screen of Rejections," *Lake County Times* (Hammond, IN), June 17, 1907.

61. "Had Many Writers," *Rock Island (IL) Argus*, January 25, 1906.

62. "Died," *New York Times*, May 26, 1919.

63. "Grants Landmark Status to Site of Eleanor Roosevelt's Childhood Home," Hempstead Town Board Meeting, Hempstead, NY, April 30, 2014. The location is the corner of Salisbury Park Drive and Valentines Road, Westbury. Students at the Woodland Middle School in East Meadow assisted in locating the homestead.

64. Cook, *Eleanor Roosevelt*, 1:50.

65. Theodore Roosevelt, *Strenuous Life: Essays and Addresses* (Mineola, NY: Dover, 2009), 74.

66. "William R. Travers Dead," *New York Times*, March 28, 1887.

CHAPTER THREE

1. Meadow Brook Club, Stewards' Report, January 23, 1891.

2. Meadow Brook Club, Stewards' Report, March 28, 1889.

3. "Cross Country Hunting," *New-York Tribune*, March 28, 1889.

4. Foxhall Keene and Alden Hatch, *Full Tilt: The Sporting Memoirs of Foxhall Keene* (New York: Derrydale, 1938), 102.

5. Ibid.

6. "Society Topics of the Week," *New York Times*, September 28, 1890.

7. "Louise Mary Eustis Married," *New York Times*, August 28, 1891.

8. "No Doubt About This Milk," *New York Times*, July 5, 1894.

9. "Around Town," *Ashville (NC) Daily Citizen*, December 24, 1891.

10. Meadow Brook Club, Stewards' Minutes, December 22, 1891.

11. "Gotham Tales," *Fort Worth (TX) Gazette*, November 19, 1891.

12. Harry S. Page, *Over the Open* (New York: Charles Scribner's Sons, 1925), 49.

13. Frank G. Griswold, *Horse and Hounds* (New York: Dutton's, 1926), 116.

14. "Death after the Hounds," *New York Sun*, October 14, 1892.

15. Page, *Over the Open*, 61–62.

16. "Killed in the Hunt," *New York Times*, October 14, 1892.

17. Page, *Over the Open*, 61–62.

18. "Time to Call a Halt," *New York Times*, October 15, 1892.

19. "Hunting Accidents," *New York Times*, October 15, 1892.

20. "The Meadow Brook Hunt," *New York Times*, March 17, 1893.

21. "Master of the Hounds," *New York Sun*, March 8, 1888; Van Urk, "Rockaway Hunting Club," in *Story of American Foxhunting*, 2:219–20.

22. Meadow Brook Club, Constitution, Article X, as amended April 2, 1885.

23. Alexander Mackay-Smith, *Masters of Foxhounds* (Boston: Masters of Foxhounds Association, 1980), 11.

24. Keene and Hatch, *Full Tilt*, 101–02.

25. "Frank G. Griswold," *New York Times*, March 31, 1937.

26. "Many In at the Kill," *New York Times*, April 2, 1893.

27. Hunting a bagged fox was banned long ago, but it was legal in the 1890s.

28. "Reynard Feeding on Ducks," *Brooklyn Daily Eagle*, August 17, 1890.

29. "Down on Long Island," *Brooklyn Daily Eagle*, March 4, 1894.

30. This was probably due to the "stiff fences" in Meadow Brook country and to the wealth of the young men in America at this time.

31. Capt. E. Pennell-Elmhirst [Brooksby, pseud.], quoted in Griswold, *Horse and Hounds*, 69–70.

32. "Nearing Close of the Hunting Season," *Brooklyn Daily Eagle*, April 13, 1895, 7.

33. Van Urk, *Story of American Foxhunting*, 2:220.

34. "Nearing Close of the Hunting Season."

35. "Meadow Brook's Opening Run," *New York Times*, March 22, 1896.

36. Ralph N. Ellis, "Fox Hunting and Drag Hunting," in *Book of Sport*, ed. William Patten (New York: J. F. Taylor, 1901), 181–215.

37. Ellis, "Fox Hunting and Drag Hunting," 181–215.

38. "Golf Players Robbed," *New York Times*, October 22, 1895.

39. "Society," *Brooklyn Life*, October 26, 1895.

40. Casper Whitney, "The Evolution of the Country Club," *Harper's Monthly*, December 1894, 32.

41. "Golf Players Robbed."

42. "Society," *Brooklyn Life*, October 26, 1895.

43. "Clever Rogues at Meadow Brook," *Brooklyn Daily Eagle*, October 22, 1895.

44. "Duke Hunts and Is Dined," *New York World*, October 25, 1895.

45. "Society," *New York Times*, October 11, 1896.

46. "A Cross Country Run," *Brooklyn Daily Eagle*, March 24, 1897.

47. "A Famous Amateur Sportsman," *Brooklyn Life*, July 13, 1901, 13.

48. "W. C. Whitney's Many Acres," *New York Times*, January 24, 1896.

49. "Millions to Wed," *Fort Wayne (IN) News*, August 1, 1896.

50. Theodore Roosevelt, *The Rough Riders* (New York: Charles Scribner's Sons, 1899; repr. Charleston, SC: CreateSpace, 2014), 20.

51. "Rough Riders to See Him," *New York Times*, May 19, 1910.

52. "Henry W. Bull, 84," *New York Times*, August 8, 1958.

53. Fred Astaire, *Steps in Time* (New York: Harper Collins, 1959), 265.

54. Page, *Over the Open*, 62 (states it was Charles's thirty-first birthday). Rawlins's age appears in his obituary, "R. L. Cottenet," *New York Times*, March 31, 1951. Fannie's age appears in her obituary, "F. L. Cottenet, Philanthropist," *New York Times*, February 13, 1956.

55. "Fine Country Mansions," *Brooklyn Daily Eagle*, September 30, 1894, 21.

56. "Meadow Brook's Fine Thoroughbreds," *Brooklyn Daily Eagle*, August 14, 1898.

57. "R. L. Cottenet Now a Florist," *New York Times*, November 2, 1893.

58. "Florist and Usher Took," *New York World*, August 24, 1896.

59. "Vanderbilt to Reopen New York House," *Brooklyn Daily Eagle*, December 29, 1905.

60. Emma Louise Trapper, *Musical Blue Book of America, 1915* (New York: Musical Blue Book, 1916), 245.

61. "R. L. Cottenet, 85, Opera Executive," *New York Times*, March 31, 1951.

62. "The Friends of Music Open Their Season," *Brooklyn Daily Eagle*, October 26, 1930.

63. The house no longer exists, but the grounds are persevered as a park honoring Olmsted.

64. "Sidelights upon Roosevelt's Life," *Boston Post*, January 21, 1919.

65. Harvard University, *Secretary's Report: Upon the Twenty-Fifth Anniversary of Graduation, Harvard College, Class of 1880* (Cambridge, MA: Riverside Press, 1905), 22; Spinzia and Spinzia, *Prominent North Shore Families*, 1:245; "Buys 88-Acre Tract: F. Ambrose Clark Adds to His Estate at Old Westbury," *New York Times*, February 15, 1946.

66. "Frank G. Griswold," *New York Times*, March 31, 1937.

67. "Mrs. F. G. Griswold: Social Leader Here," *New York Times*, September 30, 1937.

68. "Thomas Hitchcock Dead," *New York Times*, June 21, 1910.

69. Nelson W. Aldrich Jr., *Tommy Hitchcock: An American Hero* (Fleet Street, 1984), 12.

70. Van Urk, *Story of American Foxhunting*, 2:132.

71. Gerard Gagliardo, general manager, National Golf Links, e-mail message to author, November 3, 2014.

72. "Hunting on Long Island," *Illustrated American*, October 3, 1891, 293–97.

73. Aldrich, *Tommy Hitchcock*, 244.

74. Roosevelt, *The Rough Riders*, 16.

75. Ibid., 42.

76. Ibid., 227.

77. "Capt. Woodbury Kane Dies of Sudden Attack," *New York Times*, December 6, 1905.

78. "Famous Punch Pony Dead," *New York Times*, May 23, 1910.

79. "Banker Drowned at Sea," *New York Times*, February 24, 1896.

80. "Believe Ladenburg Dead," *Washington Post*, January 4, 1908.

81. "Loveliest Widow," *Postville (IA) Review*, November 7, 1896.

82. "Yankees Girls' Feet," *Boston Sunday Globe*, September 28, 1902.

83. "American Civilization," *Lake County Times* (Hammond, IN), November 17, 1906.

84. "Ladenburg Guests See a Knockout," *New York Times*, November 1, 1909.

85. "Court Gets Horse Lore from Mrs. Ladenburg," *New York Times*, May 7, 1904.

86. "Deaths: In Memoriam," *New York Times*, August 11, 1937.

87. "How Women Shall Ride," *Topeka (KS) Advocate*, September 4, 1895.

88. Purdy, "Cross-Saddle for Women," 464.

89. Roger D. Williams, *The Horse and Hound* (Lexington, KY: privately printed, 1905), 64.

90. "Mrs. Ladenburg Creates Comment," *Danville (IN) Republican*, November 6, 1902.

91. "Samuel S. Sands, Jr. Buried," *New-York Daily Tribune*, March 25, 1889.

92. "Mr. George Tiffany, Formerly of Baltimore," *Frederick (MD) News*, June 17, 1886.

93. "Rough Riders in Glory, Fighting at the Front," *New York World*, June 26, 1898.

94. "Local Briefs," *Newport (RI) News*, May 17, 1897.

95. "Tiffany's Death," *Boston Sunday Post*, November 20, 1898.

CHAPTER FOUR

1. "Fox Hunt at Meadow Brook," *New-York Daily Tribune*, January 21, 1900.

2. "Took Nearly Sixty Fences," *Brooklyn Daily Eagle*, October 14, 1900; "Drag Hunt Cross Country," *Brooklyn Daily Eagle*, Octo-

ber 28, 1898; "Meadow Brook's Long Run," *Brooklyn Daily Eagle*," March 18, 1897.

3. "Society Sees Motor Show," *New York Times*, November 6, 1900.

4. "Speed Limit for Motor Vehicles," *New York Times*, September 8, 1900.

5. "Meadow Brook May Elect a Mistress of the Hounds," *Syracuse (NY) Post Standard*, December 29, 1901.

6. "What Is Doing in Society," *New York Times*, October 29, 1901.

7. "Crushed by His Hunter," *New-York Daily Tribune*, November 17, 1901.

8. Ibid.; "Meadowbrook Huntsman Did Not Fracture Skull as Supposed," *Brooklyn Daily Eagle*, November 18, 1901.

9. "Interest Lagging in Meadow Brook Hunt Club Runs," *Brooklyn Daily Eagle*, November 27, 1901.

10. "Meadow Brook May Elect a Mistress of the Hounds," *Syracuse (NY) Post Standard*, December 29, 1901.

11. "Mr. Keene to Succeed Mr. Ellis," *Brooklyn Life*, January 4, 1902.

12. Keene and Hatch, *Full Tilt*, viii–ix.

13. "Mr. Keene to Succeed Mr. Ellis."

14. "Ellis Withdraws Resignation," *New-York Daily Tribune*, January 29, 1902.

15. "Packs of Hounds at Hempstead," *New-York Daily Tribune*, November 4, 1902.

16. Williams, *Horse and Hound*, 2; Mackay-Smith, *Masters of Foxhounds*, 25–26.

17. Mackay-Smith, *Masters of Foxhounds*, 12.

18. Keene and Hatch, *Full Tilt*, 122.

19. Ibid.

20. "Foxhall Keene's Famous Foxhounds and Hunters," *Brooklyn Daily Eagle*, August 28, 1904.

21. Keene and Hatch, *Full Tilt*, 123.

22. "Poison Kills Fox Hounds," *Brooklyn Daily Eagle*, March 12, 1903; "Opening of Spring Hunting," *Brooklyn Life*, March 21, 1903.

23. After determining that a fox is not in a hole, a hunter might block the entrance with rocks or debris to prevent the fox from going to ground.

24. "Hunting the Fox on Long Island," *Brooklyn Daily Eagle*, March 11, 1902.

25. "Whipper-in Wants His Money," *Brooklyn Daily Eagle*, November 1, 1904.

26. Keene and Hatch, *Full Tilt*, 124.

27. "Clubs and Clubmen," *New York Times*, January 31, 1904.

28. "Foxhall Keene's Famous Foxhounds."

29. "Echoes from Clubland," *New York Times*, May 22, 1904.

30. "Foxhall Keene Resigns," *Brooklyn Daily Eagle*, August 23, 1904.

31. "Whipper-in Wants His Money."

32. "Good Prices for F. P. Keene's Hunters," *New York Times*, September 30, 1904.

33. "Society at Home and Abroad," *New York Times*, September 4, 1904.

34. "Great Foxhunters on Long Island," *New York Sun*, December 18, 1904.

35. Ibid.

36. "Meadow Brook Hunters Had a Great Day," *Brooklyn Daily Eagle*, November 9, 1904.

37. "Long Island 'Tenantry' Dodged Smooth Floors," *New York Times*, November 11, 1904.

38. Alexander Henry Higginson and Julian Ingersoll Chamberlain, *The Hunts of the United States and Canada: Their Masters, Hounds, and Histories* (Boston: Frank L. Wiles, 1908), 79.

39. "Meadow Brook Hunts," *Brooklyn Daily Eagle*, November 12, 1905.

40. "Trailed Two Foxes," *Brooklyn Daily Eagle*, October 18, 1906.

41. "P. F. Collier, M.F.H., Resigns," *Brooklyn Daily Eagle*, December 23, 1906; "Master of Hounds Resigns: P. F. Collier Withdraws Shortly before Meadow Brook's Annual Meeting," *Washington Post*, December 23, 1906.

42. "No Meadow Brook M.F.H.," *New York Times*, January 24, 1907.

43. "Ride to the Hounds: Meadow Brook Pack Has Its First Run of the Spring Season," *New York Times*, March 29, 1908.

44. "The Gentleman Farmer Fad," *New York Times*, July 9, 1905.

45. "The Week in Society," *Brooklyn Life*, November 16, 1907.

46. "Ex-Actress Appears as Willets's Wife," *New York Times*, July 7, 1908.

47. "Young Mr. Willets Explains," *New York Times*, July 8, 1908.

48. "Young Mr. Willets Vanishes," *New York Times*, July 9, 1908.

49. "Willets Will Cuts Off Son," *New York Times*, December 23, 1909.

50. "Rabid Cur Spoils Fox Hunt," *New York Times*, September 27, 1908.

51. "Harry Page Breaks Collarbone in Race," *New York Times*, November 4, 1908.

52. "Mr. Bacon Leads Hunt," *New York Times*, November 4, 1908.

53. "First Drag Meet," *Brooklyn Daily Eagle*, March 18, 1909.

54. Sally Spanburgh, *The Southampton Cottages of Gin Lane* (Charleston, SC: History, 2012), 125–28.

55. "Peter Collier Dies of Apoplexy," *New York Times*, April 24, 1904.

56. Edwin Lefevre and Jon D. Markman, *Reminiscences of a Stock Operator* (Hoboken, NJ: John Wiley and Sons, 2010), 72.

57. Finis Farr, "The Fabulous World of Foxhall Keene, Part I," *Sports Illustrated*, February 16, 1959, 66.

58. Marian Burros, "The Entree That Wouldn't Die," *New York Times*, June 14, 1989.

59. "A Splendid Display," *New York Sun*, November 18, 1892.

60. Finis Farr, "The Fabulous World of Foxhall Keene, Part II," *Sports Illustrated*, February 23, 1959, 57.

61. Keene and Hatch, *Full Tilt*, 169–70.

62. "Weddings Yesterday," *New York Times*, January 29, 1892.

63. Kelley Kazek, *Forgotten Tales of Tennessee* (Charleston, SC: History, 2011), 105–06.

64. "Meadowbrook Hunters Incensed," *New York Times*, May 10, 1895.

65. "Sports of the Amateur," *Brooklyn Life*, May 18, 1895.

66. "J. L. Kernochan Beaten," *New York Times*, February 24, 1896; "J. L. Kernochan Mobbed," *Brooklyn Daily Eagle*, February 24, 1896.

67. "Jas. L. Kernochan Beaten," *New-York Tribune*, February 24, 1896.

68. "Hooted at His Overcoat," *New York Times*, January 26, 1897.

69. "James L. Kernochan Dead," *New York Times*, October 6, 1903.

70. The label of Rough Rider was used in the Civil War and in Buffalo Bill's Wild West Show, predating Theodore Roosevelt's famous troop in 1898.

71. "Riding After the Hounds," *Cedar Falls (IA) Semi-Weekly Gazette*, October 23, 1896.

72. "Mrs. Kernochan's Engagement," *Brooklyn Daily Eagle*, December 9, 1905.

73. "Hunting Set Interested," *Brooklyn Daily Eagle*, December 11, 1905.

74. "$150,000 Christmas Gift," *Brooklyn Daily Eagle*, December 22, 1906.

75. "Married," *New York Times*, November 15, 1907.

76. "Social and Personal," *Washington Post*, October 19, 1907.

77. William Faulkner, *The Reivers* (New York: Vintage Books, 1962), 163.

78. "Paul J. Rainey Dies of Stroke at Sea," *New York Times*, September 20, 1923.

79. "Memorial Gates Accepted by Zoo," *New York Times*, June 15, 1934.

80. "Mrs. Willets, Twice Divorced, Is Happy," *New York Times*, February 1, 1914.

81. "Saml. Willets Marries Mrs. Ida M'Kinney," *New York Times*, January 23, 1917.

82. "Garrick's Stock Good Start," *New York Sun*, February 13, 1906; "Horse Through the Stage," *New York Times*, February 14, 1906; Harvard University, *Secretary's Report: Upon the Twentieth Anniversary of Graduation, Harvard College, Class of 1892* (Boston: Fort Hill, 1912), 72–73.

83. "Plays and Playfolk," *Washington (DC) Herald*, April 26, 1908.

84. "Mlle. Genee's Debut," *New York Times*, January 21, 1908; Barbara Naomi Cohen-Stratyner, *Biographical Dictionary of Dance* (New York: Schirmer Books, 1982), s.v. "Adiline Genee."

CHAPTER FIVE

1. "J. E. Davis Meadow Brook Master," *New York Times*, May 6, 1910.

2. Social Register Association, *Social Register, New York, 1916* (New York: Social Register Association, 1915), 163.

3. New Baltimore lies about four miles east of Warrenton, Virginia.

4. The articles about Allison when he retired in 1951 reported that he was at Meadow Brook for forty-two years. That means he arrived in 1909, but Joe Davis did not become Master until May 1910. It may be that Allison did not actually come until 1910 or 1911. Charles Plumb, the succeeding huntsman, told the author that Allison did not

want to retire in 1951; he'd hoped to remain huntsman at Meadow Brook a few years longer. Therefore, the dates have been left somewhat muddled, because the author doesn't want to shorten his tenure even by an additional year or two.

5. Betty Babcock, "Thomas Allison, Huntsman," *Chronicle (of the Horse)* (Middleburg, VA), June 8, 1951, 18–19.

6. Ibid.

7. Ibid.

8. Ibid.

9. Ibid.

10. "Master of Hounds Absent," *New York Times*, February 23, 1913.

11. Lida L. Fleitmann, *Hoofs in the Distance* (New York: Van Nostrand, 1953), 4.

12. Meadow Brook Club, Annual Report, 1915.

13. Meadow Brook Club, Stewards' Report, February 23, 1916.

14. Masters of Foxhounds Association, "Meadow Brook Hounds," 1917, MS.

15. Meadow Brook Club, Minutes of the Board of Stewards, December 8, 1917.

16. Meadow Brook Club, Stewards' Meeting Minutes, April 12, 1916. (The parenthetical comment is in the original text.)

17. Ibid.

18. Ibid.

19. Meadow Brook Club, Stewards' Meeting Minutes, April 11, 1917.

20. Van Urk, *Story of American Foxhunting*, 2:147.

21. Francis R. Appleton Jr., *List of Meadow Brook Club Members Serving in WWI, 1918*, Appleton Family Papers, Trustees of Reservations, Sharon, MA.

22. Francis R. Appleton Jr. to B. Balding, February 25, 1919, Appleton Family Papers, Trustees of Reservations, Sharon, MA.

23. Smits, "Aviation on the Hempstead Plains," in *Nassau, Suburbia, U.S.A.*, 79–119.

24. "Business to Stop in Silent Tribute," *New York Times*, January 8, 1919.

25. Meadow Brook Club, letter from Subscription Committee, October 31, 1919, Appleton Family Papers, Trustees of Reservations, Sharon, MA.

26. Meadow Brook Club, Annual Report for the Year 1920.

27. Masters of Foxhounds Association, "Meadow Brook Hounds."

28. Peters, *Just Hunting*, 142.

29. *Members* were the foxhunters who belonged to the Meadow Brook Club and could use all the club facilities; *subscribers* paid an annual fee to only foxhunt, without a club membership.

30. Peters, *Just Hunting*, 152.

31. Meadow Brook Club, Stewards' Minutes, April 20, 1922.

32. Masters of Foxhounds Association, "Meadow Brook Hounds."

33. Van Urk, *Story of American Foxhunting*, 2:147–50.

34. "C. W. Fisk Unhorsed, Killed in Fox Hunt," *New York Times*, October 21, 1923.

35. "Stevenson Suffers Brain Concussion," *New York Times*, September 14, 1924; "Invaders Are Outplayed," *New York Times*, September 14, 1924; "Stevenson Much Better," *New York Times*, September 15, 1924.

36. Peters, *Just Hunting*, 174.

37. "Prince at Fox Hunt Takes All Barriers," *New York Times*, September 12, 1924.

38. Christopher Weeks, *Perfectly Delightful: The Life and Gardens of Harvey Ladew* (Baltimore: Johns Hopkins University Press, 1999), 31.

39. Ibid.; "Prince May Quit Syosset Today," *Brooklyn Eagle*, September 20, 1924.

40. Francis R. Appleton, "Benedictus Benedicat!," January 31, 1925, Appleton Family Papers, Trustees of Reservations, Sharon, MA.

41. Harvey Ladew, "Meadowbrook," n.d., MS, Ladew Topiary Gardens, Monkton, MD; Weeks, *Perfectly Delightful*, 43.

42. Nicholas F. Weber, *The Clarks of Cooperstown* (New York: Knopf, 2007), 251.

43. Ibid., 254.

44. "Fire Destroys Long Island Mansion Used by State U. College," *New York Times*, April 18, 1968.

45. "Joseph E. Davis, Sportsman, Dies," *New York Times*, May 18, 1955.

46. "Richest Man in Army," *Burlington (IA) Hawk-Eye*, November 28, 1917.

47. Ladew, "Meadowbrook."

48. Weeks, *Perfectly Delightful*, 51.

49. Ibid., 165.

50. "Miss Elise Ladew Bride at Elsinore," *New York Times*, April 19, 1914; Weeks, *Perfectly Delightful*, 38–39.

51. W. Russell G. Corey, Alan Corey, *Nine Goals* (privately published, 2012); telephone interview, March 6, 2014.

52. Babcock, "Thomas Allison, Huntsman," 19.

53. Weeks, *Perfectly Delightful*, 44.

54. "C. W. Fisk Unhorsed, Killed in Fox Hunt."

55. "Derby Medal" in *Green Vale School Alumni Directory* (Chesapeake, VA: Harris Connect, 2006), viii.

56. Carlyle J. Coash, William Simonds, and Christine Pell, *The Green Vale Story* (Glen Head, NY: Green Vale School, 1998), 22.

CHAPTER SIX

1. Peters, *Just Hunting*, 113–14.

2. Marjorie McDonald, interview by the author, Mill Neck, NY, December 29, 1981.

3. Peters, *Just Hunting*, 26.

4. Ibid., 29.

5. Ibid., 30.

6. Ibid., 30.

7. Ibid., 35.

8. Ibid., 24–25.

9. Ibid., 10.

10. Betty Babcock, "November 7, 1935," in *Betty Babcock's Hunting Diary: Meadow Brook Hounds, Season 1935–1936* (Woodbury, NY: privately printed, 1936), n.p.

11. Peters, *Just Hunting*, 106.

12. Ibid., 133.

13. Ibid., 141. A hare pie hound is a light-colored dog (cream or fawn), with the ears and back shading into brown and the tip of the hair being lighter than the base.

14. Babcock, "Thomas Allison, Huntsman," 19.

15. Peters, *Just Hunting*, 135.

16. Ibid., 137.

17. Meadow Brook Club, Annual Membership Book, 1946.

18. "Incidental Beneficiaries of Wealth," *Brooklyn Life*, June 12, 1926.

19. Robert A. Caro, *Power Broker: Robert Moses and the Fall of New York* (New York: Vintage Books, 1975), 161–71.

20. Peters, *Just Hunting*, 235.

21. "Mrs. F. R. Dick Dies in Hunting Accident," *New York Times*, November 3, 1926.

22. Meadow Brook Club, Report of the Board of Stewards, May 11, 1927.

23. Meadow Brook Club, Report of the Board of Stewards, May 9, 1928. The report also commended the hounds for their wins at the annual hound shows.

24. Harry T. Peters, Letter to Members and Subscribers, Meadow Brook Club, September 1, 1928.

25. McDonald, interview.

26. Francis R. Appleton Jr. to Francis R. Appleton Sr., November 30, 1928, Appleton Family Papers, Trustees of Reservations, Sharon, MA.

NOTES

27. "Miss Manville Wed in Military Pomp," *New York Times*, December 2, 1928.

28. Caro, *Power Broker*, 299.

29. Ibid., 301.

30. McDonald, interview.

31. Elizabeth Thompson "Betty" Babcock, interview by the author, Woodbury, NY, December 27, 1981.

32. Betty Babcock, "Meadow Brook's Great Day," originally published in *Polo, The Magazine for Horsemen*, April 1933, and quoted in Peters, *Just Hunting*, 64–67.

33. Meadow Brook Club, Stewards' Meeting Minutes, May 23, 1933.

34. Meadow Brook Club, "Agreement between Meadow Brook Club and Smithtown Hunt Club for Joint Operation 1933–1938 of Meadow Brook Hounds, Organized 1877 and Smithtown Hunt, Organized 1900," May 23, 1933; "Hunt Clubs Merged on Long Island," *New York Times*, June 1, 1933.

35. "Spirited Fox Hunt Held at Westbury," *New York Times*, October 13, 1933.

36. Meadow Brook Club, Meadow Brook Hounds, Report to Stewards, March 31, 1934.

37. Meadow Brook Club, "Agreement between Meadow Brook Club and Smithtown Hunt Inc., June 1934 as of April 1934, Fourth Revision," December 17, 1934.

38. Betty Babcock, Letter to the Secretary of the Meadow Brook Club, January 2, 1972, author's collection.

39. Babcock, "October 5, 1935," in *Hunting Diary, 1935–1936*, n.p.

40. "Meadow Brook Hunt Holds First Meet," *New York Times*, October 6, 1935. Betty Babcock's diary noted that there were seventy-three riders that day, not one hundred.

41. Betty Babcock to Secretary, Meadow Brook Club, January 2, 1972.

42. "Weigh Meadow Brook Club as Mitchel Field Addition," *Brooklyn Daily Eagle*, July 9, 1940.

43. Harry Peters, M.F.H, Meadow Brook Hounds, to Joseph Jones, clerk, Masters of Foxhounds Association, March 2, 1942, MFHA Meadow Brook Hounds correspondence file.

44. Jones to Peters, March 3, 1942, MFHA Meadow Brook Hounds correspondence file.

45. Peters to Jones, July 21, 1942, MFHA Meadow Brook Hounds correspondence file.

46. Jones to Peters, July 24, 1942, MFHA Meadow Brook Hounds correspondence file. After the war, Jones returned to work at the MFHA, retiring in 1973.

47. "It's Horses, Horses, Horses Now as Society Goes Back to Dobbin," *New York Times*, February 7, 1942.

48. Ibid.

49. Harry T. Peters and Harvey D. Gibson, Letter to the Members and Subscribers of the Meadow Brook Hounds, Meadow Brook Club, September 2, 1942.

50. Charles Plumb, interview by the author, Cochranville, PA, November 22, 1981.

51. Van Urk, *Story of American Foxhunting*, 2:146–47.

52. Peters, *Just Hunting*, 198.

53. Riders who did not subscribe to the hunt could participate a limited number of times during a season, but they had to pay a capping fee to the hunt secretary each time they were in the field.

54. "Rider Badly Hurt in Meadow Brook Hunt," *New York Times*, October 4, 1908.

55. McDonald, interview.

56. "Anthony Garvan," *Philadelphia Inquirer*, January 11, 1992.

57. Ibid.

58. "H. D. Gibson Dies of Heart Ailment," *New York Times*, September 12, 1950.

59. Arthur Liese, "No One Could Portray Dogs and Horses Like Marguerite Kirmse," *Chronicle of the Horse*, September 20, 2002, 24–30.

60. Sean Corcoran, Curator of Prints and Photographs, Museum of the City of New York, email to author, January 28, 2015.

61. Van Urk, *Story of American Foxhunting*, 2:222.

62. Peter Winants, *The Sporting Art of Franklin B. Voss* (Lexington, KY: Eclipse, 2005), 17.

CHAPTER SEVEN

1. "Children Continue Long Island's Tradition of Fox Hunting," *New York Times*, January 4, 1942.

2. "Horse Show Proceeds to Purchase Sirens," *New York Times*, August 24, 1942.

3. "R. E. Tod, Ex-Banker, Commits Suicide," *New York Times*, November 10, 1944.

4. Barbara Conolly, telephone interview by the author, January 20, 2015.

5. Robert Winthrop to Joseph Jones, Masters of Foxhounds Association, December 27, 1946, MFHA Meadow Brook Hounds correspondence file.

6. Joseph J. Jones, clerk, MFHA, to Marjorie Hewlett, June 20, 1949, MFHA Meadow Brook Hounds correspondence file.

7. Marjorie McDonald, scrapbook, 1949, held by her daughter, Barbara Conolly.

8. Some accounts of the Meadow Brook Hounds recorded Marjorie as Mrs. J. A. Hewlett and then, after September 1950, as Mrs. J. J. McDonald, which led to some confusion.

9. Meadow Brook colors were still robin's egg blue, but incorrect description was picked up by other writers and "postman blue" was repeated often.

10. "Fox Hunt on North Shore," *New York Times*, November 12, 1949.

11. Meadow Brook Club, Annual Report, 1946, 16.

12. "Community Takes Name of Levitts," *New York Times*, January 4, 1948.

13. Amory, *Who Killed Society?*, 87.

14. *United States v. 50.8 Acres of Land, etc.*, 149 F. Supp. 749, 751 (E.D.N.Y. 1957).

15. "Pipelines," *Locust Valley (NY) Leader*, July 6, 1950.

16. Marjorie McDonald, scrapbook, 1951–1952, held by her daughter, Barbara Conolly.

17. "Pipelines," *Locust Valley Leader*, September 8, 1949.

18. Cora Cavanagh, Secretary's Report, October 31, 1952, in Marjorie McDonald, scrapbook, 1952–1953, held by her daughter, Barbara Conolly.

19. Clipping, n.p., n.d., in McDonald, scrapbook, 1952–1953.

20. Katrina Hickox Becker, interview by the author, Aiken, SC, March 28, 2014.

21. "Ellis Withdraws Resignation," *New-York Daily Tribune*, January 29, 1902.

22. Charles W. Hickox to William Almy Jr., secretary, MFHA, June 28, 1956, MFHA Meadow Brook Hounds correspondence file.

23. Charles W. Hickox to Joseph J. Jones, clerk, MFHA, September 18, 1957, MFHA Meadow Brook Hounds correspondence file.

24. Hickox to Jones, January 2, 1958, MFHA Meadow Brook Hounds correspondence file.

25. Jones to Hickox, January 6, 1958, MFHA Meadow Brook Hounds correspondence file.

26. Meadow Brook Hounds Pony Club, *Twenty-Fifth Anniversary Journal* (Huntington, NY: Direct Press, 1981), 12–15.

27. Cora Cushny, interview by the author, Lexington, KY, March 12, 2014.

28. Peters, *Just Hunting*, 235.

29. Barbara Conolly, interview with author, April 8, 2014.

30. Sara Cavanagh Schwartz, telephone interview by the author, February 10, 2014.

31. Charles Plumb, interview by the author, Cochranville, PA, November 22, 1981.

32. Schwartz, interview.

33. Meadow Brook Hounds Pony Club, *Twenty-Fifth Anniversary Journal*, 13.

34. Schwartz, telephone.

35. Plumb, interview.

36. Crowell Hadden, telephone interview by the author, January 27, 2015.

37. Mollie Eckelberry, interview by the author, Roslyn, NY, April 8, 2014.

38. Jane McDermott and Mike McDermott, interview by the author, Oyster Bay, NY, March 7, 2014.

39. Cora Cushny to MFHA, December 21, 1966, January 10, 1967, and January 26, 1967, all MFHA Meadow Brook Hounds correspondence file; Cushny, interview.

40. Mrs. Richard S. "Jesse" Emmet, honorary secretary, Meadow Brook Hunt, to MFHA, October 9, 1968, MFHA Meadow Brook Hounds correspondence file.

41. Sara Schwartz, email message to author, January 30, 2015.

42. Cushny, interview.

43. McDonald, interview.

44. Griswold, *Horses and Hounds*, 4.

45. Hadden, interview.

46. "Mrs. C. B. Spaulding Weds C. V. Hickox," *New York Times*, April 26, 1930.

47. William Halliar, "Innovation at Its Finest," *Michigan City (IN) Beacher*, December 4, 2014.

48. "Edward Keefer, a Surgeon, Is Dead at 84," *New York Times*, April 16, 2000.

49. "Devereux Milburn, 82, Sportsman and Lawyer," *New York Times*, January 15, 2000.

50. Devereux Milburn, M.F.H., to Joseph Jones, MFHA, August 17, 1968, MFHA Meadow Brook Hounds correspondence file.

51. "Mary Plumb of Cochranville," *Philadelphia Inquirer*, June 2, 1994.

52. "Sir Ashley Sparks, 87, Is Dead, Ex-Chief Cunard Representative," *New York Times*, May 22, 1964.

53. "Robert Winthrop, 95, a Banker, Philanthropist and Sportsman," *New York Times*, September 30, 1999.

54. Following their divorce in 1941, Theodora married Dr. Archibald Cary Randolph in Upperville, VA, where she became M.F.H. of the Piedmont Hunt.

CHAPTER EIGHT

1. Harry Page, *Between the Flags* (New York: Derrydale, 1929), 13.

2. Harry Page, *Over the Open*, 112.

3. Ibid., 114–15.

4. Peter Winants, *Steeplechasing: A Complete History of the Sport in North America* (Lanham, MD: Derrydale, 2000), 30.

5. "Meadow Brook Races," *Brooklyn Daily Eagle*, April 28, 1882.

6. "Old Nags," *Brooklyn Daily Eagle*, December 20, 1882.

7. "The Meadow Brook Races," *Brooklyn Daily Eagle*, May 20, 1883.

8. Bombast was the winner of a different race the prior year, 1882.

9. "The Meadow Brook Races," *Brooklyn Daily Eagle*, May 20, 1883. The only other horse in the race fell and did not finish the race. Neither the horse nor jockey sustained injury, but the horse was not caught in time to continue.

10. "The Meadow Brook Races," *Brooklyn Daily Eagle*, May 20, 1883.

11. Ibid.

12. "Over Timber," *Brooklyn Daily Eagle*, March 22, 1885.

13. "Opening the New Track," *Brooklyn Daily Eagle*, May 10, 1885.

14. Benjamin R. Allison and James P. MacGuire, *The Rockaway Hunting Club at 125* (Lawrence, NY: privately printed, 2004), 71.

15. "The Jumpers," *Brooklyn Daily Eagle*, April 5, 1887.

16. "Ponies Race for Purses," *Brooklyn Daily Eagle*, May 3, 1891.

17. Page, *Between the Flags*, 11–12.

18. Ibid., 22–24.

19. Page does not explain exactly which meets were included each year.

20. Page, *Between the Flags*, 39–40.

21. Allison and MacGuire, *Rockaway Hunting Club at 125*, 17–18; "To Amend the Racing Law," *New York Times*, February 18, 1896.

22. Page, *Between the Flags*, 42–43.

23. "Long Island Train Lost Going to the Races," *New York Times*, May 6, 1906.

24. Ibid., 44.

25. "Society Riders in Muddy Going," *Washington (DC) Times*, April 10, 1906.

26. "Jumpers Entertain at Meadow Brook," *New York Times*, May 9, 1915.

27. Winants, *Steeplechasing*, 85–86.

28. "Meadow Brook Cup to Be Run Today," *New York Times*, September 26, 1931.

29. Winants, *Steeplechasing*, 84–85; "Mrs. Clark Back, Says She Will Not Enter Kellsboro' Jack in Grand National Again," *New York Times*, April 25, 1933.

30. Winants, *Steeplechasing*, 140.

31. Ibid., 161; "Two Leaders Fall at Last of Twenty-six Jumps," *The Washington Post*, December 7, 1930.

32. "Two Leaders Fall at Last of Twenty-six Jumps."

33. Meadow Brook Hounds, Annual Report, 1967–1968.

34. The author was one of these pony clubbers—the ones who couldn't draw a horse.

35. Arthur C. Liese, "Paul Brown: A Genius with Pen and Brush," *The Chronicle of the Horse*, May 25, 2001, 8–9.

36. "Herbert Cup Matches," *New York Tribune*, August 10, 1922.

37. "Death of Mrs. Whitney," *New York Times*, February 5, 1893; "Mrs. W. C. Whitney Injured," *New York Times*, February 22, 1898; "New Track Planned," *New York Times*, November 6, 1898; "Gentlemen as Jockeys," *New York Times*, November 9, 1898; "Mrs. Wm. C. Whitney Dead," *New York Times*, May 7, 1899; "William C. Whitney Passes Away," February 3, 1904.

38. "Frank Work," *The Brooklyn Daily Eagle*, March 17, 1911.

39. "Who has not seen him in Delmonicos?" *Brooklyn Life*, April 4, 1896.

40. "Hewitt Divorced and Remarried," *New York Times*, December 20, 1918.

41. "Work's Millions to Grandchildren," *New York Times*, April 29, 1911.

42. "Frank Work Heirs Broke Will Terms," *New York Times*, December 13, 1919.

43. "The Dowager Lady Fermoy," *New York Times*, July 8, 1991.

Glossary of Fox Hunting Terms

Cubbing: Late summer or early autumn hunting before the formal season begins.

Drag hunt: A hunt in which the hounds track an artificially laid scent.

Field: The group of people riding to the hounds, excluding the Master of Foxhounds (MFH) and staff.

Field Master: A person who is designated by the MFH to lead the field.

Huntsman or Huntswoman: The staff member in charge of raising, training and hunting the hounds.

Line: The scent trail of the fox.

Master of Foxhounds (MFH): The person in charge of the hunt.

Whipper-in: A staff member, who assists the Huntsman or -woman in controlling the hounds.

Bibliography

Albrecht, Donald and Jeannine Falino, eds. 2013. *Gilded New York*. New York: Monacelli Press.

Aldrich, Nelson W. Aldrich Jr. 1984. *Tommy Hitchcock: An American Hero*. Privately published: Fleet Street.

Allison, Benjamin R., and James P. MacGuire. 2004. *The Rockaway Hunting Club at 125*. Lawrence, NY: privately printed.

Amory, Cleveland. 1960. *Who Killed Society?* New York: Harper.

Appleton Family Papers, Trustees of Reservations, Sharon, MA.

Armstrong, Virginia Winmill Livingston. 1977. *Gone Away with the Winmills*. Privately printed.

Astaire, Fred. 1959. *Steps in Time*. New York: Harper Collins.

Babcock, Betty. 1951. "Thomas Allison, Huntsman," *Chronicle (of the Horse)* (Middleburg, VA), June 8, 1951, 18–19.

———. 1936. *Betty Babcock's Hunting Diary: Meadow Brook Hounds, Season 1935–1936*. Woodbury, NY: privately printed.

———. 1937. *Betty Babcock's Hunting Diary: Meadow Brook Hounds, Season 1936–1937*. Woodbury, NY: privately printed.

Balding, Bruce E. 2007. *When America Owned the World and We Owned America*. New York: Palm Beach Journal.

Biscotti, M. L. 2001. *Paul Brown, Master of Equine Art*. Lanham and New York: Derrydale Press.

Bishop, Chip. 2014. *Quentin & Flora*. Charleston: CreateSpace.

Black, David. 1981. *The King of Fifth Avenue: The Fortunes of August Belmont*. New York: Dial, 1981.

Boegner, Peggie Phipps, and Richard Gachot. 1986. *Halcyon Days*. New York: Old Westbury Gardens and Harry N. Abrams.

Caro, Robert A. 1975. *Power Broker: Robert Moses and the Fall of New York*. New York: Vintage Books.

Coash, Carlyle J., William Simonds, and Christine Pell. 1998. *The Green Vale Story*. Glen Head, NY: Green Vale School.

Cohen-Stratyner, Barbara Naomi. 1982. *Biographical Dictionary of Dance*. New York: Schirmer Books.

Corcoran, Sean, Curator of Prints and Photographs. Museum of the City of New York, email to author, January 28, 2015.

Corey, W. Russell G., and Alan Corey. 2012. *Nine Goals*. Privately published.

Delin, John. 2008. *Syosset People and Places*. Charleston: Arcadia.

Ellis, Ralph N. 1901. "Fox Hunting and Drag Hunting." *Book of Sport*, edited by William Patten. New York: J. F. Taylor.

Farr, Finis. 1959. "The Fabulous World of Foxhall Keene, Part I." *Sports Illustrated*, February 16: 64–72.

———. 1959. "The Fabulous World of Foxhall Keene, Part II." *Sports Illustrated*, February 23, 1959, 56–64.

Faulkner, William. 1962. *The Reivers*. New York: Vintage Books.

Fleitmann, Lida L. 1953. *Hoofs in the Distance*. New York: Van Nostrand.

Fraser, Steve, and Gary Gerstle. 2005. *Ruling America*. Cambridge: Harvard University Press.

Gray, David. 1912. *Gallops I*. Vol. I, New York: Derrydale Press.

Green Vale School. 2006. "Derby Medal" in *Green Vale School Alumni Directory*. Chesapeake, VA: Harris Connect.

Griswold, F. Gray. 1926. *Horses and Hounds, Recollections of Frank Gray Griswold.* New York: Dutton.

Halliar, William. 2014. "Innovation at Its Finest." *Michigan City (IN) Beacher,* December 4.

Harvard University. 1899. *Seventh Report of the Class Secretary of the Class of 1874.* Boston: Geo. H. Ellis.

———. 1905. *Secretary's Report: Upon the Twenty-Fifth Anniversary of Graduation, Harvard College, Class of 1880.* Cambridge, MA: Riverside Press.

———. 1912. *Secretary's Report: Upon the Twentieth Anniversary of Graduation, Harvard College, Class of 1892.* Boston: Fort Hill.

Head, John J. 2006. *With Brush and Bridle: Richard Newton, Jr. Artist and Equestrian.* Washington, VA: Ellerslie Press.

Higginson, A. Henry, and Julian Ingersoll Chamberlain. 1908. *The Hunts of the United States and Canada; Their Masters, Hounds and Histories.* Boston: F. L. Wills.

"Hunting on Long Island." 1891. *Illustrated American,* October 3: 293–97.

Kazek, Kelley. 2011. *Forgotten Tales of Tennessee.* Charleston, SC: History.

Keene, Foxhall, and Alden Hatch. 1938. *Full Tilt; the Sporting Memoirs of Foxhall Keene.* New York: Derrydale Press.

Ladew, Harvey. 1960. *Random Recollections.* Privately printed.

Lefevre, Edwin, and Jon D. Markman. 2010. *Reminiscences of a Stock Operator.* Hoboken, NJ: John Wiley and Sons.

Liese, Arthur. 2002. "No One Could Portray Dogs and Horses Like Marguerite Kirmse." *Chronicle of the Horse,* September 20: 24–30.

———. 2001. "Paul Brown: A Genius with Pen and Brush." *The Chronicle of the Horse,* May 25: 8–9.

Long Island Museum of American Art, History, and Carriages. Collection. Stony Brook, NY.

MacKay, Robert, Anthony Baker, and Carol A. Traynor. 1997. *Long Island Country Houses and Their Architects, 1860–1940.* New York: W. W. Norton.

Mackay-Smith, Alexander. 1980. *Masters of Foxhounds*. Boston: Masters of Foxhounds Association.

McDonald, Marjorie. Scrapbook, 1949–1950, held by her daughter, Barbara Conolly.

———. Scrapbook, 1951–1952, held by her daughter, Barbara Conolly.

———. Scrapbook, 1953, held by her daughter, Barbara Conolly.

———. Scrapbook, 1954–1955, held by her daughter, Barbara Conolly.

———. Scrapbook, 1956, held by her daughter, Barbara Conolly.

Meadow Brook Club. Annual Reports and Steward's Reports, and Minutes of Meetings. Jericho, New York.

Meadow Brook Hounds Correspondence File, Masters of Foxhounds Association. Millwood, Virginia.

Mateyunas, Paul. 2012. *Long Island's Gold Coast*. Charleston, SC: Arcadia.

———. 2007. *North Shore Long Island, Country Houses 1890–1950*. New York: Acanthus Press.

McCullough, David. 1982. *Mornings on Horseback*. New York: Simon & Schuster.

Meadow Brook Hounds Pony Club. 1981. *Twenty-Fifth Anniversary Journal*. Huntington, NY: Direct Press.

Morgan, Edwin D. 1938. *Recollections for My Family*. New York: Charles Scribner's Sons.

Morris, Edmund. 1979. *Theodore Rex*. New York: Coward, McCann & Geoghegan.

———. 2001. *Theodore Rex*. New York: Random House.

Murphy, Betsey. *Jericho, The History of a Long Island Hamlet*. Jericho, NY: Jericho Public Library.

National Sporting Library and Museum, Middleburg, VA.

Page, Harry. *Between the Flags*. 1929. New York: Derrydale.

———. *Over the Open*. 1929. New York: Charles Scribner's Sons.

Patterson, Jerry E. 2000. *The First Four Hundred*. New York: Rizzoli.

Peters, Harry Twyford. 1935. *Just Hunting*. New York: C. Scribner's Sons.

Planchyk, Richard. 2007. *A History of Westbury, Long Island.* Charleston, SC: This History.

Potts, Allen. 1912. *Fox Hunting in America.* Washington: The Carnahan Press.

Purdy, A. Belmont. 1905. "The Cross-Saddle for Women," *Outing*, July 31: 463–64.

Roosevelt, Theodore. 1886. "Riding to Hounds on Long Island." *Century Magazine*, July 1: 335–41.

———. 1899. *The Rough Riders.* New York: Charles Scribner's Sons. Reprint 2014. Charleston: CreateSpace.

———. 1913. *An Autobiography.* New York: Scribner's Sons. Reprint. 2014. Kentucky: CreateSpace.

———. 2009. *The Strenuous Life; Essays and Addresses,* Mineola: Dover.

———, and Laura Ross, ed. 2012. *A Passion to Lead.* New York: Sterling Signature.

Seymour, Harold, and Dorothy Seymour Mills. 1960. *Baseball: The Early Years.* New York: Oxford University Press.

Smits, Edward J. 1974. *Nassau, Suburbia, U.S.A.: The First Seventy-five Years of Nassau County, New York, 1899 to 1974.* Syosset, NY: Friends of the Nassau County Museum.

Social Register Association. 1915. *Social Register, New York, 1916.* New York: Social Register Association.

Spanburgh, Sally. 2012. *The Southampton Cottages of Gin Lane.* Charleston, SC: History.

Spinzia, Raymond E., and Judith A. Spinzia. 2006. *Long Island's Prominent North Shore Families: Their Estates and Their Country Homes.* College Station, TX: VirtualBookworm.com Pub.

Trapper, Emma Louise. 1916. *Musical Blue Book of America, 1915.* New York: Musical Blue Book.

Watson, Frederick. 1931. *Hunting Pie.* London: H. F. & G. Witherby.

Weber, Nicholas Fox. 2007. *The Clarks of Cooperstown.* New York: Knopf.

Weeks, Christopher. 1999. *Perfectly Delightful: The Life and Gardens of Harvey Ladew*. Baltimore: Johns Hopkins University Press.

Whitney, Casper. 1897. "Cross Country Riding." *Harper's Monthly*, May: 821–38.

———. 1894. "The Evolution of the Country Club." *Harper's New Monthly*, December: 16–35.

———. 1895. "Fox-hunting in the United States." *Harper's Monthly*, March: 495–511.

Wiesen Cook, Blanche. 1993. *Eleanor Roosevelt, 1884–1933*. Vol. 1. New York: Penguin Books.

Williams, Roger D. 1908. *Horse and Hound*. Lexington, KY: Privately published.

Winants, Peter. 2005. *Sporting Art of Franklin B. Voss*. Lexington, KY: Eclipse.

———. 2000. *Steeplechasing: A Complete History of the Sport in North America*. Lanham, MD: Derrydale.

Van Urk, John Blan, and Gordon Grand. 1940. *The Story of American Foxhunting: From Challenge to Full Cry*. Vol. 2. New York: Derrydale Press.

Acknowledgments

I was introduced to the Meadow Brook Hounds through Music. When I was about four years old, a hound trotted up our driveway. The hound befriended our dogs and spent the afternoon trailing behind my brother and me. My parents called us in so that our visitor would leave and find her way home. But it grew dark and began to snow, and the hound huddled on our porch. After several phone calls, my father spoke with someone at the Meadow Brook Hounds kennels. The result was that the hound, whose name we learned was Music, was invited inside to spend the night in front of our fire. I snuck down and slept on the sofa next to her.

The next morning a big chestnut horse stood on our snow-covered lawn with Charlie Plumb on her back. Charlie thanked us and said Music had a habit of wandering off to play with children. Then he blew his horn, and the trio departed. The sight and sounds were magical. I knew then and there that I wanted to foxhunt. After hours of riding lessons at Barney Balding's stable in Brookville, I began foxhunting, a sport I would enjoy for the next four decades. I hunted regularly with Meadow Brook and, after moving to Virginia, with Farmington, Fairfax, and Middleburg. I have never once been out when a fox was killed, but this book is not a defense of past practices any more than a tome recounting the battle of Gettysburg is an acclamation of war. My purpose is to record the history of a foxhunt, and in so doing, take a backward glance at the people and places on Long Island that existed for almost one hundred years.

Many people assisted me in this endeavor. They have taken time to share their memories, photographs, and works of art. In the early 1980s, I had the foresight and good fortune to interview Betty Babcock, Marjorie McDonald, and Charlie Plumb for the book "I hoped to write." I am most grateful for the time they spent with me. Bob Winthrop, Raymond Brown, and Dot Balding Brown responded to my letters and sent me materials to include. More recently I have received encouragement and assistance from Eileen Bliss Anderhazy; Bruce Balding; Katrina Hickox Becker; Shelby Bonnie; Lillian Pyne Corbin; Russell Corey; Cora Cavanagh Cushny; Penny Denegre, Master of Foxhounds, Middleburg Hounds; Peter E. Doane; Mollie Eckelberry; Norman Fine; Lynn Merrill Gray; Jane Greenleaf; Cokie Hadden; Betty Keefer; Elizabeth "Libby" Keefer; Arthur Liese; Lee Bradley Mackay; Robert MacKay; Paul Mateyunas; Mike and Jane McDermott; Patricia Corey Montgomery; Katie Emmet Peterson; Keith Rehberger; Ken Reigner; Turner Reuter; Sarane Hickox Ross; Peter Schiff; Sarah Cavanagh Schwartz; Jeanne Stockman; and Charles and Elinor Von Stade. I owe a special debt to Katrina Becker and Barbara Conolly who loaned me their wonderful scrapbooks and numerous photographs, and also to my writing group, Teddi Ahrens, Terry Jennings, and Kim Waxman, who never knew they wanted to read about foxhunting.

I received and am grateful for assistance from Appleton Farms and The Trustees of Reservations; Bryant Library in Roslyn; Chisholm Gallery; *The Chronicle of the Horse*; Elkridge-Harford Hounds; Friends of Sagamore Hill; Glen Cove Public Library; Green Vale School; Hicksville Public Library; Historical Society of the Westburys, Westbury Library; Houghton Library, Harvard University; Ladew Topiary Gardens; Long Island Museum of American Art, History & Carriages; Masters of Foxhounds Association of America; Meadow Brook Hounds Pony Club; Museum of Hounds & Hunting of North America; Museum of Polo & Hall of Fame, Lake Worth, Florida; National Sporting Library and Museum; Locust Valley Public Library; Red Fox Fine Art, Middleburg, Virginia; Sporting Gallery and Bookshop, Inc.; Rockaway Hunting Club; Theodore Roosevelt Association; and Ed Watkins Photography.

I am deeply indebted to the Board of Governors and officers of the Meadow Brook Club, who gave me access to their records and art collection. The club's general manager, Dennis Harrington, and his staff provided me every courtesy and responded to my requests with thoughtfulness and good humor.

I appreciate my family members who have shown great fortitude and patience in listening to endless conversations about the Meadow Brook Hounds spiced with tidbits about Long Island that only I found interesting. And finally, I thank my parents who often rose before dawn to drive me to meets, my riding instructor Barney Balding, my fellow riders at Uncle Barney's and Libby Keefer who made a day's hunting so much fun, and Mitzie and Spring Fever who carried me across the fields and over the fences of Meadow Brook country.

$\mathcal{I}ndex$

Page references for figures are *italicized*.

Buckram Beagles, 169, 218

Bull, Henry Worthington, 57,
70–73, *72*, 79, 86, 88–89,
100

Bull, Mrs. Henry Worthington.
See Baker, Phyllis Livingston

Bulldags, 57–59, *58*, 70–71, 75,
86, 229

Burden, James A., 132, *135*,
136, 138

Burden, Mrs. James A. *See*
Sloane, Florence Adele

Burke Roche, J. 14

Burke-Roche, James Jeffrey, 246

Burrill, Middleton S., 26, 164,
188, 195

Bywater, Colonel, 122

Caffyn, Edgar, 102

Cameron, Walter "Scott," 89,
94–95, *94*, 106–7

Camp Albert L. Mills, 128

Campbell, Douglas, 129

Cary, Margaret L. (Mrs. Elliott
Zborowski), 16

Caumsett Farm, 202

Cavanagh, Cora (Mrs.
Theodorus V. W. Cushny),
193, 198, 201, 208–9, *209*,
213–14, 216, 220

Cavanagh, Elise "Mouse" (Mrs.
James F.), 197, 199, 201, 214

Cavanagh, James F., 199, 201,
214

Cavanagh, Sara Schwartz, 198,
201, 203, *203*, 209, 214

Cavcote, 214

Center, Robert "Bob," 5–9, 15

Chase, Dr. Henry, 240

Cheever, Jack, 24

Clark, Ambrose, 123, 136,
139–40, 142, 168, 231–33,
233, *234*

Clark, Ann, 240

Clark, Florence (Mrs. Ambrose),
203, 233

Clar, Frederick Ambrose. *See*
Clark, Ambrose

Clark, Grenville, 157

Clason, *3*

Coatsworth. *See* Cotesworth

Coe Estate, 159, 188

Collier, Peter Fenelon, 89, *100*,
100–3, 108, 113

Columbia Stock Farm, *135*, 188

Connett, Eugene, 178, 242

Conolly, (Mrs. Joseph). *See*
Hewlett, Barbara

Corcoran, William W., 55

Corey, Alan, 144, 199

Corey, Mrs. Alan. *See* Grace,
Patricia

Coster, Charles, 107

Cotesworth, E. Robert "Ned,"
96, 98–99

Cotsworth, see Cotesworth

Cottenet, Charles L. "Little
Minch," 57–59, 73, 229